living and learning in two languages

living and learning in two languages

Bilingual-Bicultural Education in the United States

Frances Willard von Maltitz

McGraw-Hill Book Company
New York   St. Louis   San Francisco
Düsseldorf   London   Mexico
Sydney   Toronto

**Library of Congress Cataloging in
Publication Data**

Von Maltitz, Frances Willard, date
  Living and learning in two languages.

  Bibliography: p.
  1. Education, Bilingual—
  United States. I. Title.
LC3731.V66   37.9′71   74-23960
ISBN 0-07-067609-7

1 2 3 4 5 6 7 8 9 0 BPBP 73210987654

to
H.v.M.

Contents

Acknowledgments

I should like to express my gratitude to all the many persons who have facilitated my investigations into the progress and development of bilingual education in the United States. These have included officials of state departments of education, specialists in the field of language teaching, school principals and other administrators, and the directors, classroom teachers, aides, and secretaries responsible for the operation of bilingual projects in many different parts of the country. I have found them unfailingly kind and hospitable to an observer previously unknown to them, whose attitudes and intentions they had no way of predicting. Their willingness to respond to my questions, in writing and in conversation, to permit me to visit their schools and to observe teachers and pupils in bilingual classes, to provide me with pertinent information, and to discuss freely any aspect of the subject I chose to bring up has been of enormous value to me.

Though space does not permit a complete listing of all those who have been of assistance to me in the course of my research and writing, I should like to thank especially the following persons for the contributions they have made in one way or another to my knowledge of bilingual-bicultural education: Dr. Theodore Andersson, Austin, Texas; Edward Booth, Department of Education, State of Maine; Jack Chen, Center for International Studies, Cornell University; Robert Fournier, Department of Education, State of New Hampshire; Edward Costa, Department of Education, State of Rhode Island; Hernan LaFontaine, Office of Bilingual Education, New York City Board of Education; Ernest Mazzone, Bureau of Transitional Bilingual Education, State of Massachusetts; Robert Rebert, Language Arts Branch, Bureau of Indian Affairs, Albuquerque, New Mexico; and Meredith Ring, Indian Educator, State of Maine.

For facilitating visits to their schools I thank the following persons: John Correiro, Onésima Almeída, João Botelho, Fall River, Massachusetts; Luis Cartagena, Wildon Rodriguez, P.S. 25, New York City; Helen Hanges, Irene Kellogg, Dazne Sajous, P.S. 9, New York City; Rosa Inclan, Gretchen Worden, Illuminata Valle, John Moore, Dade County Schools, Miami, Florida; Dr. Wayne Holm, Agnes Holm, Dr. Elizabeth Willink, Paul Rosier, and members of the Navajo Community

School Board, Rock Point, Arizona; Dr. E. Roby Leighton, Kathy Moyes, Meredith Pike, Rough Rock Demonstration School, Arizona; Larry Lew, Marina Jr. High School, Victor Low, Commodore Stockton School, San Francisco; John Lilly, Judith Kennedy, Carew School, Gerry Fortier, Junior High School, Springfield, Massachusetts; Virginia Lity, Tomás Miranda, Bridgeport, Connecticut; Cyrin Maus, Miccosukee School, Tamiami Trail, Miami, Florida; Adele Nadeau, Nestor School, Project Frontier, Chula Vista, California; Wayne Newell, Abnaki (Passamaquoddy) School, Dana Point, Maine; Ann O'Donnell, Lowell, Massachusetts; Normand Robitaille, Martha Kelber, Robert Paris, Greenville, New Hampshire; Hal Schultz, Acomita Day School, New Mexico; Robert Tharp, P.S. 2, New York City; Paul White, Haverhill, Massachusetts; Paquita Viñas de Vasquez, Francisca Ayala, Mary Barker Cora, Department of Education of Puerto Rico, and the principals and teachers in several towns and cities on the Island who so graciously welcomed me as visitor and observer in their classrooms.

I would not wish to suggest by acknowledging my indebtedness to any of the above-named persons that their views necessarily coincide with mine, or that they are responsible for any inadequacies or errors which may be found in the text. Responsibility for the contents of the book rests with the author alone.

My thoughts at this time also turn to the many students, adult and adolescent, to whom at one time or another I have taught English as a new language, and to the myriad elementary school children I have observed or tutored in the past fifteen years as a volunteer in the public schools in New York City and Bridgeport, Connecticut, most recently, during the preparation of this book, the Spanish-speaking pupils in Mrs. Badr's ungraded, transitional class in an elementary school in Bridgeport. Their bilingual-bicultural charm and high spirits have been a constant source of renewal, in my weekly meetings with them, of my interest in bilingual education and my belief in its value.

Frances Willard von Maltitz

Definitions and Abbreviations

Acculturation
In the context of bilingual-bicultural education the term *acculturation* is used to indicate the gradual loss by newly arrived immigrants (or members of a minority group within a society) of their distinctive cultural characteristics, and the adoption of the cultural traits and social patterns of another (usually the dominant, majority) group.

Anglo
A person, not necessarily of Anglo-Saxon blood or background, whose first (family) language is English.

Assimilation
This term suggests a two-directional process: the larger society receiving and absorbing into itself the lesser or minority group, the minority group developing greater resemblance to the majority and merging with it.

Barrio
A Spanish word, meaning "neighborhood," used to refer to a section of an American city inhabited by Spanish-speaking persons, usually Puerto Rican or Mexican American.

Bilingual-Bicultural Education
Teaching pupils in two languages and from the point of view of the cultures of which the languages are a part and an expression. In the United States, one of the languages will be English, the other the mother tongue of the particular pupils involved who are not native speakers of English. Both of the languages will be studied, and both will be used as media of instruction. Emphasis is also placed on developing a knowledge and understanding of the differences in manners, mores, history, and cultural characteristics and values of the two (or more) groups.

ESAA
*E*mergency *S*chool *A*id *A*ct, a federal act, passed in 1972, that provides money for certain programs in public schools.

ESEA
*E*lementary and *S*econdary *E*ducation *A*ct, a federal act passed by

Congress in 1965 to provide funds and guidance to local school districts in order to improve educational opportunities for pupils. The various Titles (sections such as Title I, Title III, Title V) were addressed to different problems faced by the schools, including the special needs of disadvantaged children, the improvement of library facilities, the training of teachers, and so forth.

ESL

Acronym for *E*nglish as a *S*econd *L*anguage, a definition devised to differentiate the teaching of English to pupils who are not native speakers of the language from the normal English classes for English-speaking students. It is in some ways an unfortunate choice of terminology, since it leads to misunderstandings and is sometimes interpreted by uninformed persons as suggesting that English is considered of secondary importance in the school or program concerned. The term ESL developed as a substitute for *English to Foreigners*, the words *foreign* and *foreigners* being considered generally unacceptable in the public school setting, since many of the pupils in public schools today who do not speak English are not necessarily foreigners. (Puerto Ricans and many Mexican Americans, who are Spanish speaking, are citizens.)

ESOL

Acronym for *E*nglish for *S*peakers of *O*ther *L*anguages, a description or designation of a course in English for pupils who speak some other language as a mother tongue.

FLES

Acronym for *F*oreign *L*anguages in *E*lementary *S*chool, a concept which gained popularity and was put into practice in many schools in the 1950s. It calls for teaching foreign languages to young children, starting usually at the third- or fifth-grade level, based on the conviction that the younger pupils are, the more easily they will learn a second language.

Indian Education Act

Title IV of the Higher Education Amendments Act of 1973, which provided money for the education of Indian children in schools throughout the United States.

Johnson O'Malley Act

Often referred to as "JOM" (P.L.874), the Johnson O'Malley Act was enacted in 1936 to provide money for services to meet the special needs of American-Indian children. The original intent of the act was to give financial support to public school districts serving students from non-taxable Indian land.

TEFL
Acronym for *T*eaching *E*nglish as a *F*oreign *L*anguage, a term used in language departments at the college (and sometimes secondary school) level, but not usually in public school bilingual-bicultural programs.

TESL
*T*eaching of *E*nglish as a *S*econd *L*anguage, a variant of the term ESL.

TESOL
Acronym for *T*eaching of *E*nglish to *S*peakers of *O*ther *L*anguages. There is a national TESOL organization that publishes a quarterly and an occasional newsletter containing articles and information of interest to specialists in the field.

Title VII
The so-called "Bilingual Education Act" (P.L. 90-247) was added to the ESEA in 1967 and signed into law by the President in January 1968. Title VII determined policy and provided money for the establishment of bilingual-bicultural educational projects in public schools, thus shaping the ideology and giving impetus to the bilingual education movement in the United States.

living and learning in two languages

Introduction

The term *bilingual*, whether applied to a person or a group, usually carries with it the implication of at least some degree of *biculturalism*. Implicit in the concept of bilingual education, as it comes under discussion in the present book, is the importance of exposing members of one ethnic and linguistic group to the traditions and values, the ways of thinking and feeling, of another. The word *bicultural* is often added to the name or description of the bilingual projects being carried on in the public schools in the United States today. When it is omitted for the sake of brevity, it is generally to be understood. Furthering a knowledge among pupils and teachers, parents and administrators, and the community at large, of the different cultures in which the languages in question have developed is considered to be an integral part of the bilingual programs. And this furthering of understanding is two-directional. Both majority and minority groups, it is hoped, will learn about and from each other.

One of the objectives of bilingual-bicultural education—it is, of course, more accurate to call it *multi*lingual *multi*cultural—is to offer information about the cultures of minority groups, to present something of their history—the part they have played and the contributions they have made in the development of the American nation. The purpose of this, also, is twofold: to instill in children from those minority groups, who have often been subject to prejudice, a pride in their own language and culture and to promote among persons from other segments of the population an understanding and a respect for Americans who may be different from themselves.

The stereotype of the "ugly American abroad" has its counterpart at home. Persons who are insensitive to the reactions of members of a different cultural group often offend, sometimes unintentionally; those ignorant of the manners and mores of a society varying markedly from their own can leap to unhappy and unwarranted interpretations of what may be considered normal and expected behavior in that other group.

It might be pointed out that the cultural conflicts and misunderstandings between different national or linguistic groups are in some respects extensions or magnifications of the variations that occur even within a monolingual Anglo society. Any New Englander who has lived in the South or a Southerner who has moved North knows about the surprises in store for new arrivals in both areas, if they are not attuned to the sometimes subtle, sometimes obvious, differences in attitude and pace. A Southerner will interpret a New Englander's "coming to the point" and "not beating about the bush" as abrupt and unmannerly; to a Northerner, circumlocutions may smack of insincerity. What is thought of in one place as being "courteously not late" for appointments may be considered in another as "overly and inconveniently prompt." Even if one doesn't want slavishly to follow the precept "When in Rome, do as the Romans do," it is usually helpful, if one wishes to live harmoniously in a new setting or with people different from oneself, to adapt oneself to the prevailing habits of life. In order to do that, one has to know what they are.

Some of the differences between one ethnic group and another, of course, go much deeper than superficial variations in manners and habits. Underlying some of them are attitudes toward life and death, love and family relationships, concepts of time—not in the meaning of hours and minutes but in the larger sense. There are also different views concerning the way man should conduct his life, motivated by a competitive, acquisitive spirit or guided by an acceptance of what fate brings. The attitude toward land—man's use of the earth—also varies, with Indian societies traditionally favoring communal rather than individual ownership. Teachers and school administrators need to understand all of these varied aspects of the cultural backgrounds of the pupils whose education is entrusted to them. A study of the cultural roots of the various segments of the American nation is considered to be an important part of the bilingual-bicultural movement in public education.

In the actual planning and organization of the bilingual projects, providing members of the school community with the chance to become better acquainted with other cultures means incorporating into the curriculum units on the history and cultural characteristics of Puerto Ricans, Mexican Americans, Afro-Americans, and other ethnic groups; it may mean the celebration of holidays with special significance for one group or another—the beginning of a new year according to the Chinese calendar, Three Kings' Day for Puerto Ricans, or Columbus Day (now claimed by both Italian and Spanish-speaking). It means becoming acquainted with the manner of expression of the artistic impulse of a particular group, in music, dance, and the graphic arts. It will include fiestas, with Spanish, Greek, Portuguese, or some other national food, music, and dance. In addition, it means the continuation of the celebration of Thanksgiving, Washington's and Lincoln's birthdays and studying the beginnings of American history and the development and growth of the nation's governmental system from its inception in the original colonies, which have always been part of the curriculum and activities of the schools. In the teaching of the two languages, the mother tongue of the pupils and English, it means using both languages as media of instruction and as subjects to be studied.

The major thrust of bilingual-bicultural projects is the same as the goal of education in general: the promotion of learning and the fullest development of each child to the extent of his potential, but in this case, by using first the language a pupil knows and by creating an atmosphere in which a child can feel confidence in himself, whatever his background. The curriculum must, of course, be basically in conformance with state requirements as established by law. As for the choice of specific materials, the placement of pupils in one type of class or another, and the organization of the actual programs there is, and inevitably must be, great variation from school to school, from city to city, and from state to state because of differing circumstances. It is impossible to draw a diagram of a bilingual-bicultural program that is appropriate for all places and all groups. One can describe goals and principles that they will all presumably have in common, but it must be left to the local school boards, administrators, and teachers to work out the pattern that best suits their situation.

The subject of "educational politics" will be left largely untouched in this treatment of bilingual-bicultural programs. Politics, in its prime definition, "the science or art of political government,"[1] is, of course, involved in providing money for public education and establishing priorities for its distribution. The political process comes into play in local affairs in the approving of town budgets, the setting of mil rates on property values and the election of school boards; at the national level it is involved in the action congressmen take in supporting or opposing legislation relating to education. But politics in its lesser definitions ("the use of intrigue or strategy in obtaining any position of power or control, as in a business, university, etc.,"[2] or "intrigue within a group"[3]), as it is played in some of the bilingual-bicultural projects and presumably throughout the educational scene, will not be explored here. This decision is made not because the author is unaware of the existence of political intrigue within the educational bureaucracy. There is jockeying for position and prestige within both high governmental offices and local school districts. One can read between the lines, in proclamations and public materials released by those involved in bilingual projects, and guess at infighting and petty politics. Even during brief visits to schools one can sense or sometimes be told outright of conflicts of interest and clashes of personality or ideology within the staff of a bilingual project, or between them and other school personnel. But no one who is not an active participant closely enough involved to know all the facts and predisposing factors that lead to the infighting can judge who or which side is "in the right" or "better." The most one can say is that it is regrettable when "playing politics" in school affairs results in mismanagement, waste, or the sabotaging of any program, the sole purpose of which ought to be giving the children in that classroom or that school a better educational opportunity.

As for the specific actions of ethnic pressure groups, the "politics of ethnicity"—if one may characterize it in these terms—is a worldwide phenomenon. It is manifested in many countries at this particular period in history, in different ways, and to varying degrees, whether as a separatist movement for the Basques or the revival of the Breton language as evidence of resentment in Brittany against the highly centralized French government seated in Paris.

Ethnic politics have certainly played a role in the United States in getting bilingual education under way, influencing decisions about the nature and locations of the bilingual-bicultural programs and the choice of recipients of the limited funds available. Claims sometimes heard of the "cruel" treatment received in the past by minority children in public schools seem exaggerated to the nonpartisan observer, but there is little doubt that new approaches in education for minority children were sorely needed. And it is a truism that the squeaky wheel receives the grease. It does sometimes appear that opposing groups vying for funds do themselves and the entire movement some damage by the stridency of their voices and by their actions in working against rather than with each other. But where political pressure has been required to bring about necessary changes in education, it is likely to be used again. Wherever radical political activism, however, is involved in the process of developing bilingual education in the public schools, it should not be permitted to overshadow the more important fact that it is children, and not the radical politicians, who are, or ought to be, the reason for the very existence of the schools and the focus of what goes on in them.

Notes

1. *Random House Unabridged Dictionary*, 1966.

2. Ibid.

3. *American Heritage Dictionary*, 1969.

A Review of the Origins:
Some Historical and
Sociological Perspectives

Among the many innovations introduced in public schools in the United States during the past decade, one of the most controversial but potentially significant is the establishment of bilingual classes for pupils whose dominant or mother tongue is a language other than English. Beginning usually at the kindergarten or first-grade level but continuing in succeeding grades, some of these children are being taught basic concepts—reading, writing, and some subject matter—first in the language they know best, the one they speak at home, while they are making their first acquaintance with English or becoming more proficient in it. At the same time in many of the bilingual programs, English-speaking pupils are also beginning to learn the other, to them "foreign," language spoken by so many of their schoolmates. (This was the situation during the years of operation of Title VII of ESEA, the Bilingual Act of 1967. In July 1974, however, Congress passed an Education Amendments Act [signed by President Ford on August 21, 1974], that amended the earlier legislation. Though the act ensured continuing federal financial support for bilingual education through 1978, it contained a new policy statement regarding bilingual education programs, one sentence of which reads: "In no event, shall the program be designed for the purpose of teaching a foreign language to English-speaking children." See Chapter 9 for a discussion of the implications of the new policy statement.) The concept of bilingual-bicultural education appears startling, even revolutionary, in a country where it was until recently illegal in many states to teach in any language but English. But this concept is gaining acceptance and proving its worth, in many locations and situations, as an educational philosophy and technique.

There is considerable variety in the types and magnitude of the bilingual projects in different sections of the country, since the planning and developing is done locally to suit the needs and characteristics of the particular community involved. However, all the projects have as their ultimate aim improving the educational achievements and subsequent social adjustment of the large numbers of children among minority groups in the United States today who have a less-than-adequate command of English when they arrive at school because they speak some other language as their mother tongue. An equally important objective of bilingual education in public schools is the according of respect and dignity to the language and cultural traditions of the various ethnic and linguistic groups that have always contributed to, and been an integral part of, the rich diversity of the American nation.

In one of the early bilingual programs at the Fox Point School in Providence, Rhode Island, for instance, 250 children in the first five grades began their school day by reciting the words: "Eu prometo a minha lealdade á bandeira dos Estados Unidos da America, a o paíd que representa, uma naçao, indivisiel, sob o poder de Deus, com liberdade a jústiça para todos," the familiar pledge of allegiance translated into Portuguese. They also gave the pledge in English. Some of the children were from Portuguese-speaking families; others were "Anglos," as English-speaking pupils are now being referred to in public schools. During the rest of the day, for these selected students, some lessons were conducted in English, some in Portuguese, with new subject matter introduced in the native language for each group, but with Anglos learning some Portuguese and Portuguese children setting about mastering English.

Similar classes, using some language in addition to English, have been in progress all over the United States, usually on a voluntary basis. In most cases parents enroll their children in a bilingual program only if they want to, though as a rule there are more pupils wishing to' participate in bilingual classes than there are classes available for them. The other language in these bilingual programs may be French (Canadian in New England, Cajun or Creole in Louisiana, Haitian in New York or Boston); Chinese (in port cities on the East and West coasts); Italian, Greek, or some other Southern or Central European language (if a community has a high percentage of residents of such national origin); or it may be a tribal American-Indian language (in schools on or near Indian reservations). In the majority of all instances of dual language classes, however, the other language will be Spanish, with Cuban overtones in Florida, Puerto Rican in major urban centers in the North and East, and Mexican American in Western and Southwestern states.

These bilingual classes represent not only significant innovations in the philosophy and techniques of teaching but also a major change in attitudes toward children in American schools whose first language is not English. Adult Mexican Americans who attended school in Texas or the Southwest in their childhood tell stories of having had to forgo recess in order to write 500 times, "I will not speak Spanish in school," if they had broken this ironclad rule. Some still feel bitterness at the insensitive, unfair treatment they received; others with greater resiliency or humor recall how they solved the problem by starting on the writing chore the minute they arrived at school in the morning so that when assigned the prescribed punishment for having succumbed to the temptation to communicate with their friends in the language that came naturally, they could gleefully hand over their 500 written promises not to speak Spanish and race out to the schoolyard with the others.

The concept of teaching in two languages (or in a language other than English) is not a completely new idea in the history of education in the United States. Some bilingual public schools existed here before the Civil War and flourished in various places thereafter. In localities with heavy concentrations of German-speaking families, such as Cincinnati, Cleveland, and Milwaukee, there were schools in which at least part of the curriculum was taught in German; in an earlier era, French was used in public schools in Louisiana, and Spanish in New Mexico. Parochial schools, of course, have often used the language of their parishioners as a medium of instruction. Various ethnic groups, through community organizations or religious institutions, have also provided after-school language classes in such languages as Chinese, Greek, or Hebrew, so that children who were learning only English in public schools could maintain their traditional family language.

But because bilingual education, or teaching in any language but English in *public* schools, did not conform to the melting-pot philosophy (and, on occasion, for additional reasons, such as the United States' being at war with Germany), it fell into disfavor and in many states was declared illegal. The resurgence of interest in bilingual teaching, which came about in the decade of the 1960s, was fostered by two factors: the growing determination of various ethnic minorities (especially the two major Spanish-speaking ones—Puerto Ricans and Mexican Americans) to maintain their ancestral languages and life-styles and the schools' inability to educate many of the children from these ethnic groups (who were often from the lowest socio-economic segment of the nation's school population), when using a language that the pupils had not yet mastered as the only medium of instruction.

Most of the bilingual projects now in operation in public schools are the direct result or an outgrowth of the so-called "Bilingual Act of 1967." This was the addition in that year of Title VII to the federal Elementary and Secondary Education Act (referred to as "ESEA"), which Congress had passed in 1965 to help local school districts solve some of the myriad problems that were overwhelming them and upgrade the educational opportunities for certain groups of students who were not doing well or dropping out altogether. Earlier in the decade there had been a highly successful experiment in bilingual teaching in the Dade County schools in Florida, conceived to handle the influx of Cuban pupils into the Miami area at that time. After Castro came to power in 1959 and revealed his adherence to communism in 1961, with the subsequent disastrous Bay of Pigs episode and then the Missile Crisis involving the Soviet Union in 1962, Cuban families poured into Florida. Their children enrolled in public schools there, and the county was faced with the problem of how best to teach large numbers of children who spoke only Spanish. With money made available from Cuban-refugee funds, a bilingual program was set up at the Coral Way Elementary School in Miami, which has flourished ever since. Materials and techniques were developed which have served as models and sources for subsequent bilingual projects in other parts of the country. After its successful use at Coral Way, teaching in two languages was introduced in other schools in the Dade County system. Today some degree or type of bilingual teaching goes on in all the elementary schools in the county, and the program has been expanded to include junior, and in some cases senior, high schools.

Towns and cities in Texas soon followed suit or on their own initiative were already developing new approaches and materials for teaching their Spanish-speaking students, who were mostly of Mexican origin. In 1964 bilingual classes were introduced at the Nye School outside of Laredo in Webb County; in the San Antonio Independent School District special methods were devised for teaching reading to Spanish-speaking pupils, which eventually developed into bilingual programs. Similar projects for Mexican-American children were started in 1965, 1966, and 1967, before the existence of the federal Bilingual Act, in other locations in Texas, in Pecos and Las Cruces in New Mexico, and in Calexico in California,[1] to name a few. To serve the needs of Puerto Rican pupils, bilingual classes were started in Hoboken, New Jersey, and plans for a bilingual school, P.S. 25, were initiated in the Bronx in New York City. The first steps toward bilingual education for American-Indian children were also taken at Rough Rock, Arizona, using the Navajo language.

But it was the creation of the federal Bilingual Act in the course of 1967 (signed into law in January 1968), with the funds it provided and the attention it focused on the widespread need for teaching children in a language they understood and could handle, that sparked a vigorous new movement toward bilingual-bicultural education in many parts of the United States. In the words of the legislators:

> The Congress hereby finds that one of the most acute educational problems in the United States is that which involves millions of

children of limited English-speaking ability because they come from environments where the dominant language is other than English; that additional efforts should be made to supplement present attempts to find adequate and constructive solutions to this unique and perplexing educational situation; and that the urgent need is for comprehensive and cooperative action now on the local, State and Federal levels to develop forward looking approaches to meet the serious learning difficulties faced by this substantial segment of the Nation's school age population.[2]

As a congressional declaration of policy, Sub-chapter IV-A, "Bilingual Education Programs," continues:

In recognition of the special educational needs of large numbers of children of limited English-speaking ability in the United States, Congress hereby declares it to be the policy of the United States to provide financial assistance to carry out new and imaginative elementary and secondary school programs designed to meet these special educational needs. For the purpose of this sub-chapter, "children of limited English-speaking ability" means children who come from environments where the dominant language is other than English.[3]

Title VII of ESEA, with its subsequent amendments, authorized the appropriation of funds amounting to $15 million for the year ending 1968, $30 million for 1969, $40 million for 1970, $80 million for 1971, and $125 million for 1973 (though, with the not uncommon discrepancy between amounts authorized and those finally appropriated, the figures for funds actually appropriated and distributed had reached only $25 million in 1971–72 and $35 million in 1972–73). How the funds were to be allotted was spelled out in the following way:

In determining distribution of funds under this sub-chapter, the U.S. Commissioner of Education shall give highest priority to States and areas within States having the greatest need for programs pursuant to this sub-chapter. Such priorities shall take into consideration the number of children of limited English-speaking ability between the ages of 3 and 18 in each State.[4]

School districts wanting to apply for federal monies to finance bilingual projects were required to submit carefully worked out plans and objectives to the U.S. Office of Education (Department of Health, Education, and Welfare [HEW]–Division of Bilingual Education), and those projects approved for funding had to be evaluated at the end of each school year in order to be eligible for continued or increased funding. The maximum period of federal financial support for any project would be five years from the date of the project's inception. At the end of that time it was the expectation or hope that local school districts would assume the costs of those bilingual programs which were considered successful and which had won the approval of local communities and school boards. This is already happening to a certain extent in many projects, with costs being partially absorbed by the local district and the salaries of some of the bilingual staff being paid out of regular school budgets.

All the federally financed bilingual projects were expected to include the following four objectives: actual bilingual instruction (devising techniques and methods for teaching in two languages); acquisition of materials (preparing or locating texts, tapes, films, pictures, and other materials suitable for use in the bilingual classes); staff development (training of bilingual teachers and other personnel); and community involvement (encouraging parents and other members of the linguistic and ethnic community to participate actively in the program, contributing in some way to the planning and implementing of the project. Their participation could include taking language lessons themselves).

The Bilingual Act, as enacted, was to be in effect for five years. The vagaries of political and economic life being what they are, however, the fate of the Bilingual Act was in doubt for a time early in 1973. The sweeping reorganization of governmental departments under the Nixon administration resulted in the elimination of some "poverty" and educational programs or in their placement under different governmental authorities. Congress did take action, however, to continue the Bilingual Act on a one-year basis; bilingual projects already in operation and approved for continuation were assured of receiving funding for the 1973–74 school year, though no applications for new programs were to be accepted.

The number of federally financed bilingual projects under Title VII for 1973–74 was 220, and they served over one hundred thousand children—a small percentage of those across the nation who might be expected to benefit from bilingual teaching. Since the passage of ESEA in 1965, there have been numerous supportive activities relating to the operation of public schools financed under other Titles of the act which have a bearing on bilingual education. Money was provided for teacher training programs, the acquisition of materials, library supplies, and equipment, and for special services for disadvantaged children. In addition to the federally financed projects, there are now bilingual programs of various types in operation in public schools, paid for out of local or state funds. Massachusetts passed a state Bilingual Act in October 1971—the first in the country—with mandatory provisions for transitional bilingual teaching in certain situations. Moves are afoot in many other states to enact similar legislation concerning recommendations or requirements, and in some cases reimbursement, for bilingual teaching of pupils with a limited knowledge of English.[5]

The largest language group being served by the presently evolving movement toward bilingual-bicultural education in public schools is the approximately 10 million Spanish-speaking persons in the United States, made up of two major segments, Puerto Ricans and Chicanos, as Americans of Mexican descent now often choose to call themselves.

Many persons have asked why bilingual teaching should be necessary or desirable in the United States today when in the past, immigrant children from different countries, speaking a variety of languages, who were tossed into the melting pot of the public schools usually managed to learn English and in the long run were able to take part in a largely English-language dominated society. There are cogent and compelling reasons for turning to bilingual education today, reasons rooted in the geographic and historical genesis of the presence of Puerto Ricans and Mexican Americans as participants in the American society.

The circumstances concerning language use that affect public education today are very different from those of the past in two respects: the magnitude of the language problem within the school population and the fact that it involves mainly one language, Spanish. It is one thing to put three or four children, each speaking a different language, into a class of thirty who speak English. In such a situation, English will probably prevail, and the few who speak different languages will learn the dominant one of the classroom, English. But when a minority becomes a numerical majority and more pupils in a class speak Spanish than English, it is unlikely that the Spanish-speaking children will automatically "pick up" English.

There may have been other elements encouraging assimilation or adjustment in past years, such as greater linguistic sophistication among certain immigrant groups who came from Europe, a continent where many people spoke more than one language and the idea of learning a new language did not necessarily connote losing their old one. But it is basically the sheer numbers of Spanish-speaking pupils in the school population that have forced the issue of bilingual education and made it a necessity in some areas.

The situation of Puerto Ricans and Mexican Americans is very different from that of earlier immigrants who came from Europe or Asia to make a new life in a new land. Puerto Ricans, when they come to the continental United States, are not moving to a foreign country. They are American citizens and have been since 1917. In December 1898, under the terms of the Treaty of Paris, which ended the Spanish-American War, Puerto Rico was ceded to the United States (though the war had been started over the issue of Cuba). The Jones Act of 1917, which established a certain amount of self-government for Puerto Ricans, also granted them United States citizenship. As long as ships were the only means of transportation, few Puerto Ricans availed themselves of their new status to move to the continental United States, even though economic and living conditions were far from ideal for many of the island's inhabitants. The advent of the jet plane changed all that. In recent decades, planeloads of Puerto Ricans have descended on cities in the Northeast. (It is true that not all Spanish-speaking travelers coming from San Juan are the Puerto Ricans they claim to be. It is widely reported that a good many immigrants from the Dominican Republic, and a few from other Spanish-language countries to the south, filter into the United States via San Juan, and "pass" as Puerto Ricans. English-speaking Americans are unable to spot them, though Puerto Ricans say they can detect who is a native Puerto Rican and who is not.) In any case, those Puerto Ricans who board a plane for the relatively cheap, short flight to New York come in search of a job or a better life than they have had in Puerto Rico, but most of them have a deep attachment to their tropical island and many of them expect to return, for visits, for brief periods of residence, and, in some cases, for good. Even if they intend to remain and realize that they will have to learn English, a little to survive and a lot to prosper, they have no intention of giving up Spanish altogether, no matter how fluent they may become in their new, second language.

Many of the older generation of Puerto Ricans have spoken no English on arrival; some have had little schooling and have been illiterate even in Spanish. This is not to suggest that there are not many people in Puerto Rico who have a high level of education and can speak English well, but they are the least likely to migrate to the continental United States looking for work. Children from the more poorly educated families, if they learn only English at school but continue to speak Spanish at home, are likely to remain illiterate in their first language, their mother tongue. In the opinion of many people—both educators and persons who have gone through the experience themselves—this can be detrimental later to the development of verbal and linguistic skills in the second language learned. Bilingual education offers Puerto Ricans the opportunity to become literate in Spanish *and* English, instead of remaining fundamentally, or functionally, illiterate in both, as sometimes happens if they get a poor start in both languages.

The situation of Mexican Americans in the United States is different from that of Puerto Ricans and in many ways more complex. Chicanos who are born in any of the Southwestern or Western states are, of course, United States citizens, and most of them are Spanish-speaking. Those who cross the border from Mexico, legally or surreptitiously, are entering a foreign nation, but the United States Southwest does not necessarily look or feel like alien country to them. The landscape is the same on both sides of the border—the territory was once part of Mexico—and in whichever direction they go, they are surrounded by Spanish place names, from El Paso to Las Cruces, Santa Fe, San Antonio, Del Rio, Colorado, Nevada, Los Angeles, and San Francisco, echoing the history of that part of the continent.

Most Easterners, if they have ever heard of the Treaty of Guadalupe Hidalgo, probably don't remember what it was all about. But to Mexicans and Mexican Americans it signifies an event of historical importance, the end of the Mexican-American War and the ceding by Mexico in 1848 of about two-fifths of its territory to the United States (with a payment of $15 million indemnity by the United States government making the treaty more binding). The territory acquired by the United States in this way was California, most of New Mexico, and parts of Arizona and Colorado. The Gadsden Purchase in 1853, for another $10 million, added a strip of what is now southern New Mexico and Arizona, finally establishing a clearly defined border.

Texas had its own early history, first as a province of Mexico that was gradually populated by newcomers from the United States who settled in Texas under grants originally obtained from local Spanish authorities and later confirmed by the Mexican government. In 1836 these settlers declared their independence from Mexico and established Texas as a republic. It was then accepted into the Union as a slave-holding state in 1845. (It was the annexation of Texas by the United States that was a major cause of the war with Mexico.) After going through the vicissitudes of the Civil War, Texas rejoined the Union in 1870. Since it had once been part of Mexico, Texas had always had many Spanish-speaking inhabitants of Mexican origin. As part of the United States, Texas has shared a border with Mexico, and in the course of the twentieth century, many Mexicans have made the decision to move across that border to look for work or to join friends, families, or people to whom they feel related by virtue of sharing the same ethnic and linguistic roots.

Some of the feelings of dispossession and discrimination that lead to complications in present-day relations between impecunious Mexican-American residents of the Southwest and wealthier Anglo landowners go back to the question of old Spanish land grants. Under the terms of the Treaty of Guadalupe Hidalgo, these land grants were to be honored even after the territory came under the jurisdiction of the United States.

Article VIII of the treaty reads, in part, as follows:

> Mexicans now established in territories previously belonging to Mexico, and which remain for the future within the limits of the United States, as defined by the present treaty, shall be free to continue where they now reside, or to remove at any time to the Mexican Republic, retaining the property which they possess in the said territories, or disposing thereof, and removing the proceeds wherever they please. . . .
>
> In the said territories, property of every kind, now belonging to Mexicans not established there, shall be inviolably respected. The present owners, the heirs of these, and all Mexicans who may hereafter acquire said property by contract, shall enjoy with respect to it guarantees equally ample as if the same belonged to citizens of the United States.[6]

In many instances properties belonging to Mexican families were lost because of what some members or heirs of formerly landholding families consider trickery, cheating, or taking advantage of poor or poorly educated Spanish-speaking Mexicans, who because they didn't understand the language being used, signed away their rights or gave up lands for a fraction of their worth.

In California, which was the goal of land-hungry settlers from the 1850s on, the situation was especially complicated by the passage of the Federal Land Act of 1851, which required the validating of titles to land acquired under Spanish or Mexican grants. Many of the "Californios" (people of Spanish or Mexican birth or background who settled in the province during the Spanish or Mexican eras) lost their ranchos because they lacked the resources or the expertise to validate the titles to their lands, or were financially ruined by the prolonged litigation in which they became entangled in trying to establish their claims.

Historians writing of California always emphasize the problems arising from the Spanish and Mexican land grants. As Andrew Rolle puts it:

> By the time of the American conquest, almost fourteen million acres in all had been granted by Spanish and Mexican officials. . . . Although the Treaty of Guadalupe Hidalgo had guaranteed resident Californians protection and security in the "free enjoyment of their liberty, property and religion," increasing dissatisfaction over the . . . grants was expressed by settlers who had arrived more recently, especially the Americans. . . . From the standpoint of the American pioneer, it was intolerable that a "few hundred despised Mexicans" should control vast tracts of the most fertile and desirable lands. . . . During that . . . period [of Land

Commission hearings] rancheros searched their homes for original grants . . . ferreted maps out of the Surveyor General's . . . archives, called on friends to testify to their long tenure on the land, and consulted lawyers—all to justify their titles. The burden of proof remained on them. They were at a disadvantage in other respects too. None of the land commissioners spoke or read the Spanish language. . . . A fairly contemporary assessment of all this confusion over land, that of Henry George's *Progress and Poverty* (1871) stated: "If the history of Mexican grants of California is ever written, it will be a history of greed, of perjury, of corruption, of spoliation, and high-handed robbery, for which it will be hard to find a parallel."[7]

Though many Chicanos are relatively recent immigrants who lay no claims to land in the United States, the experience of earlier Mexican residents is part of the whole picture of the position of Mexican Americans in the United States Southwest. To most Americans, especially in other sections of the country, these events are part of a long-ago past. A lot of water has gone over the dam since the signing of the Treaty of Guadalupe Hidalgo and one can't replay history. But one must take account of it, if one wants to understand some of the underlying reasons for the attitudes and feelings of the Spanish-speaking people of the Southwest regarding their rights, their language, and their cultural heritage.

Though Mexican Americans speak the same language as Puerto Ricans and though they inherited that language from the same kind of Spanish explorers, conquerors, and converters who crossed the Atlantic from Spain in the sixteenth century to the newly discovered hemisphere, their racial and ethnic characteristics are somewhat different. Puerto Ricans evolved as a people from the mixture on their island crossroads of the Spanish adventurers, the Negroes who were brought to the West Indies as slaves, and what was left of the Taino Indians of the island, after their encounter with the Spanish colonizers.

Chicanos—or their progenitors in Mexico—developed from the merging of the Spanish invaders and the Indian inhabitants of Mexico at the time of the European conquest, the Aztecs, a people who had a high degree of civilization, an astonishing understanding of astronomy, a written (picture) form of their history, and a mythology that contributed to their downfall, since they took the arrival of the white man to be the predicted return of their god, Quetzalcoatl.

Though *Hispano* has been used as a name for a Spanish-speaking person in some parts of the Southwest, especially in New Mexico, Mexicans in the area have often referred to themselves as "Españoles-Mexicanos," adding the second word to emphasize their Indian blood, as the original Mexicans. The term *Chicano* is derived from their (or the Nahuatl Indian) pronunciation of *Mejicano* as Me*sh*icano, or Me*ch*icano, shortened to Chicano.[8]

In usage the term *Chicano* has gone through various stages, in its connotations and its acceptance. It has been considered pejorative when used by Anglos to refer disparagingly to poor or poorly educated Mexican immigrants in Texas and other parts of the Southwest. For a time early in the century it seems to have been the term employed by Mexican Americans, themselves, to mean recent immigrants as contrasted with *Pochos*, persons of Mexican background who either had been born within the confines of the U.S. or had lived this side of the border long enough to have lost some of their Mexicanness and to have acquired a certain knowledge of things American. (Pocho literally means "faded" or "bleached.") Today, however, Pocho seems to be used chiefly in referring to the mixed Spanish-English dialect spoken by many Mexican Americans in the *barrios*. In any case, *Chicano* has now assumed for many Mexican Americans a connotation of pride in their race, serving to indicate their Mexican-Indian roots. In case of doubt, an Anglo should probably refrain from using the term and speak of Mexican Americans but recognize the respect and pride the term *Chicano* implies when used by Mexican Americans to refer to themselves. Some Mexican Americans also refer to themselves as "*La Raza*," after an old expression predating the Spanish conquest, when the Mexicans called themselves "the sacred race."

In numbers Chicano pupils are often in the majority in both urban and rural schools in the Southwest, as are Puerto Rican children in cities in the East. The total Mexican population in the United States rose from about 1.3 million in 1930 to more than 5 million in 1969, and in 1971 had reached 5.6 million, with 5 million living in the five Southwestern states (California, Texas, Arizona, Colorado, and New Mexico). The figures for 1974 are believed to be much higher, but accurate data are unavailable. This increase reflects both a high birth rate and continuing immigration. The *barrios* of Los Angeles constitute the third-largest Mexican city in the world—only Mexico City and Guadalajara have greater Mexican populations.

The Puerto Rican population in the United States fluctuates, with a good deal of movement back and forth between the island of Puerto Rico and the continental United States, the direction of the flow depending on economic conditions in both places. In 1969 it was estimated that there were about a million and a half Puerto Ricans living in the United States, with New York City accounting for 969,700. According to statistics given the author in August 1973 by the Migration Division (in New York City) of the Commonwealth of Puerto Rico, in

1972 there were 2,782,300 Puerto Ricans on the island of Puerto Rico and 1,800,000 living in the United States, with San Francisco accounting for 20,500; Chicago, 120,000; Boston, 30,000; Philadelphia, 45,000; Bridgeport, Connecticut, 30,000; Hartford, 35,000; Newark, 40,500; and New York City 1,280,000. It is difficult to maintain an accurate count, and these figures differ widely from other estimates, but they serve to give some idea of the size of the Puerto Rican population in some of the major urban areas of the United States.

No matter how many Puerto Ricans choose to return to their native island, there are always others coming to the United States for the first time, usually with little or no knowledge of English. Partly as an off-shoot of the bilingual movement, however, new programs in teacher training are being set up in Puerto Rico. New approaches and techniques will no doubt result in an improvement in the teaching and learning of English in the schools there.

Mexican Americans may be factory workers in cities like Los Angeles, but in many areas they are likely to be engaged in agricultural work, migrant or permanent. Some Puerto Ricans are found doing migrant farm labor, but the majority of them are in the cities, working in factories or in service jobs of one kind or another. Whatever their differences, what both groups have in common—as Spanish-speaking Americans—is their wish to preserve their language and their specific identities as ethnic minorities with distinct and distinguishing characteristics.

The location and linguistic type of the federally funded bilingual projects has reflected the concentration of Spanish-speaking people in the United States. Of the 164 federally supported bilingual programs in operation in 1971, 130 were exclusively for Spanish-speaking students. These programs were largely centered in Texas and California, with New York State having the next highest number. However, other languages used in Title VII bilingual projects have included Portuguese, Chinese, Russian, and French as well as Eskimo Yuk and twelve tribal American-Indian tongues.[9]

Addressing the 4,000 people attending the First International Multilingual-Multicultural Conference in San Diego, California, in April 1973, Albar Peña, the then acting director of the Division of Bilingual Education of the U.S. Office of Education, summarized the statistics and accomplishments of the federally supported bilingual projects from the time of their inception to the spring of 1973. In 1969 the Bilingual Division of the Office of Education had received $7½ million, with which it had sponsored 76 projects. Of these initial experiments, 72 were continued the following year, and 39 new ones were added, with Congress providing in all $21¼ million for that second year. Congress appropriated $25 million for 1971 and $35 million for 1972, with the cumulative figure topping $88 million by 1972. At the time of Mr. Peña's report to the conference, there were 217 projects in operation in 29 states. It had been hoped that funds for the 1973–74 school year might be increased to $41 million, but with the uncertainties about the future of many of the social and educational programs financed by the federal government, the figure was held at $35 million. As a result of the continuing resolution passed by Congress in 1972, bilingual programs already in operation were to be funded again for 1973–74, but the preliminary proposals received by the Office of Education for 130 new projects could not be acted upon. These would have to be held in abeyance until Congress appropriated more than the $35 million already committed to the earlier projects.

Mr. Peña pointed out that, by the end of five years after their inception, the first 72 projects would be phased out as far as federal support was concerned and that this might free funds for new projects. The Office of Education requested funding for Bilingual Education for three more years and was hopeful that support would be forthcoming. Mr. Peña also mentioned that Title VII was not being put under Revenue Sharing, as some federal programs were, but suggested that the Title might at some time in the future be included in an omnibus bill. Though the beginnings might seem meager, in the actual percentage of children enrolled in bilingual programs throughout the country, Mr. Peña indicated his belief that the spin-offs from the projects had been tremendous and that the future potential of bilingual education in the United States was great.

Mr. Peña's optimistic predictions were borne out by the passage, after long debates in both houses of Congress, of the "Education Amendments of 1974." Section 105 of Title I of that Act provided for continued federal financial support for bilingual education through the end of fiscal year 1978. In addition to special funds for bilingual vocational programs, the amended Bilingual Education Act authorized the appropriation of $135 million for fiscal year 1975, $140 million for 1976, $150 million for 1977, and $160 million for 1978.

Notes

1. Theodore Andersson and Mildred Boyer, *Bilingual Schooling in the United States*, Southwest Educational Development Laboratory, Austin, Texas, 1970, pp. 18-19.

2. "Congressional Findings," Section 701, P.L. 90-247, Title VII, ESEA.

3. Ibid.

4. Ibid.

5. See Chap. 7 for list of states which have enacted legislation relating to bilingual education.

6. Ruth S. Lamb, *Mexican Americans: Sons of the Southwest*, Ocelot Press, Claremont, Calif., 1970, p. 68.

7. Andrew Rolle, *California, A History*, Thomas Y. Crowell, New York, 1963, pp. 299-306.

8. Personal communication from Professor George Sanchez, University of Texas. Also the *Encyclopaedia Britannica*, 13th ed., London, New York, 1926, vol. 18, p. 329, which traces the derivation of the word *Mexico* to the name of the Aztec war god, *Meh-sheet-li*, and notes that the Aztec tribes in the area of what is now Mexico were Meh-shi-ca (Mehshi-catl in the singular). The Spanish, in transliterating the name of their newly conquered land into their language spelled it *Mexico* (or Mehico), and pronounced it *Mehico* instead of Me*sh*ico or Me*ch*ico, as the Indians did.

9. The tribal Indian languages being used in bilingual projects in 1971-72 were Navajo, Pomo, Ute, Passamaquoddy, Crow, North Cheyenne, Cree, Keresan, Zuñi, Cherokee, Choctaw, and Lakota Sioux plus Eskimo and Indian languages in Alaska. Other native languages being used in programs were Chamorro on Guam, and Palau in the Trust Territory of the Pacific.

Opposition to Bilingual Education:
Arguments For and Against

2 Opposition to the concept of bilingual-bicultural education is vigorous in some quarters, whether expressed contentiously in editorials and "Letters to the Editor," or in unspoken but subtle resistance, such as lack of support and encouragement on the part of administrators and other teachers when bilingual programs are introduced in a school. The hard fact of money also enters the picture, and if school board members, budget makers, and influencers of public opinion are not in favor of bilingual teaching, it is difficult to set up or carry on bilingual projects. Some of the stated grounds for disapproval are valid and based on legitimate concerns; others arise from misunderstandings about the nature and purposes of bilingual instruction; in some cases, undoubtedly, prejudice or self-interest play a part.

In editorials inveighing against the use of any language but English in the schools, one finds statements like the following:

> ... the drive to learn English after arriving on these shores has all but disappeared with an assist, it seems, from public officialdom. Hospital emergency rooms identify men's and women's toilets in Spanish as well as English. ... Instructions to welfare recipients can be had both ways too. (We sometimes wonder whether the one-year residency requirement for welfare eligibility went far enough. Perhaps a passing acquaintance with the language in which the welfare check is made out ought to be another requirement.)
>
> But now comes the new twist. The school authorities of the U.S., Connecticut and Bridgeport (and, presumably, those from other towns) have cooperated in financing a bilingual teaching program. ... Its long-range goal is to make the youngsters fluent in English.
>
> This newspaper takes no issue with the intent of the program.
>
> But the pedagogians who cooked it up have overlooked one undeniable fact: Hundreds of thousands of youngsters from Europe, Asia and intermediate locations came to this country and became fluent in English without benefit of a multi-lingual

teacher. . . . In our opinion, the new program . . . amounts to a frill. . . . And, as such, the program is a waste of money.

Moreover, one might expect school authorities to be more concerned with imbuing a sense of pride in their new home country and its language in Spanish-speaking students, instead of tacitly encouraging them not to be in any great hurry to learn it.[1]

Such attitudes reveal a lack of knowledge of the particular circumstances that apply to the two major groups of Spanish-speaking residents in the United States today, little understanding of the way bilingual teaching functions, and a failure to comprehend the not necessarily reprehensible wishes of some members of ethnic minorities to retain to some degree their linguistic and cultural heritage.

There are teachers, administrators, and school board members who sincerely question the advisability of teaching children in two languages simultaneously, fearing confusion and inhibition in verbal expression and an impairment of cognitive development. Many also feel that since English is of paramount importance for full participation in life in this country, no time should be wasted on continuing at school with the child's first language (if it is not English) but that all effort should be concentrated on mastering English, realizing that the pupils will be speaking their mother tongue at home and with their companions all the other hours of the day. Attempts are being made through various types of research projects in different parts of the country to ascertain, by observation and testing, whether children who are learning English in bilingual classes acquire less of the new language than pupils learning English in the traditional all-English setting. It is difficult to make accurate measurements of comparative degrees of language learning, but most persons intimately involved in bilingual teaching believe that children in bilingual classes make as fast progress in learning English as those enrolled in the other classes. A paper presented at a language-teachers' convention in San Juan, Puerto Rico, in May 1973, by a representative of the Illinois Bilingual Education Service Center reported on an experiment conducted with mixed Cuban, Mexican-American, and Puerto Rican Spanish-speaking pupils in Illinois. An abstract of the findings contained the following favorable summary of the results of bilingual teaching for elementary school children:

Children enrolled in an Illinois bilingual program typically are exposed to approximately 25% less English during the school day than their counterparts in traditional school programs. This raises fears among some educators and parents that enrollment in a bilingual program might retard the learning of English as a Second Language (ESL). To probe this, data were collected in three cities during a five month interval in 1972 on the ESL achievement of 213 kindergarten through third grade Spanish-speaking children taught ESL within the context of a half-day bilingual program and 104 similar children reseiving ESL instruction as part of the traditional school curriculum. Analyses indicate no statistically significant difference in ESL achievement between the two groups. The implication of these results is that half-day bilingual programs do not inhibit English language achievement in primary-aged children.[2]

In other words, in addition to whatever positive advantages the bilingual classes offered in permitting the children to maintain and develop their knowledge of Spanish, there were no indications that a bilingual curriculum was detrimental to the children's acquisition of English. These findings are also in conformity with one theory of language (vocabulary) acquisition[3] namely, that what is important for children in increasing vocabulary is the learning or understanding of new ideas and concepts and that once this is accomplished, it is relatively easy to learn a new name for the concept, in another language. A corollary to this finding is that a person who has a wide vocabulary in one language is more likely to acquire the same type of vocabulary in another language. The converse of this theory has often been propounded in discussions regarding the desirability of developing fully a command of one's first language; many supporters of bilingual education believe that a limited vocabulary and poor verbal capacity in one language are likely to be repeated in the second language learned.

A comment sometimes heard about bilingual programs is that parents who want their children to be literate in their native tongue should take care of it themselves by organizing after-school classes (as some ethnic minorities do) and not expect the public schools to do it for them. This view ignores the fact that in the majority of cases, the parents of the children involved in the bilingual classes in public schools today are not in a position, for many reasons, economic or educational in nature, to arrange for this type of supplementary teaching. It is precisely because the parents or community cannot provide training toward literacy in the mother tongue that it may be desirable and in the public interest for the schools to do so.

As to the objection often made regarding the additional cost of bilingual teaching, it is true that, in the initial stages, a good deal of money is invested in organizing the programs, training staff, and preparing materials. Some administrators feel that the same amount of money spent on additional personnel for the regular curriculum or for more supplementary English classes might produce results equal to those of the bilingual classes, or better. One of the benefits of the five years of federal funding of bilingual projects should be a backlog of materials and trained personnel to carry on in those schools that elect to continue or increase their efforts in bilingual-bicultural teaching. It is possible, nevertheless, that planning and teaching a curriculum in two languages may well continue to be more costly than conducting classes solely in English. The ultimate criterion will have to be whether bilingual-bicultural education is carried out effectively and is worth the extra expense.

It is the opinion also of many persons, both within school systems and in society at large, that encouraging ethnic minorities to assert their differences and their special identities, in language use and distinctive cultural characteristics, tends to foment political divisiveness rather than to strengthen a feeling of national unity. The last thing America needs is problems like Italy's Alto Adige or Belgium's conflicts between French-speaking Walloons and Dutch-speaking Flemish. But in many cases of political animosities between different ethnic or linguistic groups around the world, it is the lack of consideration or respect given to members of minority groups by the larger society and their poorer economic condition that often cause the dissension, as the separatist movement in Canada attests. In situations where there already exists some feeling of estrangement between groups from differing linguistic and cultural backgrounds, a rapprochement can often be better accomplished by according status to minority groups as well as the power to make decisions affecting the society they live in, instead of trying to deny their existence or insisting that they submerge themselves within the majority group.

When a letter to the editor appeared in *The New York Times* during a period of controversy over bilingual education, deploring the movement as "a serious threat to the tranquillity of our city and an obstruction to the acceptance of our Puerto Rican neighbors into the mainstream of the life of our community,"[4] a Puerto Rican educator was heard to exclaim, "Tranquillity! What city has he been living in?" And to those old enough to remember a less-troubled era, it seems a very long time ago indeed that WNYC, the radio station of New York City, announced the time of twelve noon (and twelve midnight) with chimes and the words:

> Twelve noon [or midnight] by the century old chimes of historic City Hall. This is New York, the city of opportunity, where nearly eight million people live in peace and harmony and enjoy the benefits of democracy.

During a period of ethnic antagonisms and racial conflict, the phrasing was modified to "where nearly eight million people seek peace and harmony." And at some time before the present era, the chimes and the accompanying optimistic claim were quietly dropped altogether.

Other worries, sometimes legitimate and sometimes unfounded, have to do with the simple but fundamental problem of holding onto one's job. There is fear on the part of some English-speaking teachers that their jobs will be in jeopardy if bilingual teachers are hired. They reason that there are only so many jobs to go around, and if some are taken by special (often not fully certified) bilingual staff, their own positions are threatened. There is also the tendency on the part of parents and school board members from ethnic minorities to give preference to "their" people when they have the opportunity to hire personnel. In some cities and school districts, notably in New York City, this is an important issue; in others, it appears to be insignificant.

One suggestion, proposed by teachers-union representatives, which is certainly—inherently—not feasible, is that English-speaking teachers should be retained but trained to become bilingual, as though one could wave a wand over an adult monolingual teacher and by means of a few language lessons make such an English-speaking person proficient enough in a new language to be able to teach in it. It would not be a bad idea, indeed, for all teachers to know something of the language spoken as a mother tongue by their pupils and there are native English-speaking teachers who have studied other languages intensively and developed an extraordinary facility in them. Many such linguistically gifted persons are to be found working in the recently established bilingual projects. But it takes a considerable amount of time and effort, in addition to talent, to become anything approximating bilingual, if one begins the study of a new language as an adult.

Some of the objections to bilingual-bicultural education are petty or demagogic in nature, expressive of resentment on the part of members of earlier immigrant groups, whose attitude is, "nobody did this for *us. We* made it in English. Let *them* do it." There is certainly no dearth of examples in the highest positions in all areas of national life of successful and contented persons whose families have chosen the path of total assimilation into the Anglo-dominated society of the majority; in most periods and situations in American history in the past this has appeared to be an appropriate and desirable goal for the nation, and for most of the individuals concerned. But there is a growing awareness that the results of this melting-pot philosophy have not always been perfect or happy solutions for all members of the minority groups involved. When one acquires a wide acquaintance among the teachers and administrators who are working most enthusiastically and idealistically in the field of bilingual education, one is struck by how many come from earlier immigrant ethnic minorities who were not encouraged to maintain their ancestral language and now regret it. Many of them indicate that they don't want to see happen to today's immigrant children what happened to them or their parents.

It is interesting to note how many of the smaller ethnic minorities —now that the barrier of prejudice has been breached and it is no longer suspect to demonstrate affection for one's "foreign" roots—are showing revived interest in their ancestral languages and cultures. Increasing participation in ethnically oriented churches such as the Ukrainian, Rumanian, Greek, and Armenian is being attributed more to the attraction of their cultural aspects than to religious devotion. And the study of some of the more obscure languages is being pursued where pockets of their former nationals exist. Arlington and Watertown, Massachusetts, for instance, at the instigation of the Armenian communities, in 1971 included Armenian as one of the foreign languages taught in high school, with 41 students in Watertown and 18 in Arlington studying the language in 1973. On the university level, the University of California at Los Angeles has established courses in Armenian civilization and language, granting both master's and doctor's degrees in the field.[5]

Some sociologists and observers of the acculturation process among various ethnic minorities in the United States have noted that, traditionally, the second generation of immigrant families have rejected or ignored their linguistic and ethnic origins, while the third generation often shows renewed interest in its ancestral heritage. The proponents of bilingual-bicultural education tend to believe that this "generation gap" can be avoided and that there is no need for anyone to deny or reject his parents' background while becoming assimilated, to whatever degree he wishes, into the larger picture of the national society. It should also be remembered that for the two major Spanish-speaking groups in the United States today, there are always the special circumstances that reinforce the ties to their ethnic and linguistic origins; for Mexican Americans, the proximity of their (or their forebears') homeland; for Puerto Ricans, the constant renewal of attachment to their native island by frequent visits or return migration.

On the subject of teaching Anglo children a foreign (or second) language, claims are sometimes made that the FLES (Foreign Languages in Elementary School) programs, put into practice in many schools in recent years, can do a better job than the bilingual classes. It is still too early to tell how successful the bilingual projects will be, in the long run, in their goal of giving Anglo pupils fluency in a second language. It is relatively easy, under either system—FLES or bilingual programs—for young children to acquire a good pronunciation and a familiarity with simple expressions in a new language. But it takes continuity and progression in language teaching and language learning for pupils to develop a knowledge in depth of a new language if they are not living in an environment where it is the dominant language of the society and essential to them in daily life. The majority of the bilingual projects to date have started in kindergarten classes and progressed to third or fourth grade and have involved chiefly pupils in the lowest grades. The Anglo pupils of this age group seem to be making a good start on learning Spanish, French, Portuguese, or whatever other language they are being exposed to, but only time will tell whether they will continue to build on the foundation which they have acquired and increase their knowledge of their second language.

FLES classes have usually been offered to fifth- and occasionally third-grade pupils. Some school systems begin the study of foreign languages in the seventh grade. Any evaluation of the relative effectiveness of FLES and bilingual programs must take into account the fact that not all the pupils who enroll in FLES courses continue with them for a second or third year. Sometimes it appears that all that is accomplished is to take the bloom off the idea of learning a new language, leaving the student with less enthusiasm to take it up at a later date. From the point of view of continuity and relevance, it may be that bilingual classes have an edge over the FLES approach—though bilingual classes, too, are subject to attrition from the high mobility of the pupil population found in many of the areas where bilingual projects are in operation.

One mistake made in many FLES programs was to believe that, since babies acquire their first language by imitating what they hear (disregarding for the moment the more complex theories of language acquisition put forward by abstract theoreticians), all that was necessary to assure that Anglo pupils would learn a *second* language was for them to listen to and memorize typical dialogues in the language. In many cases, the realization came all too late that repeating certain set phrases and sentences—of which the students understood neither the structure nor the meaning—was not sufficient to develop in nine, ten, or eleven-year-old pupils comprehension of a foreign language and the ability to communicate in it. Out of this misconception concerning language learning after babyhood arose the often-quoted joke about the FLES student traveling abroad in the country of his newly acquired foreign language. Chided by his mother for not being able to speak or understand the language or to communicate with the natives, he complained, "It's not my fault. None of these people know the other half of the dialogues !"

Within the ranks of bilingual teachers, there are variations in attitudes and procedures, and in the degree of commitment they exhibit in regard to teaching Anglo children a second language. Some of the teachers indicate that their major concern is the well-being of the children from the minority group, especially if these children come from particularly disadvantaged backgrounds. In certain cases the teachers feel they should devote most of their time and attention to the children who have the greatest need, believing that the generally more privileged Anglo children will have future opportunities to study foreign languages. The majority of bilingual teachers, however, seem eager to promote the knowledge and use of "their" language among Anglo pupils, and achieve a good deal of success in pursuing this goal. One major problem is maintaining in the bilingual classrooms balanced proportions of children whose dominant language is English and of those who speak the "other" language, whatever it may be. Initially, federal guidelines emphasized the desirability of including Anglo pupils in all bilingual classes with those from other ethnic groups; however, many schools where bilingual projects have been established have few English-speaking pupils on their rosters, and if Anglo children do not exist, they can hardly be placed in the bilingual classes. There is some busing of children to schools where bilingual programs are in operation, but in most cases this is done to bring in pupils who don't speak English and urgently need either intensive ESL (English as a Second Language) or bilingual teaching rather than to place Anglo children in the programs. One also discovers that among the pupils classified as "English-dominant" in bilingual classes there are many who are not monolingual and not from Anglo families. They are children who speak English, and, to some extent, the native language of their parents but are more fluent in English.

It should also be mentioned that FLES classes are usually restricted to a limited and carefully selected number of pupils—those with high academic credentials. In the bilingual classes there is no such restriction, and, in fact, the makeup of the (federally funded) bilingual classes is supposed to represent a cross section of the school population. The bilingual projects, therefore, offer to some Anglo children who would probably not otherwise be enrolled in a foreign language course an opportunity to be exposed to and learn, to the best of their ability, the other language spoken by so many of their schoolmates.

There has always been variation in the degree of success achieved in FLES (as in most foreign-language) classes, accounted for—one can speculate—by the gifts (including charisma) and qualifications of the teachers as well as the caliber of the students. Since motivation is an especially important factor in learning a second language, much depends on the ability of a teacher to maintain the interest of pupils when the first easy acquisition of a few key phrases is over with and the going gets rougher, requiring concentration, determination, and persistence. The same conditions apply, to be sure, to pupils learning languages in bilingual classes, and the success achieved varies from program to program.

Regarding the role of the teacher in motivating pupils to study foreign languages, Dr. Leo Benardo, chairman of the department of foreign languages for the New York City school system, had words of caution and advice for teachers attending a gathering of the Association of Foreign Language Teachers of Connecticut in New Haven in the spring of 1973. Dr. Benardo pointed out that any teacher who subscribes to the theory—ever more prevalent in educational circles—that true learning results from a pupil's desire to learn, rather than from a teacher's insistence on teaching, must guard against the temptation to "show off" in the classroom, that is, using the classroom as a platform for displaying extraordinary linguistic talents and holding center stage before an admiring audience of students. These tendencies Dr. Benardo confessed to having shared until fairly recently in his teaching career with many teachers of foreign languages. Though the histrionic approach can be effective and has probably stimulated certain types of students in many situation to emulate their teacher (it is common knowledge that gifted linguists often have a bit of the "ham actor" in them), Dr. Benardo pled the cause of shaping the curriculum and instructional methods to suit the actual needs, capacities, and interests of the particular students involved in any foreign-language class—even when this means forsaking long-cherished standards or preconceived notions of what students should be *made* to learn. Dr. Benardo admitted that he had reached these conclusions only after much soul searching as to what might be best and proper for the students; he assured his listeners that if they thought he or other traditionalists in language teaching had been able to arrive at such decisions without a hard struggle of conscience, they were greatly mistaken.

Though Dr. Benardo's responsibilities do not involve the bilingual programs in New York City, his remarks have application to the concepts underlying bilingual-bicultural education. There is likely to be immediacy and relevance in the class work for pupils learning a second language in a bilingual setting. And since most teachers in the bilingual programs are native speakers of the languages they teach, they tend to be natural in their use of it and less likely to substitute the charismatic approach for sounder and soberer ways of helping students. (If the new policy statement appearing in the Bilingual Act of 1974 results in revised guidelines prohibiting or discouraging the teaching of a second language to English-speaking pupils enrolled in federally funded bilingual projects, all the above considerations will become—most regrettably, in the opinion of this author—purely academic and irrelevant.)

One complaint sometimes heard about bilingual teachers in the public school programs is that they have an inadequate command of the English language or a poor standard of pronunciation. There is often justification for this criticism. Even though such teachers are not responsible for the English components of the curriculum, the children do hear them speak the language, and often they don't provide a satisfactory model. This is a problem which should receive greater attention, with increased emphasis on more training in the English language for those bilingual teachers who are deficient in it.

On this point, a stickler for purity in language might justifiably note that many a monolingual Anglo teacher today also falls short of what a few decades ago would have been considered an acceptable standard in syntax, style, and diction. At one time, candidates for college degrees were required to meet certain minimum requirements in language use, both written and spoken, and to take remedial courses if they failed to pass muster. It was a usual practice for prospective teachers, as well as other persons training for professional careers, to attend classes in public speaking, and if necessary, in "speech correction." An ability to speak one's native language correctly and effectively was considered essential. The concept of "standard" English, or indeed a standard form of any language—on which such requirements were based—has fallen into disrepute as smacking of elitism (now a word with only pejorative connotations) or discrimination based on social-class distinctions. The widely held, and perfectly tenable, position that one regional accent or idiom is as good as another and that such variety enriches a language has been misconstrued or misapplied to suggest that anything goes and that there should be no standards of excellence whatsoever applied to language use.

The subject of variant or non-standard types of language and what to do about them in a school setting is a touchy one, whether it concerns the mixtures of Spanish and English called Spanglish (when spoken by Puerto Ricans) and Pocho (in the case of Mexican Americans); a Cajun, Creole, or Canadian French patois; or even the contemporary concept of "Black English" as a distinct language. In the sociological climate that prevails at present, anyone who attempts to discuss the subject objectively and with anything less than total acceptance or permissiveness toward the use of non-standard forms of language in any and all situations runs the risk of being attacked as socially snobbish, politically undemocratic, and educationally autocratic. Nevertheless, it is a subject that should be brought up and explored, since most teachers and directors of bilingual programs in public schools in the United States have to make decisions as to how best to deal with the variant types of native languages spoken by many of their pupils. What these variant forms are and how project directors and teachers handle them will be discussed in greater detail in later chapters, those devoted to descriptions of the bilingual programs for specific ethnic and linguistic groups. Whatever the dialect—or type of non-standard language used by children—the most prevalent attitude in the bilingual projects under discussion here seems to be, "We accept it. We don't criticize a child for using it, but we don't *teach* it in the classroom." There are, however, occasional, wide deviations from this approach, with the degree of insistence on granting equal value and status to the dialect form of the language frequently being in direct proportion to the sociological militancy of the proponents.

This author, while visiting a Spanish-English bilingual classroom in a town in Arizona, noticed the word *Pocho* written on the blackboard and was told that during one half hour of the school day, the pupils were allowed and encouraged to speak this language of the *barrio*. The variations from standard Spanish included not only the use of English words interspersed with the Spanish vocabulary but also the use of English verbs conjugated in the Spanish manner *(yo fixo, tu fixes, el fixe)*. It was a bit startling and brought to mind the disapproval normally felt in the past for such grammatical bastardy in speaking German-English as, "Die cow has über die fence gejumped and has die potatoes gedamaged." Professor Ernesto Galarza in his touching and informative book about his childhood, *Barrio Boy*, describes his mother's insistence that he avoid such mixing of languages. "But at *pocho* talk my mother drew the line. . . . Such words as *yarda* for yard, *yonque* for junk, *donas* for doughnuts, *borde* for meals shocked her and I was drilled to avoid them"[6] (when speaking Spanish). Referring to the distinctions made at that time (early in the century) between the terms *pochos* and *chicanos*, he explains that the latter were new arrivals from Mexico and that the former were partially Americanized Mexicans, immigrants of longer standing, or Mexicans born in the United States.

> Crowded as it was the *colonia* found a place for these *chicanos*, the name by which we called an unskilled worker born in Mexico and just arrived in the United States. The *chicanos* were fond of identifying themselves by saying they had just arrived from *el macizo*, by which they meant the solid Mexican homeland, the good native earth. . . . They remained, as they said of themselves, *pura raza. . . . pochos* were Mexicans who had grown up in California, probably even been born in the United States. They had learned to speak English of sorts, and could still speak Spanish, also of sorts. They

knew much more about Americans than we did. . . . The *chicanos* and the *pochos* had certain feelings about one another. Concerning the *pochos*, the *chicanos* suspected that they considered themselves too good for the barrio, but were not, for some reason, good enough for the Americans. Toward the *chicanos*, the *pochos* acted superior, amused at our confusions but not especially interested in explaining them to us. In our family when I forgot my manners, my mother would ask me if I was turning *pochito*."[7]

In handling the problem of non-standard dialects in school situations, two diametrically opposed principles seem to be involved: one, that great care must always be taken not to damage a child's self-esteem or lessen his respect for his family and community by indicating that the language he has learned from them is unacceptable and the other, that, if one of the purposes of public education is to increase the knowledge of students and to broaden their horizons so that they will be at ease and able to function effectively not only within the limits of a particular neighborhood but also in a wider and more complex world, then, at school, children should be given every opportunity to gain a command of the standard, universally accepted and understood forms of whatever languages they are learning. If they wish to use Spanish, for instance, in all the countries where it is spoken, the less regional their accent and syntax and the more widely prevailing their vocabulary, the better it will serve them. If they substitute *el lunche* for *el almuerzo* (lunch) or *el rufo* for *el techo* (roof), in a country where English is not spoken, they may not be understood. If some non-standard type of French such as Haitian Creole or Louisiana Cajun is the mother tongue of the pupils, then, using that as a basis, they should be encouraged to acquire a knowledge of the kind of French that is widely used in the French-speaking parts of the world. If a student whose mother tongue is Canadian French responds to *merci* with *bienvenu*, instead of *de rien, il n'y a pas de quoi* or *je vous en prie*, he should at least be aware that this idiom in the Canadian patois is a translation into French of the English phrase, "You're welcome," and that it is not used in most other French-speaking countries, where *soyez le bienvenu* represents the other meaning of the English word, as in "You are welcome here, we are glad to see you." The crucial factor would seem to be knowledge about the kind of language one is speaking so that the speaker can make conscious decisions.

It might be pointed out that no matter what kind of language one is using, there are always many different styles or degrees of formality adopted as a matter of course in speaking or writing, depending on the situation and the personal relationships of the people involved. Everyone uses a different style of language in addressing a father, a child, a superior in authority, a lover, a companion, a stranger, or an audience in a formal situation. A presentation of these aspects of language can be one approach to teaching children the possibility of using different types of language.

The director of a successful and highly regarded bilingual project for Puerto Rican pupils in Springfield, Massachusetts, when asked how she handled the problem of mixing up Spanish and English vocabulary, responded that she didn't criticize the children while they were doing it but tried to set the proper example herself, avoiding being too rigid. Though the pupils often referred to *el lunche* instead of *el almuerzo*, she almost always used *almuerzo*, but once in a while, with a twinkle in her eye to show she was doing it for fun, she would also say *el lunche* in talking to the children.

Theodore Andersson, a respected authority on bilingual education and a professor of romance languages whose credentials are impeccable at all levels of teaching from graduate-level university courses to early childhood education, when asked his opinion about how to draw the line between failing to set proper standards for pupils in language use, on the one hand, and doing damage to their self-esteem on the other, had no hesitation in replying that in case of doubt with young children he would always opt for forgetting the rigid standard, temporarily, rather than risk undermining a child's confidence. The secret probably lies, as in so many other situations in teaching, in the exercise of tact, the possession of real liking and affection for the students, and applying common sense to the situation at hand. Children from the best-educated families, no matter what language they speak, constantly make mistakes in grammar and word usage as they are learning to talk, and parents can either correct the mistakes gently by providing the proper model for the children to follow or create inhibitions and emotional problems by commenting in only a negative way. We have all seen children who have been confused or made into stutterers by constant nagging criticism of the way they speak, from insensitive parents. But it is quite simple, and usually effective, if a child says, for instance, "I *breaked* it," for a parent to say, "Oh, you *broke* your toy; that's too bad. Here's something else to play with," or some such uninsistent presentation of the correct past tense of an irregular verb. It is perfectly possible for a teacher to do the same kind of thing in a classroom, with young pupils.

Whatever the attitudes and opinions of bilingual teachers and project directors on the subject of non-standard language, whether the decision is merely to accept it from young children or to encourage or discourage its retention for use in certain settings, it seems to this writer that there can be no doubt about the necessity of setting as a goal for students in bilingual classes developing a command of the standard, generally accepted form of both English and the other language being used and taught. If one of the justifications, as well as aims, of bilingual teaching in public schools is to develop a reservoir of competent speakers of many different languages in the United States by taking advantage of the linguistic resources represented by the varied ethnic groups in the country, surely attention should be paid to setting standards which will assure that students will be able to speak and write a type of language which will be understood and accepted in other parts of the world. Only thus equipped would they be able to work successfully abroad.

Similar comments can also be made about Black English and the controversy concerning the extent to which it should be accepted as a substitute for, or equal partner of, standard English for some black Americans in the United States. Whatever the merits of Dillard's[8] research and theories on the subject (and many of his beliefs are certainly open to question) and admitting the fascination and fun of any kind of linguistic detective work, an objective observer must say that a good deal of nonsense is being bandied about in some academic circles concerning Black English. At a language-teachers' conference in San Juan, Puerto Rico, in May 1973, one workshop panel was devoted to, or taken over by, a proposal put forth by several (black) teachers—all speaking standard English—that Black English should be permissible and accepted at all stages and levels of academic work up to and including the writing of Ph.D. theses and that it should be left up to the students to decide themselves whether and when they would choose to use standard English. The proposition was concurred in and encouraged by a white college professor who was leading the workshop. This idea was proposed not as a beginning step for young children in making an adjustment and transfer in their early school years but as a substitute at any time for the standard form of the language, ignoring the fact that standard, not Black, English is the lingua franca of the English-speaking world. A disinterested eavesdropper could only wonder why the teachers who were composing their manifesto in standard English, which they could handle effectively, wished to deny to less-privileged black pupils the advantages that they themselves possessed by having a command of the English language.

There are worldwide precedents for an educated person's retaining fluency in a regional or class dialect while at the same time possessing a knowledge and command of a standard version of the same language. In Italy the variations in language are great from province to province; Neapolitan or Sicilian dialects will not be understood by northern Italians. It may be that an educated Sicilian or Neapolitan will be able to understand and perhaps to speak the regional dialect if he wishes, but he will certainly also speak the classic kind of Italian that is understood by educated Italians everywhere. An *un*educated Sicilian or Neapolitan probably will not, though television and radio are having an impact in increasing the familiarity of all Italians with a more standard, though not necessarily Tuscan, version of Italian. In Germany many well-educated persons speak a strongly regional dialect at home or with persons from the same province but have a perfect command of "high German," which they use with people who do not understand their provincial language. German-speaking Swiss, also, always speak Schwyzertütsch with family and friends but will switch at a moment's notice to the use of standard German with any other German-speaking person who is not Swiss. (In both of the latter cases the written languages are identical, except for some variations in vocabulary; the non-standard aspect is the pronunciation.) Many educated Viennese, too, can switch from standard German (with Austrian overtones) to a widely variant Viennese dialect when they are talking with uneducated persons who speak the dialect.

In the long history of immigration in the United States, a great percentage of those coming to this country have been drawn from among the poorer and therefore less well educated segments of the population in the countries of their origin. With the exception of political refugees, this has usually been the reason for their emigrating. They have looked to the United States as a place where they might have a chance for a better life. Because of their geographic or social origins, they have often spoken a strongly regional or non-standard kind of language. And learning a standard form of language has traditionally been one of the factors aiding upward social mobility here, as in all countries.

If upward mobility, too, has become suspect in some circles today as indicating disloyalty to one's origins or the assumption of the worst kind of materialistic false "values" often attributed to or blamed on the middle class, in a truer educational or developmental sense, upward mobility can be viewed as healthy and desirable. It is basically what learning is all about. To those for whom the term or concept has acquired a bad connotation, it might be suggested that we are all engaged in a kind of upward mobility—not necessarily social, but human—from infancy on, in gaining control over our own lives. Ignorance is the barrier, and knowledge the key, to the better life, not necessarily in the acquisition of possessions but in the ability to make informed choices about how one wants to live. A baby who can walk has the advantage over one who can't. One who can dress and feed himself is in a better position than one who hasn't yet reached that stage of development. It is always hoped that the process of education will result in a broadening of knowledge, a deepening of understanding, and a refining of perceptions—and perhaps the acquisition along the way of enough wisdom to help in shaping one's life to suit one's particular needs and desires. It should not be considered treason to one's origins to take advantage of educational opportunities to try to make a better or fuller life for oneself than one's parents may have had. Most parents who have had little schooling are happy to see their children given a chance for more, and they are often the most positive in wanting the schools to set standards of excellence for their children to meet.

It may well be that the future of bilingual education in the United States will depend on what kind of standards are set for pupils in the bilingual classes. The amount of support, financial and theoretical, for bilingual teaching will be determined by what the results appear to be; the academic accomplishments of the students in subjects which they have been taught through the medium of bilingual settings and techniques; and how well those students speak, read, and write the two languages they have been learning—their mother tongue and English.

Notes

1. *Connecticut Sunday Herald,* September 1971.

2. K. Balasubramonian, "Do Bilingual Education Programs Inhibit English Language Achievement? A report on an Illinois Experiment," pre-publication draft, paper presented at the Seventh Annual Convention, Teachers of English to Speakers of Other Languages (TESOL), May 9–13, 1973, San Juan, Puerto Rico.

3. Suggested by the Johnson O'Connor Research Foundation, Human Engineering Laboratory, Bulletin 106, 347 Beacon Street, Boston, Mass. 02116, but also a theory widely held by others.

4. *New York Times,* 2 September 1972.

5. *Wall Street Journal,* 11 July 1973.

6. Ernesto Galarza, *Barrio Boy,* University of Notre Dame Press, Notre Dame, Ind. 1971, p. 235.

7. Ibid., pp. 200, 207.

8. J. L. Dillard, *Black English,* Random House, New York, 1972.

A Glimpse into Some
Bilingual Classrooms

3 Bilingual classes for public school children whose common language heritage is French are or have been in operation in such geographically and culturally disparate environments as Madawaska, Maine; Greenville, New Hampshire; and Derby, Vermont; Breaux Bridge and Lafayette, Louisiana; and Haitian enclaves in New York City and Boston. Not only are the communities in which these students live very different in history and development but so is the kind of French spoken by these widely separated groups, varying greatly in type and degree of dialect. In northern New England the children are white and the patois is Canadian, with its seventeenth-century overtones in vocabulary and pronunciation and the many omissions, abbreviations, and distortions that differentiate it from the language spoken in France. In Louisiana there are both black and white pupils who speak either Cajun (Acadian), Louisiana Creole, or a Negro dialect referred to as *"Gumbo,"* while black Haitian immigrants have their own version of Creole French.

The fathers and grandfathers of the French-speaking pupils in northern New England left Canada in the nineteenth or early twentieth century to work in textile mills or other factories in Maine, New Hampshire, and Vermont, sometimes recruited by the mills, brought in by the busload, and housed in mill-owned properties. Though many of the mills have closed, the families remain. Most of the children of these originally French families speak some French and some English but often have a limited command of both, which in the view of many teachers and educational specialists has often been a handicap in their intellectual development and academic achievements in the past. French-Canadian pupils have tended to drop out of school earlier, and fewer of them have gone on to college or to advanced university study compared with the school population as a whole.

Though there have never been serious problems of discrimination or hostility against French-Canadian Americans, their language has set them apart from English-speaking residents in New England communities. In small towns where much social life revolves around church affiliations, the division into Catholic and Protestant has also emphasized the separation. French-Canadian families have often felt not fully accepted, though Anglos are not always aware of this and would deny any such conscious intent on their part. In any case, inadequate or accented English has marked French-Canadian Americans as "different." One of the aims of the bilingual program in Greenville, New Hampshire, which was the first federally funded (Title VII) French-English bilingual project in the United States, started in the fall of 1968, was to encourage the French-speaking children to take pride in their ancestral language and to preserve and improve their command of French, while at the same time instilling respect among Anglo students for bilingualism.

Greenville, New Hampshire, is a small town of about 2,000 inhabitants, with 175 children in the first four grades. (From fifth grade on, pupils are bused to a regional school in a neighboring town, New Ipswich.) About one-third of the pupils have two French-speaking parents, one-third have one parent of French-Canadian extraction, and the remaining third are Anglos, or completely English-speaking, whatever their original ethnic classification may have been. In 1971 all 175 children in the first four grades were enrolled in bilingual classes and French and English-speaking pupils alike were learning in and studying two languages. Some children in the town formerly attended Sacred Heart parochial school, which has gone out of existence as a Catholic educational institution, though the white clapboard building, still bearing the name Sacred Heart, now houses some of the public school classes.

A visitor to the Greenville schools in the winter of 1971 could drop into a fourth-grade classroom and listen to a lesson in New England geography being conducted in French—with students discussing the mountains, seacoast, borders to the north and south, and the resources and products of the area—and then writing about their lesson in French. The teacher, being bilingual, could explain a point in English to any Anglo pupil who had trouble understanding the French, though most could understand since they had had bilingual teaching for the previous three years. A third-grade class, on the same morning, had been taken over by a special teacher, a young Anglo woman who had studied French and spoke it well, for a lesson in music. While the English-speaking teacher observed, the bilingual teacher displayed and talked about musical instruments (the oboe or hautbois was a logical choice) and then led the class in singing traditional French and American folk songs and rounds (*"Il était une Bergère,"* "Row, Row, Row Your Boat," "Oh Susanna," *"Frère Jacques,"* and the like). Up in the Sacred Heart building, on top of a little hill, a kindergarten class enthusiastically greeted a young man, a graduate student at a college in the area, as he strode into the room with big round color cards under his arm, sat on the floor, and gathered the children around him. He then taught the children the names of colors and how to make simple questions and answers about them in French by playing guessing and hiding games with the cards. The children were obviously delighted by their language lesson. The English-speaking classroom teacher was of French-Canadian origin, but had been doubtful of her qualifications to teach in French. She was learning techniques and gaining confidence in her own ability to make use of her knowledge of French by observing an experienced bilingual instructor.

The director of the Greenville bilingual program was born in Canada, came to the United States at the age of 18, and attended college in Denver. He has lived and taught French in Colorado, Connecticut, and several other places. When asked his origin, he replied with humor, "Oh, yes, I'm a Canuck." He understands children who feel uncomfortable about being French-speaking and of Canadian origin in an Anglo-dominated society and indicated that he was happy to be involved in a bilingual teaching project, which he believed would do much to counteract prejudice while also promoting a knowledge of French. One of the teachers, a French war bride from Bayonne, recalled some of her difficulties in adjusting and being accepted on her arrival. She has been an enthusiastic teacher of French to her mixed classes of French and Anglo pupils and has expected Anglo teachers also to seize every opportunity to help students improve their knowledge of English.

In addition to the bilingual teaching program, there has also been in Greenville a federally supported project, which was established in 1971 to provide liaison among the several French-English bilingual programs in different parts of the country. The director of this *Service de Liaison des Projets Bilingues Français-Anglais*, was born in the United States of French-Canadian parents and grew up speaking both French and English. He claims that even at the university level, at Harvard, he was aware of prejudice against Canadian French and that it was not until he had eliminated all trace of his Canadian accent that knowing French became an asset rather than a liability. He has taught modern languages and literature at several colleges, but, being interested in the concept of bilingual education for younger children, he has enjoyed being involved in the work of the liaison office. He has organized conferences in Louisiana, New Hampshire, and northern Maine at which project directors and teachers have been able to exchange ideas and to listen to lectures by specialists in the field of bilingual education.

The offices of the two federally financed projects in Greenville in 1971 shared quarters in a new small shopping complex in the middle of town where they were very visible, with signs on the door, *Mascenic Bi-lingual*

Project (Mascenic being a composite name made up at the time of the consolidation of the upper grades of Greenville with those of neighboring towns), and *Service de Liaison des Projets Bilingues Français-Anglais.* When English classes were scheduled for parents (conducted on a voluntary basis by the teachers in the program), announcements were also posted here. Greenville is a rather attractive place, with the usual mill pond and small dam found in most New England factory towns, but it is hilly with streets that climb and curve instead of the one straight main road leading in and out of town, characteristic of so many small American towns. There are several attractive old red-brick houses, once the residences of the mill owners or other well-to-do people, now converted for double or triple occupancy but still retaining their former outward appearance. Whatever the French heritage in Greenville, it does not seem to extend to the public eating places, where cheeseburgers are more readily available than specimens of *la cuisine française.* One priority of the bilingual program perhaps should have been to organize cooking classes in the schools as part of the cultural aspect of the project and to recruit some of the French-Canadian grandmothers to teach them.

The bilingual projects involving the largest number of pupils from French-speaking families anywhere in the country are those in Aroostook County in northern Maine, where during the 1973–74 school year nearly one thousand children were enrolled in bilingual classes. Franco-Americans, as American-resident French Canadians are sometimes called, make up as much as 95 percent of the population of some towns, such as Madawaska, Maine, just across the border from Canada, at the end of the bridge spanning the St. John River—the boundary line between the two countries at this point. In 1970 bilingual teaching was initiated in Maine schools in Frenchville, St. Agathe, and Madawaska and was extended to Caribou and Van Buren in succeeding years.

One of the important aspects of the Title VII projects here, as in other parts of the United States, has been the preparation of materials in the two languages of the program, dealing with the history and the life of the section of the country in which the pupils live, to be used as reading primers, supplementary social studies texts, mathematics workbooks, and the like. Books have been written by staff members dealing with maple-sugar production, potato farming, tobogganing and skating, and the history of the French and English involvement in the area, including the forced emigration of the French-speaking Acadians to Louisiana. (Some local French families trace their ancestry to the Acadians who went only as far as this part of Maine.) Included are also a few songs and dialect stories with the French-Canadian pronunciation transcribed phonetically.

In the activities going on in the bilingual classrooms, one sees many examples of individualized and self-directed instruction. Children use the "Language Master" in practicing reading by inserting cards with words printed on them and listening to the spoken versions of the cards, which come from the machine; they handle filmstrip projectors, which illustrate a story as it is being told, in either French or English; they tape their own voices and play them back, or spell out words and sentences on typewriters. Federal funds have made it possible for the schools to purchase such equipment. In many similar projects in different parts of the country, classrooms are being transformed from teacher-dominated enclosures, where all students are exposed to the same one-track lesson, to places where much self-directed learning is going on.

Aroostook County, Maine, unlike the part of the state immediately west and south of it, which is heavily forested, is mostly rolling farm country with potato fields stretching far and wide. The population ranges from fairly prosperous to rural poor, and most of the schools have a healthy mix and variation in the socio-economic backgrounds of the pupils. In this potato country, school begins in mid-August for grades 7 through 12 in order to permit a three-week break during the potato harvest in September so that pupils can help in the fields. This is not, as some commenters from afar have proclaimed in shocked tones, the exploitation of the young and an example of unacceptable child labor "in this day and age," but comes closer to what many observers of American life indicate is missing in the growing-up process for youth in America—a chance to participate in the work of the community. The hard digging is done by machine, the potatoes gathered by hand and placed in baskets left beside the field rows to be hauled away by tractor truck. The gatherers come from all kinds of families, and the entire community is involved in the harvest during the relatively short period when extra hands are needed. Young people have a chance to earn some money, working only as many hours as they wish or their parents permit. As a system for solving a short-term need, it is surely more reasonable and socially healthy than importing migrant farm laborers for the brief harvest time.

Classes resume after the "potato recess," as it used to be called before the fancier term "harvest vacation" was coined, and everyone settles down again to the business of learning. The atmosphere in the classrooms in both lower and upper grades in the area, as in other New England towns, seems more conducive to learning than in many large urban schools, with order, though not rigidity, being the normal state of affairs. Staffing the bilingual classes are many teachers of French-Canadian background, those who overcame whatever handicap their language duality may have held for them at the time when the use of

French was discouraged. There are also a good many Catholic sisters teaching in the schools, who as certified teachers were hired by the public school system when parochial schools closed down.

The aim of the bilingual programs in the St. John Valley is, like those in other parts of the United States, to help pupils preserve and improve their knowledge of their ancestral tongue while at the same time gaining a firm command of English. In those towns where Anglos make up a substantial part of the population, the goals are also to develop respect for bilingualism, a knowledge of French on the part of the English-speaking students, and an understanding and appreciation of the history and the cultural traditions of both groups.

The recent Haitian immigrants, who have settled in New York City, Boston, and other urban centers in the East, come from a cultural and linguistic background very different from that of the New England speakers of French. They vary among themselves in their command of standard French, but, in any case, no matter what their educational and social backgrounds, they all know and at times use Haitian Creole, a language that evolved from French but is markedly variant in syntax, vocabulary, and pronunciation from its original source. It is incomprehensible to an Anglo who speaks "school French" and probably to any native of France today, as well. Haitian Creole contains some of the same archaic vocabulary found in the Canadian patois, such as *fret* for *froid*; has an admixture of Spanish, English, and some African words (some researchers, e.g., the Comhaires, claim to have found as many as 4,000);[1] and makes use of extreme abbreviations and distortions. A standard French sentence, such as, "Elle est la mère du professeur de mes enfants" ("She is the mother of my children's teacher"), would be rendered in Haitian Creole—according to a Haitian aide in one of the bilingual classes who wrote down the phonetic transcription—as "Cé manman professeu ti-moun moin yo" (*ti* comes from *petit*; *moun* from *monde*). This is decipherable as "It is mama teacher little person mine," with the *yo*, according to sources consulted later, coming from an African plural suffix. It is what an amateur linguist might call "pidgin" French. (Some linguists distinguish between a pidgin and a creole, defining as creole a pidgin that has been taken over by a group and developed as its mother tongue.)[2]

Coming from a tropical island, the Haitian children, who are black, find themselves in Northern cities where few people speak French, where no one outside of their enclaves understands Haitian Creole, and where black-skinned persons are a minority rather than a majority—as on their native island—and are often subject to discrimination. The first French-English bilingual project aimed at helping Haitian pupils in their new school situation was set up at P.S. 9, an elementary school on the upper West Side of Manhattan in 1971. In its first year of operation about 35 children, in one kindergarten and one first-grade class, were involved. The classes were located in adjacent rooms, one intended and equipped for French instruction, the other for English. The children moved from one room to the other on alternate days, studying math and science in English; social studies in French; and art, music, and language arts in both languages, taught by Haitian and American teachers and aides, all of whom spoke both French and English. In the second year of operation of the bilingual project, a second-grade class was added, and in the fall of 1973, the bilingual teaching program was advanced to the third-grade level. The scenes in either the French or English class periods are reminiscent of any first-, second-, or third-grade classroom, except that the pupils learn to read first in French, if they are more fluent in that language, and continue to study some of the curriculum in French and some in English. They sing songs, play games, and listen to and retell stories in French and English to develop verbal skills. In one corner of the first-grade room, small groups of children—three or four at a time—sit with the teacher, learning to sound out French syllables. Others make a train on the floor of French word cards, which read *dans, est, l'avion, il, rouge*, and so forth, laying the cards out in proper sequence to form correct sentences, such as, "Il est dans l'avion rouge et marron," which they then read to an aide. In another room, while the teacher and the aide work with individuals or small groups of pupils, other children paint, play games, and match number cards with word cards showing the spelled-out form for the numerals, in French or English.

A Haitian-born French teacher, who speaks standard French, excellent English, and also the Creole dialect, stresses the point that her pupils speak Creole and standard French to varying degrees but that they all need to gain a better command of a formal, universally understood form of French. In helping them develop their verbal skills, first orally and then in writing, she is teaching them many things about the French language. In the English-language components of the curriculum, the pupils acquire fluency and competence in English, though in most cases they do not begin to read in English until they have learned to read in French. Though the children will continue to speak Creole in settings in which it is the common language, at home or with other Haitians, it is for the most part eliminated in their school situation; in the bilingual classes they are learning to speak "standard" French.

A mixed first- and second-grade class, in the "French day," was divided into four reading groups: two were completing written exercises in workbooks styled like comic books with dialogue enclosed in balloons; at another table the teacher was helping the slowest readers sound out syllables; and in another corner the aide was listening to individual pupils reading in French. The walls of the room were gaily decorated with pictures and clippings about Haiti under the heading *Images de Haiti*. One corner was identified as *Le Coin des Artistes*, and some of the pupils' art work was posted under *Peinture, Dessin, Collage, Modelage*, and *Sculpture*. Another part of the room was labeled *Le Coin des Mathématiques*, with examples of *Addition, Soustraction, Multiplication*, and *Division*.

In a second-grade class the teacher reported that the majority of her pupils were learning to read in both French and English, though a few were continuing to read in just one language until they had mastered the technique well enough to move on to the other. Some of the pupils were new arrivals from Haiti, others had been in the United States for a year or two. With the usual problem of mobility of the student population in big cities, some of the pupils of the previous year had left Manhattan for Boston or other boroughs of New York City.

In the 1973–74 school year, there were some 450 Haitian elementary school pupils in Manhattan and Brooklyn enrolled in French-English bilingual classes. It was estimated that in 1974–75 the number would rise to 600. Some bilingual French-English teaching was also being carried on in Brandeis and Wingate High Schools as a transitional aid for newly arrived Haitian students of that age level. Massachusetts, by the fall of 1973, had also established programs for Haitian pupils in its public schools, financed through both Title VII of ESEA and its own state transitional bilingual act.

Since there are well-educated, professionally trained persons among Haitian immigrants (those who may have left the island for political rather than purely economic reasons), the local Haitian communities are a source of teachers and aides for the Haitian bilingual programs. Occasionally, if no qualified Haitian is available, French-English bilingual teachers of other backgrounds are engaged, but it is desirable when possible to have persons working with Haitian children who can understand and speak Haitian Creole. Among the aides in the bilingual classes are young Haitian students working for degrees at local colleges and universities as well as older members of the Haitian communities who, though not certified as teachers, can contribute much as aides.

One development, which is far from rare among those who can afford it and indicative of a relatively high educational and social level in a community, was reported as in the offing in the spring of 1973 in a Haitian section of Queens—the founding of a private lycée (where presumably French would be emphasized) for children from the more privileged families. This is one more example of a problem that plagues the public educational scene over and over—families who, because they want to give their children the best possible education, withdraw them from the public schools and send them to private institutions, thereby depriving public school classes of the diversity and challenge that children from higher socio-economic segments of the population can contribute. With the leaven of such pupils missing, public schools then show a drop in their academic accomplishments. This, in turn, encourages still more families to send their children elsewhere. This phenomenon has been occurring in the urban schools for many decades, among all kinds of ethnic and linguistic groups. It is happening, one also hears, among Cuban refugees and in Portuguese enclaves, where, as soon as new immigrants possess sufficient economic resources, they choose to send their children, especially when they reach adolescence, to private schools, parochial or nonsectarian, where the parents believe the pupils' behavior as well as their academic performance will be more strictly observed and controlled.

In Louisiana there are both black and white pupils who speak regional types of French, either Cajun (a variant of the language developed by the descendants of the Acadians, who were expelled from Canada by the British in 1775 and who settled in the bayou country of Louisiana) or a Negro patois sometimes referred to as "Gumbo," described as "a negroid jargon quite unintelligible to all but themselves or a student of their specialty. . . . It is spoken chiefly in St. Martinsville, Breaux Bridge . . . by *both* white and colored, although it had been evolved by the Negro slaves in the original settlements."[3]

One of the Louisiana dialects is also sometimes called *"Creole"*[4] though the word has different connotations in different locations and in different periods of time. The word is of Spanish derivation, *criollo* meaning "child," or "native" from *criar*—to "breed," to "raise," or to "bring up." It was originally used to refer to white children born to Spanish or French families in the New World colonies in the Caribbean, Spanish America, and Louisiana—Napoleon's Josephine was a Creole from Martinique—and by extension the word has been used at times to mean the language they spoke, if French, a patois reasonably close to that spoken in France, or at least a language used by educated descendants of French (or Spanish) families. Since today in Louisiana there are few descendants of old French families who still speak a Parisian version of the language (if, indeed, they speak French at all), Creole as used now in Louisiana[5] is likely to suggest a markedly variant type of the language.

In Louisiana during the 1972-73 school year, about 450 children —both black and white—who spoke some type of French were taught in bilingual classes in the urban schools of Lafayette and the rural setting of Breaux Bridge. In staffing its bilingual programs, Louisiana is able to take advantage of the French government's policy of permitting young men to do some alternative service, even abroad, as a substitute for military training. Over 100 *coopérants militaires*—participants in a kind of French peace corps—are teaching in Louisiana schools, some of them assisting in the bilingual classes at Breaux Bridge and Lafayette, with their expenses partly paid for by the French government.

Since the French that had been kept alive in Louisiana was largely an oral language, whether Cajun or Gumbo or Creole, many who wished to preserve it feared that in the course of time it would inevitably die out. Before the Title VII classes were established steps had been taken by some local officials to encourage its survival, including making arrangements with the French government to send French natives to teach in Louisiana schools. The federally supported Title VII French-English bilingual projects are helping pupils develop literacy in both French and English and are providing better educational opportunities to the many children who speak a mélange of the two languages.

The Cajuns pride themselves on being a vigorous and tenacious people, expressed in their capacity to enjoy life and their determination to maintain their original language and life-style. An appreciative appraisal of the Cajuns was published in the bulletin of the northern Maine (St. John Valley) French-English bilingual project, after a liaison conference in January 1972 in Louisiana for personnel from several French projects. It contained the following descriptions:

> A Cajun likes fiddles and accordions in his music, plenty of pepper in his court bouillon, shrimp in his nets, speed in his horses, neighborliness in his neighbors and love in his home.
> Little Cajun children are made of gumbo, boudin [sausage], and sauce piquante. . . crawfish stew and oreilles de cochon [pigs ears]. . . . A Cajun child is given bayous to fish in, marshes to trap in, room to grow in and churches to worship in.
> A Cajun likes to dance and laugh and sing when his week of hard work has ended. . . . And as fun-loving as he is, a Cajun can work as hard and as long as any living man. He carved out "Acadiana" by hand, from the swamp and marshes and uncultivated prairies. But when the work is done and argument is ended, a Cajun can sweep you right into a wonderful world of *joie de vivre* with an accordion chorus of "*Jole Blone*" [*Jolie Blonde*] Beautiful Blonde, and a handful of happy little words . . . five little words to be exact, "*Lessez le bon ton roulle!*" [*Laissez les bon temps rouler*]. Translated: Let the good times roll![6]

At P.S. 2 on Henry Street in lower Manhattan, for several years during the operation of a Title VII bilingual project, from 8:40 to 9:30 each school-day morning, groups of Chinese and Puerto Rican parents gathered in a room identified as theirs, by both Chinese characters and *Salon de Padres* written on a sign on the door, for English lessons taught by Chinese- and Spanish-speaking teachers assigned to the new "trilingual" program being carried on in this school. These classes for parents were a peripheral benefit to the community of this particular project, which was called *"Building Bi-Lingual Bridges."* The title of the project refers to the name given this area in the past because of the two actual bridges, the Brooklyn and the Manhattan, that dominate the skyline. The early hour of the parents' classes was for the convenience of the mothers and fathers, many of whom accompanied their little children to school. Most of the mothers had a two- or three-year-old child in tow at the class, too young to be enrolled in school or perhaps assigned to an afternoon pre-kindergarten session. There were three different classes, one for Chinese beginners, one for Spanish-speaking beginners, and a mixed class for intermediate students.

While their parents studied English, the pre-school-age children played with toys laid out for them and ate breakfast brought in on individual trays by the Community Family Assistant, who moved in and out of the room on her various duties. The atmosphere in the Parents' Room was one of hopeful activity, with some of the young mothers giggling like schoolgirls at their success in getting out an English sentence or commiserating with each other over mistakes in homework. They obviously enjoyed the companionship of other mothers with similar problems and preoccupations, the opportunity to study English under the tutelage of sympathetic and lively instructors, and perhaps just the opportunity to get out of the house in the morning. The Chinese characters on the door signified "Welcome, parents," and the parents seemed to take the sign at face value.

In the meantime and throughout the day, groups of Chinese and Puerto Rican pupils in kindergarten and first grade who did not know English were participating in joint classes, with a few Anglo children included too, taught by teachers who knew the children's languages as well as English, so that the children did not need to feel lost in an alien environment nor lose out completely in their schoolwork while developing the necessary facility in English to cope with life in a society where it is the lingua franca. The ethnic composition of the school population at P.S. 2 in the early 1970s was approximately 60 percent Chinese, 30 percent Puerto Rican, and 10 percent "other" (English-speaking, both black and white). The three ethnic groups were represented in roughly the same proportions in the trilingual classes.

Mathematics was taught in English to the mixed group of pupils at P.S. 2 by an Anglo instructor, but Chinese- and Spanish-speaking teachers were present during the lessons and they moved quietly among the children helping them and explaining in their native languages anything that the pupils did not understand. One of the classroom activities popular with the children was listening to, retelling, and acting out stories illustrated by their *Giant Books*. These large-size (14- by 24-inch) picture books (developed under a federal grant, by private educational specialists) illustrate various stories, with fur and other materials added to give tactile impressions, which the children can look at and handle while their teachers read them the story—the Chinese teacher telling it in Chinese to the children of that group clustered around her, the Spanish teacher using Spanish with her Puerto Rican pupils, and the Anglo children hearing it in English. There were also tapes of the story in the three different languages, which the pupils could put on the recording machine and listen to by themselves. Later they were assigned parts and acted out the story. At some time, after retelling and dramatizing it in their native languages, all the children also told or enacted the story in English.

The director of the P.S. 2 Title VII project is an American who was born, and lived for many years, in China. He taught Chinese (Mandarin) at Yale for 15 years and was later on the staff of the Army Language School at Monterey in California. The Chinese teachers and staff were recruited from the local Chinese community; some had previously taught in the Chinese school in New York City's Chinatown; others were graduate students at local universities. Of the Spanish-language teachers, one was of Castilian-Spanish parentage, others were Puerto Rican.

The evaluator originally assigned to the project was a young Hong Kong–born graduate student, working for his Ph.D. at Fordham University in New York City, who had arrived in this country from Hong Kong only a few years earlier. He has received his doctoral degree and returned to teach at Hong Kong University. The Chinese teacher, who supervised the actual classroom instruction and also did some teaching herself, prepared materials and handled consultations with parents. A young Spanish-speaking aide functioned in various capacities, assisting in the classroom, and helping in the preparation of materials or doing clerical jobs in the office. Copies of a trilingual newspaper, *The District Reporter*, published by the school district and containing news and announcements in Spanish, Chinese, and English were available at the school for parents, teachers, and any members of the community interested in keeping up with school district affairs.

The Chinese-Spanish-English program at P.S. 2 was established in 1971. The program was originally set up at a different school in the district, but problems of one kind or another in the community made it ineffectual there. It was decided to transfer the project to P.S. 2, where it remained in operation until June 1974. A proposal for a much expanded program of bilingual education in District 2 was submitted for approval and funding under Title VII in the spring of 1974. Most of the Chinese-speaking pupils in New York City live within the area consti- tuting this school district. Before the opening of the school year in the fall of 1974, a grant of $550,000 was approved. This money was to be used to provide at least a limited amount of bilingual teaching for the Chinese-, as well as the Spanish-speaking, pupils in six elementary, one junior high, and four parochial schools in the district.

There have been other federally funded bilingual projects for Chinese-speaking children in the United States, in both the San Fran- cisco and the Los Angeles areas. With an ever-increasing number of newly arriving Chinese pupils, in the San Francisco schools especially, much more will have to be done to solve the language problems of these students.

P.S. 25, one of the elementary schools in District 7 of the New York City school system, is located on East 149th Street in the South Bronx, an area plagued by poverty, a high crime rate, and other assorted urban ills. It is known in the neighborhood, and far afield, as "the Bilin- gual School." District 7 has the highest concentration of Spanish- speaking pupils in the city. Sixty-eight percent of the 28,000 children attending its schools come from Spanish-speaking families, most of them Puerto Rican. Of the 720 pupils registered at P.S. 25, 92 percent have Spanish-language backgrounds; the remaining English-speaking 8 per- cent are black children who have chosen to enroll at a school where they will learn Spanish as well as English and have a chance to develop in a bilingual-bicultural atmosphere. (Enrollment at the school is entirely voluntary for all students.)

P.S. 25 was established as a bilingual school in 1968. Since that time some of the housing adjacent to the school has been torn down, and a good many families have moved some distance away. Many of these children have indicated a desire, however, to continue their education at the school and are given bus passes enabling them to come back to P.S. 25.

The building housing the Bilingual School is an old-style five-story structure that had been scheduled for demolition before being taken over for the experiment in bilingual teaching. What goes on inside, however, is most contemporary in both style and purpose. Teachers who believe in the advantages of the "open classroom" are permitted to follow this procedure in teaching their pupils. Those who feel more comfortable or more competent in the traditional classroom situation handle their teaching assignments in this way. All the teachers, administrators, and clerical staff are able to speak both Spanish and English, whatever their ethnic origins.

A visitor to the school on a last day before spring vacation in 1974, unannounced in advance but accompanied by a member of the administrative staff, observed a variety of activities during a morning session. In a fourth-grade classroom the teacher, a woman, was standing at the blackboard questioning pupils about a math lesson they had been working on, at this particular moment having to do with line segments. Boys at the back of the room, standing in excitement, were firing answers back to her, accompanied by such statements as, "They wanted to trick us on that one; we saw through it though." All eyes were riveted on the teacher, and it was obvious that she had the undivided attention of the class. (This lesson was being conducted in English.)

In a corridor four young children from one of the lower grades were sitting on the floor, clustered around a little record player listening to a story, interspersed with songs, all in English. From a third-grade classroom, the smell of a cake baking in a small portable oven permeated the air. The teacher, a man, said that the children, who loved to cook, could learn a good deal from it too, about measuring, halving, doubling, and so forth. A second filled cake pan was waiting to go in when the first one was done. In several rooms there were animals of various kinds in pens and boxes, a gerbil, guinea pigs, and several generations of rabbits, some of whom had been born the evening before. They were munching on food contributed by individuals or stores in the neighborhood. (The problem of caring for the animals during weekends and vacations was solved by the children's taking them home, only, of course, on condition that they brought a signed letter of permission from their mothers.)

In other classes pupils were practicing writing, perhaps copying a sentence they had dictated to the teacher and she had written for them to learn from. Others were reading in Spanish or English. Since it was close to Easter, some children were drawing and painting spring motifs, coloring eggs, and making Easter baskets. The fifth- and sixth-grade pupils were in the auditorium, attending a musical play conceived and put together by one of their teachers and performed by some of the sixth graders. A streamer around the top of the stage curtains proclaimed, "I Believe in Music," a theme around which many acitivities had been centered during that particular week. The previous day, members of a string quartet from the neighborhood had come to P.S. 25 to demonstrate their instruments and to talk to the students about their music.

During the lunch hour, several mothers came in to volunteer their services to help maintain order and keep an eye on pupils in the lunchroom. The directors of the program at P.S. 25 consider that they have good cooperation from the parents of their pupils and a good sense of community participation. As is true of most bilingual projects, there are classes for parents in both English and Spanish. It has sometimes been found advisable to recommend to parents who have signed up for English classes that they need first to learn more about Spanish and become literate in it, if they don't yet know how to read and write their native tongue.

In devising a schedule for determining how much of the instruction during the school day should be in English and how much in Spanish, the planners have to take into consideration the competency of the pupils in the two languages. The black children, on entering the school, will presumably know nothing of Spanish. The pupils from Spanish-language backgrounds will vary greatly in their relative command of the two languages, ranging from no knowledge of English whatsoever, to understanding a little but not speaking it, to understanding Spanish but perhaps being more fluent in English. Under ideal circumstances, all children would start the bilingual program in kindergarten or first grade, be placed in the proper "language dominance" grouping, and stay in the school through the sixth grade. This does not, of course, correspond to the actual state of affairs in any urban school. Some pupils enroll in the middle of a year or in whatever grade level they happen to belong when they arrive in the city or the district. The administration must try to ascertain by testing what the child's dominant language is and place him accordingly in the kind of class that best fits his needs.

The theoretical model worked out by P.S. 25 for the ratios of instruction time in native and second language, and an explanation of the reasoning behind it, follows.

The Theoretical Model[7]

A child entering the Bilingual School in the kindergarten grade and remaining in the school until graduation from the sixth grade will have experienced seven years of bilingual instruction and is expected at the end of this time to have developed sufficient proficiency in each language to be able to receive 50 percent of his instruction in English and 50 percent in Spanish. In order to achieve this proportion of native and second language instruction without subjecting the student to undue stress in functioning in a second language, it is necessary to gradually increase the percentage of second language instruction through the grades. The proposed ratios of native language instruction to second language instruction are indicated below.

Ratio of Percentage of Time Devoted to Native Language Instruction (N) and Second Language Instruction (S) in Each Grade.

Grade	N/S Ratio
Kindergarten	85/15
First	75/25
Second	75/25
Third	70/30
Fourth	60/40
Fifth	60/40
Sixth	50/50

Given the mobility of urban pupil population, changes of residence within the city and the in- and out-migration of the Puerto Rican population in particular, by no means do all the children at P.S. 25 start the bilingual program in kindergarten or first grade, or stay in the school through the sixth.

P.S. 25, like all bilingual projects receiving Title VII money, is required to submit to evaluation each year by an outside team of evaluators. The report for the 1973–74 school year had not been completed at the time of this writing but the evaluation for the 1972–73 school year was available.[8] The school had not at that time, by any means, accomplished all that it hoped to do, especially in achieving high test results in reading. It is impossible to summarize here the many findings published in the 133-page report, where all the test scores of the third, fourth, and fifth graders are tabulated.

The evaluators postulated certain hypotheses about what the students' performance would be and then tested them, making comparisons of the P.S. 25 pupils with the pupils of two other neighborhood schools (which were not operated as bilingual schools). They also tested the pupils' relative performance on tests given in their native and their second languages.

The evaluators found that the pupils at P.S. 25 had a consistently high standard of performance in mathematics. In computing the comparative performance of pupils, various factors were taken into consideration. Children who had been at P.S. 25 from their first year of schooling on were scored both separately and as part of the entire grade grouping. Scores of the entire pupil roster, including recent arrivals, were compared with total pupils enrolled in the comparison schools. P.S. 25 children's test scores in reading and mathematics were computed twice, on the basis of tests administered both in their dominant and non-dominant languages (according to which they had been placed in classes and given more instruction in the medium of the dominant language) and according to their *own* judgment of themselves as Spanish or English dominant—which was not always what they had shown themselves to be on their earlier testing for placement in classes. The children sometimes scored better when tested in what *they* considered was their dominant language, even though this had not been evidenced by the placement tests. This suggested to the evaluators that children might do better when being tested in a language in which they *felt* more confident or comfortable. (All such findings are further evidence of the slippery nature of language ability and language testing, the many factors influencing language use, and the difficulties of *proving* almost anything in the field indisputably.)

One interesting point that came to the evaluators' attention was a seeming incongruity in the pupils' knowledge of vocabulary (single words) in the two languages, and their relative scores on comprehension of groups of words or sentences. Most students, whether English or Spanish dominant, scored higher on vocabulary in Spanish and on comprehension in English. The evaluators speculated that this might indicate something about the relative difficulties of the two languages, with vocabulary acquisition being easier in Spanish, perhaps because of the phonetic spelling, and general comprehension being easier in English, because of syntactical and grammatical aspects of English. They proposed that this would be a fruitful field of study for someone to pursue. They also stated their belief that some of the dual language tests, purportedly of equal difficulty in both languages, are not always, in fact, comparable and that more work is needed to prepare testing materials that are more closely matched in their degree of difficulty in the two languages.

According to the evaluators:

> Among the findings of the present study were consistent differences among the reading subtests, in that the Spanish subtest in Vocabulary seemed to be consistently easier than the English Vocabulary subtest; the English Comprehension subtest appeared consistently easier than the Spanish Comprehension subtest. These findings were noted at both fourth and fifth grade levels, and were found when dominant or non-dominant languages were considered.
>
> It is possible to interpret these results in terms of the nature of language learning itself within each of the two languages. Spanish, as a more phonetic language, may be approached through small units—words—or vocabulary, whereas the English language may be learned through contextual cues in sentences and paragraphs. It is important to note, however, that the tests do not appear to be

equivalent in the two languages, as the publisher suggested might be the case. In fact, the current group of children in the present study, as participants in one of the most important bilingual experiments in the nation, might be considered as the most suitable subjects for studying the equivalence of forms across languages, for which bilingual subjects would be necessary.[9]

In general, the evaluators found that the third- and fourth-grade pupils at P.S. 25 performed much better on the tests than the fifth graders. They were not, however, inclined to interpret this as indicating that pupils lost ground at P.S. 25 as they moved along from grade to grade but suggested that the problem might reside in the nature of the particular group of students in the fifth grade at that time, who had also done poorly on tests the year before when they were at the fourth-grade level. The evaluators suggested only that some special attention should be given to the learning problems of those particular students. They also raised the possibility that the teachers' strike of 1968 might have had a damaging effect on this group of fifth-grade pupils.

In interpreting these results, many factors that might have affected these pupils' progress should be considered. In the fall of 1968, when these children were first graders, the teachers' strike occurred in New York City. The controversies involved were particularly acute in the community surrounding the newly organized bilingual school. At best, the current fifth graders began their educational experience in a new school amid city-wide controversy.[10]

Among the general comments and judgments made in summarizing the results of the evaluation tests of P.S. 25 pupils were the following:

The general picture (for third grade) is one of stability or of slight increase from the first third grade tested to the second. The Number test shows steady gain over the three years. Some of the gain in scores in the 1971-72 year may reflect the particular ability level of the class then in the third grade. There is also the possibility that the learning environment in P.S. 25 has been improving generally. This seems especially likely with respect to the mathematics curriculum.

With regard to fourth-grade-level findings:

A trend toward steady improvement from one year to the next is noted in these subtests. This lends some support to the idea that achievement in P.S. 25 is showing some improvement over time.

About fourth- and fifth-grade English:

> The existence of better average performance supports the conten-
> tion that P.S. 25 children are increasing their skills in English. . . .
> Modest gains in most verbal skills for the English dominant group
> in Spanish were found. . . ."

It is usually the case that Spanish-speaking pupils learn more English
than English-speaking pupils do Spanish, a not unexpected result, given
the environment and prevailing circumstances. Pupils from English-
dominant families are likely to hear more English than Spanish outside
of school.

Judgmental statements taken from different sections of the evaluation report indicate improvements in test scores compared with earlier
years (except for the fifth grade, and even their progress in mathematics
compared favorably with the other neighborhood schools). P.S. 25
pupils' scores on reading-speed subtests were lower on the whole than
those in comparison schools. Some of the comments of the evaluators are
as follows:

> The overall achievement picture for all P.S. 25 pupils, without
> consideration of the amount of time they have been in school, in
> comparison with longitudinal sample pupils in schools A and B
> (comparison schools) is generally favorable. When testing was
> carried out in dominant language, few differences were found on
> verbal tasks between P.S. 25 and comparison schools. P.S. 25
> children's superior performance on number tasks, noted in 1972,
> has been maintained and in some cases augmented.
>
> P.S. 25 children achieved significantly higher scores on the
> number tasks than did children in either of the other schools. . . .
> The differences in reading achievement between the 1972 longi-
> tudinal sample (those who had attended P.S. 25 for several years)
> and the comparison schools favored both schools A and B (the
> comparison schools). Speed of reading scores differed significantly
> favoring Schools A and B.[12]
>
> In summary, when the stable sample's achievement is compared
> with that of children enrolled in neighboring schools for similar
> amounts of time, P.S. 25 children's achievement picture is quite
> favorable, except in the area of Reading Speed. The achievement
> of the Spanish-dominant classes is worthy of note. In comparison
> with the 1972 achievement picture, the Spanish-dominant groups
> have made substantial gains relative to their peers. The English-
> dominant groups have generally maintained equivalent
> achievement with respect to children in comparison schools.
>
> When the achievement of P.S. 25 third graders was compared
> with that of a longitudinal sample of third graders in two neigh-

boring schools a generally favorable picture of the effects of the bilingual program was found. . . .

As a group then, the students in P.S. 25 performed as well in English as students in the comparison school, despite the inclusion of the scores of many newly arrived, Spanish-dominant students in P.S. 25.[13]

Any statements taken out of the full context of the testing reports may be misleading. It would be necessary to study the reports in detail to be able to interpret the significance of the scores of all classes in all areas. The evaluators suggest that much more needs to be known about how accurately test scores reveal performance and how various factors should be weighed in arriving at judgments. The final paragraph of the evaluation report, which might well be applicable to other programs, reads:

In general, this set of comparisons yields a picture of some steady increases in skills from one year to the next. Without data for other groups' achievement over time, interpretation of these gains isn't possible. These gains can only be documental at this time. There is a pressing need for appropriate normative data regarding children's language development in a bilingual instructional environment.[14]

Time did not permit the author to visit more than a limited number of the many bilingual projects now in operation in public schools throughout the country, and space does not allow a description of all those schools visited and observed in the course of the past two or three years. There are innumerable interesting bilingual programs being carried on for Puerto Rican pupils in cities in New York State, Illinois, Massachusetts, Connecticut, and Pennsylvania and for Mexican-American children all the way from Washington through California and the Southwest to Texas. Project Frontier based in the Chula Vista, California, school system, which operates in schools near the Mexican border, has been notably effective not only in teaching Spanish-speaking pupils but also in achieving a high degree of bilingualism on the part of the Anglo children participating in the program. The Chinese programs in San Francisco are making a start on the difficult problem facing the schools there of absorbing and teaching the large numbers of new arrivals swelling the city's Chinese-pupil population. There has been state funding for a three-year experimental project at San Francisco's Marina Junior High and a Title VII project for elementary-age pupils at its Commodore Stockton school. Portuguese programs have been functioning effectively at Artesia in California as well as in Eastern seaboard cities. Fall River, Massachusetts, where Portuguese immigrants have replaced French Canadians as the newest and poorest minority group, has been producing much needed curriculum materials in Portuguese for the fifth-grade level. New Bedford, Massachusetts, and Providence, Rhode Island, also have thriving Portuguese programs.

There are innumerable projects for Mexican-American pupils in Texas established under Title VII. Many of these projects, as well as the State Education Agency and the Regional Educational Agencies Project on International Education, have turned out valuable materials on the historical background and cultural characteristics of Mexican Americans in general, and Spanish-speaking Texans in particular, as well as specific teaching materials for Spanish language-classes and for teaching subject matter in Spanish. Though it is not possible to describe all the programs observed, it is possible to state that almost without exception the bilingual-bicultural classrooms looked like places where learning was going on, was being encouraged, and was being enjoyed.

It is still too early to make final evaluations and draw conclusions about the long-term effects that bilingual teaching will have in the overall progress and development of pupils. But it appears that the programs which have gone through their shakedown maneuvers, have survived the upheavals and growing pains of the first year or two of operation, and have been able to resist local prejudice or political pressures against the concept of bilingual education are making valid contributions to the educational scene and offering desirable alternatives for many of the children who have little or no knowledge of English and who have in the past suffered in one way or another because of this fact.

Notes

1. Quoted in Robert A. Hall, Jr., *Pidgin and Creole Languages*, Cornell University Press, Ithaca, N.Y., 1966, p. 95.

2. Robert A. Hall, Jr., op. cit., pp. xii-xiii.
"A Creole language arises when a pidgin becomes the native language of a speech community. When Negroes were imported from Africa to the Caribbean area, their new masters deliberately separated slaves ... from the same African tribes, ... so as to lessen the danger ... of revolt among those speaking a common language. The only language plantation slaves had in common was a pidginized variety of their masters' tongue: English, French, Spanish, or Portuguese. ... As successive generations grew up using the new language ... they re-expanded its grammatical and lexical resources ... to meet all the needs of their way of living. In the French West Indies and Louisiana, the slaves' language was called Créole ...: this term has come to be applied to any language that has undergone a similar development, growing out of a pidgin to become the first language of a speech-community.

Creolization is simply one manifestation of a broader process which for want of a better term we can call nativization. A language is nativized when it is taken over by a group of speakers who have previously used some other language, so that the new language becomes the native language of the group."

For a detailed analysis of Haitian Creole, see Hall, op. cit., passim.

3. Theodore Andersson and Mildred Boyer, *Bilingual Schooling in the United States*, Southwest Educational Development Laboratory, vol. 2, p. 172 (quoting Marius Barbeau, "Louisiana French," p. 5).

4. Robert A. Hall, Jr., op. cit., p. 16.

"Then there is Louisiana Creole, which is radically different from both the provincial standard French and Cajun (in Louisiana). It is spoken by the descendants of plantation slaves, and linguistically it is closely related to the other French-based creoles of the Caribbean area, showing the same drastic structural changes: for example, phonological simplification; loss of categories of gender, number, and person: use of aspectival and tense prefixes.

"In the Antilles there are a number of creoles close enough to Louisiana Creole to be mutually intelligible with it. The best known of these is Haitian Creole, which is spoken as a mother tongue by the entire population of the Republic of Haiti."

5. One of the clearest explanations of the *sources of confusion* in the use of the term *Creole* was given by Arlin Turner in an introduction to the stories of George Cable, *Creoles and Cajuns*, Anchor Books, Doubleday, Garden City, N.Y., 1959, p. 8. Turner writes:

"Readers outside of New Orleans have had difficulty with the word *Creole*. . . . the confusion existed . . . largely because the different uses of the word can be distinguished with precision only through long familiarity. In the strict sense a Creole would be of French or Spanish descent and of pure blood, with some implication of high social status. There could be, of course, no infusion of Negro, Indian or other blood, nor could the word be applied to the descendants of a lower class, such as the Acadians in southwest Louisiana. The confusion arises not from this restricted meaning of the word, but from the collateral, vague meanings. It was used locally (in Louisiana)—and readily understood in that use—to designate anything pertaining to the Creoles: Creole ponies, for example, Creole chickens, Creole onions, Creole gumbo, Creole songs. By extension, a slave belonging to Creoles, speaking a brand of French and displaying countless traits recognized as Creole rather than American, would be called a Creole slave or a Creole Negro, or simply a Creole when the context, his presence, or an acquaintance with him might be supposed to make the meaning clear. By a further extension, the language spoken by Creoles might be called Creole; as applied to Creoles in the strict sense, it meant the dialect of educated Frenchmen speaking English; as applied to the French-speaking Negroes and mulattoes, it meant the rude patois spoken by illiterates. In the Caribbean islands, this inclusive use of the word was commonplace and the restricted use rare—thus the confusion in the minds of people remote from New Orleans when they found the word used in its narrower sense."

6. Bob Hamm, "What is a Cajun?" Project Brave Bulletin, vol. II, no. 4, p. 2. Sponsored by Title VII, ESEA, St. John Valley, Maine.

7. Hernan LaFontaine, Carmen Rivera, and Muriel Pagan, "Model for the Implementation of the Elementary School Curriculum through Bilingual Education," p. 1. Pamphlet of The Bilingual School, P.S. 25, 811 East 149th Street, Bronx, New York 10455.

8. Elaine Chapline and Wendy Oxman (evaluation directors), *An Evaluation of the ESEA Title VII Program*, District 7, New York City Board of Education, 1972–73 school year, "The Bilingual School at P.S. 25," *Final Report*, Institute for Research and Evaluation, Regis G. Bernhardt, Director, Publication No. 73–50, July 1973.

9. Ibid., p. 124.

10. Ibid., p. 111.

11. Ibid., pp. 126, 127, 129.

12. Ibid., p. 39, 45.

13. Ibid., p. 58, 61.

14. Ibid., p. 134.

The Rationale behind Bilingual-Bicultural Education

4 In any discussion of the rationale behind bilingual-bicultural education in the United States, one should perhaps distinguish between the political pressures which have provided some of the impetus for the movement and the ideological basis—pedagogical and sociological—which would justify acceding to those pressures. There is little doubt that the increasing political strength of Spanish-speaking voters played an important part in bringing bilingual-bicultural educational programs into existence in the late sixties, for Mexican Americans in the Southwest and for Puerto Ricans in New York City and other Northeastern urban areas. It was certainly not a matter of chance that the bill resulting in a federal Bilingual Act had as sponsor a senator from Texas, where approval or disapproval of candidates and issues by Spanish-speaking residents was beginning to be felt at the polls. It is also true that certain aspects of political activism currently manifested at the local level in the promotion or management of bilingual projects are responsible for some of the resistance offered to bilingual education by a wide spectrum of opponents, ranging from militant teachers'-union leaders to political arch-conservatives. (All the opponents might also, of course, be charged with caring chiefly about protecting their own particular stake in the status quo.)

Claims are made, sometimes with justification, that what many members of minority groups who are pushing for bilingual programs in community-run schools are really interested in is getting a cut of the rich financial pie that the expenditures for public schools represent today. One often hears, as answer to such claims, "What of it? They have it coming to them. As members of a group that has been economically underprivileged for too long, why shouldn't they have the jobs or the distribution of patronage that goes with the management of the public schools?" Though there is something to be said for a balancing of the scales, this kind of answer is too facile and not basically valid educationally, unless it results, in the long run, in lasting betterment of the schools themselves and improved educational opportunities for the children attending those schools.

There have also been charges of nepotism, waste, and mis-

61

management in some of the programs being administered by persons new to duties and responsibilities incumbent on a school board. In an earlier era these duties were assumed by disinterested, unpaid school board members, the best of whom were motivated by a desire to be of service. Many of them contributed unstintingly of their time and talents to overseeing the management of the public schools with no thought of personal gain and no political axe to grind. It is not enough in response to such charges of nepotism or mismanagement merely to state bluntly, "Times have changed," though indeed they have. Consideration has to be given to the complex question of how people, as individuals and as a group, function, develop, and increase their potential for constructive action.

The concept of encouraging adult members of various ethnic and linguistic minorities to become involved in the schools attended by their children has many ramifications. If, as seems to be true, what goes on at home and parents' attitudes toward education are of vital importance in determining whether children succeed or fail in school, it is essential to see that parents are informed about what goes on in the schools, and are also encouraged to become involved to whatever degree is feasible in their children's education. If parents, in addition to other disadvantages, cannot speak or understand the language used by the "ruling majority" of a school system, it is also advisable, if not imperative, to have some people in the school scene who speak their language, both literally and figuratively.

In evaluating the effectiveness of the participation of minority-group representatives in policy making regarding their children's education and in the actual management of programs, it is well to keep in mind the sound pedagogical principle that one learns by doing. A basic tenet of many of the contemporary social programs devised to encourage initiative and responsibility on the part of persons who have not previously been in the habit of exhibiting these highly valued characteristics is that those very persons must be given an opportunity to exercise initiative and responsibility, even with the realization that one of the normal expectations in doing anything for the first time is making mistakes. This does not mean that errors in judgment or performance need to be condoned if stubbornly adhered to or repeated. But time and experience are always needed for new systems and activities and the people involved in them to function at optimum capacity. This is true in the field of education as well as in other affairs.

One of the major reasons for the original federal decision to give bilingually biculturally oriented teaching a try in educating children from some of America's ethnic and linguistic minorities, especially those from poor socio-economic backgrounds, was that their drop-out rate and their percentages of failure in school were so high. Though no one has all the answers to the puzzling question of why some children learn and others, equally intelligent, do not, almost everyone agrees that motivation is a crucial factor. The concepts and practices involved in bilingual-bicultural educational projects have as a major goal leading students to believe in themselves, in their basic worth as human beings, and in their native capacities. One important factor in reinforcing these pupils' self-confidence is having the language they speak acknowledged and respected; another is having as teachers, and models whom they can emulate, persons who use that language and stem from the same cultural community as their pupils. Though it is not necessarily true, as some community spokesmen insist, that Puerto Rican children can be taught only by Puerto Rican instructors, Chicanos by Chicanos, or Cubans by Cubans, there is no doubt that it is salutary for children who have always had as teachers only English-speaking persons from some ethnic group other than their own, to see people from their ethnic or linguistic community in influential positions in the schools as teachers and administrators. (For native American Indian children it may indeed be essential to have some teachers from their own tribes because of a number of factors unique to the Indian situation.)

Regarding the prohibition which until fairly recent times was in force against pupils' using their own language within the school complex (if it did not happen to be English), there is little doubt that it was both frustrating and demoralizing for many students, even when the intent of the regulation was not to harm the pupils but to help them in their acquisition of a new language. Temporary prohibitions against speaking one language while trying to master another can make sense for mature, sophisticated, or advanced language students but not for bewildered children who may conclude that their language is banned by the schools because it is inherently bad. Most adult college graduates will have recollections of French or Italian or German tables in the university dining rooms, or special residence houses on college campuses where it was forbidden to speak in any language but the one being studied. The so-called "immersion method" of language study is also based in part on this concept. It is a useful technique when freely accepted by mature students who understand the reason for it. But when young pupils are constantly told not to speak their language, whether they are Indian children living away from home in government boarding schools or Mexican Americans or Puerto Ricans attending the nearest public school, it is not difficult to imagine their interpretation of this rule as criticism of their language and of their families and friends who speak it.

Let it be said immediately that in bilingual classrooms and various bilingual learning situations, it is desirable to keep the two languages separate in order to avoid a scrambling of tongues. This can be accomplished in a variety of ways, by having separate classrooms, or corners of rooms, equipped and used for different languages; by having different portions of a day set aside for concentration on one language or the other; and by having different persons as instructors of the two languages. In many linguistically sophisticated bilingual families, great attention is paid to a careful separation of the languages so that children consciously or unconsciously use one language for certain situations and persons, and the other in different settings. But such divisions in language use are quite different from prohibitions, since respect is shown for both languages.

As for the logic of teaching children to read and write first by using a language they speak and understand, it seems too obvious to need explanation. But any monolingual adult who has forgotten that learning to read and write consists of decoding and encoding symbols representing the sounds of spoken language might gain comprehension of the difficulties of mastering these techniques by trying to read and write a language he doesn't know, especially one with an unfamiliar alphabet, such as Greek or Russian. First you discover the complexity of an alphabet: every letter has four forms, sometimes quite different in shape, capitals and small letters, both cursive and printed. A, in Russian, let's say, is easy— A a *A a*, like English. But B— Б б *Б б*; and as for G— Г г *Г г*. Suppose you manage to decode and sound out "ключ" (something like "kliooch"). The teacher says "Good. That's right." And you still haven't the remotest idea that what you have just said means "key." You would soon decide, if you had not yet learned the techniques of reading and writing, that it would make more sense to begin with a language you knew. If the decision is made simply to wait with reading until the child has learned to speak English, there is the possibility of a twofold loss—the child's remaining illiterate in his mother tongue and the wasting of the potential learning capacity of the young child at his particular stage of development.

Even simpler tests can remind an adult who may have had no trouble learning to read that it takes time and practice to learn to decipher and blend the sounds of separate letters to form words. Try setting the letters vertically in a column or even diagonally and you understand better what a beginning reader encounters, until he has had practice enough to grasp meaning when he sees a group of symbols forming an unfamiliar word. (We all, of course, eventually read by seeing and interpreting whole words and phrases without needing to sound them out, but one has to master the skill of decoding to be really able to read anything new.)

These are what might be called technical considerations. But there are more subtle aspects in the relationship between language use and stages in cognitive development. Elizabeth Willink, in writing about the desirability of bilingual education for Navajo children, states:

The deliberate development—not merely use—of both languages (Navajo and English) in and through all the language arts, has been emphasized . . . because we have known for a long time the intimate relationship that exists between language and thought, between language development and thought development. The relationship is complex, dynamic rather than static. A great deal about it is still unknown. Summarizing what seems to be the consensus to date among investigators of this relationship (Piaget 1959, Vygotsky 1962, Liublinskaya 1967, Amster 1965, Taba 1965), we could define thinking as structuring reality, i.e. "making sense" out of the continuous stimulation to which we are submitted by virtue of being equipped with our senses. For this structuring, that is, for thinking, actual sensory perception is used, which itself can be characterized as an active and selective mental process. In addition, the memory of previously received stimuli, and the thoughts and concepts derived from those, are used in thinking. Concepts find their expression in language, in vocabulary as well as in syntax. But besides expression language has another important function. The child "learns the world" along with, and through, his first language. The mother tongue greatly aids in *forming* concepts in the growing child. And the importance of the role of language in concept formation increases as the child grows older.

Language then not only expresses, but also forms concepts in the learner. Language learning, mother tongue learning, and conceptual development, however, don't appear to take place along neatly parallel lines and at the same rate. There is prelinguistic conceptualization and there is also a period, apparently, until about the age of twelve or thirteen, on the average (in the children of the investigator's culture, that is), during which language competence runs ahead of true concept acquisition. Yet, even this discrepancy is believed to be aiding the child in acquiring the concepts for which he has already learned the language (Vygotsky 1962).

Whatever light further investigations may shed on this complex relationship between thought and language, the educator, who cannot wait with his teaching until all the answers are in, knows, and has known for a long time, that when he speaks of his pupils' language development, he implicitly means their general mental development. . . .

To summarize the argumentation thus far presented: language development, and particularly mother tongue development where the mother tongue is the child's dominant language when he comes to school, is extremely important for thought development, and thought development is what education is about. Once the child has better learned how to think, and thereby how to learn, he is better equipped to learn anything he may need to learn—including his second language, English.[1]

Though Mrs. Willink makes reference in her article to Navajo Indian pupils, the theories of cognitive development that she is discussing are equally applicable to children of other ethnic backgrounds and cultures.

In addition to its potential value in the cognitive development of pupils, bilingual education also has a bearing on the affective domain. Encouragement of the use of mother tongues and a demonstration of respect for a child's cultural and familial roots has an effect not only on how children think, but also on how they feel. And feeling right, feeling good and confident about oneself, is usually of great importance in the motivation and the capacity of any person, child or adult, to carry out a task successfully, in school or out.

In purely practical matters also, in school administration, it can be most helpful to have bilingual persons on the staff. In the handling of discipline and attendance problems, an understanding of the ways of family life in the pupils' homes and an ability to talk things over with both parent and child in the mother tongue of the family make it easier to reach solutions. If a ten-year-old boy, for instance, stays out of school to help his mother with the marketing, to interpret for her and carry heavy packages, this may seem to him a valid reason and a worthy action. Refraining from criticizing him, even praising his good intentions, but proposing the alternative of after-school shopping, and explaining to both mother and pupil the importance of regular attendance for continuity of study, is more likely to achieve the desired end than angry denunciations of truancy.

Dr. Bruce Gaarder, a professor of Spanish who has been influential in the field of bilingual education, addressing the opening session of the Pre-Conference Workshop on Bilingual Education at the ACTFL (American Council for the Teaching of Foreign Languages) meeting in Boston, November 22, 1973, reviewed the five original reasons for establishing bilingual teaching in public schools, listing them on a sheet that was distributed to those attending, as follows:

1. Avoid retardation when child's English is not adequate.

2. Establish mutually supporting relationship between home and school.

3. Defend and strengthen child's concept of himself.

4. Exploit career potential of the non-English language.

5. Conserve cultural (including linguistic) heritage of our people.

Though Dr. Gaarder proposed a revision of the rationale for bilingual education, discussing newly emerging considerations, he indicated that all five of the original reasons were still valid. He did comment that not much was actually being done to exploit the career potential of bilingual students.

New reasons for promoting bilingual-bicultural education, which Dr. Gaarder suggested might be even more important than those originally given, were:

1. The basic right of every people to rear and educate its children in its own image.

2. The superiority of foreign *medium* instruction over foreign *language* instruction.

3. Bilingualism and bilingual education as instruments of politics.

Regarding the first point, Dr. Gaarder suggested that defensive research to justify bilingual education was inconsequential if one accepted this premise. In bringing up the second point, Dr. Gaarder was referring to the belief that students learn more of a language, and learn it better, if some subject matter is being taught through the medium of that language rather than only the grammar, and lexicon, and syntax of the language. In other words, one doesn't learn vocabulary or constructions of a language in a vacuum; they must communicate something, express something. The application of this theory to bilingual education programs would mean that Spanish-speaking pupils studying English are likely to make greater progress in learning their second language when part of the curriculum is taught in English. In addition, those Spanish-dominant pupils who need to improve their command of their mother tongue and broaden their knowledge of it can benefit by studying biology, history, or other subject matter in Spanish instead of taking just an "advanced Spanish" language course. English-speaking students are, as a matter of course, constantly learning vocabulary and developing a fuller command of their first language when they live in a predominantly Anglo environment and have their schooling in English. When they learn a second language, they will also learn more of it if it is used as a medium of instruction in other courses in the curriculum. (The best language teachers have, of course, always proceeded on this principle, but not in as fully structured a manner as Dr. Gaarder was proposing.)

In connection with the third point, Dr. Gaarder indicated his belief that in Puerto Rico bilingualism was encouraged as a means of weakening the position of Spanish, while in South Africa, bilingualism was being discouraged in order not to weaken the position of Afrikaans —interpretations not necessarily shared by everyone. In enumerating some issues beginning to be recognized as matters of concern in bilingual education, Dr. Gaarder mentioned the "self-destructive nature of bilingualism," and, as he put it, "the extent to which bilingual groups are unaware that bilingualism is an unstable phenomenon and tends to destroy itself as one of the languages displaces the other." He was thus adding his voice to some others being raised now, sometimes in unexpected places and by persons in the forefront of bilingual education, questioning whether it is possible for people to maintain two languages side by side when they live in a society in which one language enjoys greater prestige than another. (Similar doubts are expressed by some French Canadians who say they fear that once French-speaking citizens have learned English, they will forget their French, if not in the first generation, then in the second.) The implication is that bilingualism is not a natural condition and that in order to survive, the language of lesser prestige or importance in any given society must be supported by political activism or some radical means. Since these statements are usually made by persons who are fluently bi- or trilingual, it sometimes appears that such expressions of lack of confidence in bilingualism are self-contradictory or examples of an elite refusing to believe that others can do what they have done. It is true that most people do not maintain an equal degree of excellence in two or three languages simultaneously. Many bilinguals speak one language better than another or exhibit variations at different times and places in their command of the two languages, depending on which language they are hearing and using more at the time. But if one has a firm grounding in a language and is literate in it, it is always there, on tap, to be activated and brought up to a high level of proficiency when the speaker is in a situation in which that language is the prevailing one.

In any case, it seems unwise, or impolitic, for the proponents of bilingual education, now that a beachhead has been established, to proceed to wash out some of the underpinnings by making statements that run counter to some of the original reasons for establishing bilingual programs in the first place.

Whether the idea of linguistic pluralism will gain full acceptance in the United States, only time will tell. Not everyone will approve of the concept of a patchwork of separate ethnic and linguistic communities as a substitute for the now unpopular melting-pot theory. Many will feel that it could lead to too much political "separatism" and that the country would stand to lose a great deal if too narrowly based ethnic loyalties were encouraged to override the concept of a united people who have a common history and a common future, no matter how varied they may be in origin.

Those who express concern about the withering away of some mother tongues, once the members of various linguistic groups have learned English, would seem to be worrying unnecessarily. Certainly the several segments of the Spanish-speaking population in the country exhibit great determination to cling to Spanish in their family and their community lives. They are obviously going to remain Spanish-speaking when among their own. It is true that when they move outside of that particular group to participate in the broader spectrum of American society, they are going to need, and undoubtedly are going to learn, at least some English. They are going to be bilingual. The only questions are, what kind of bilingual, literate or illiterate, and how competent in both their mother tongue and English?

As for members of other language groups, whether Greek, Portuguese, Chinese, Italian, French, or whatever it may be, the recently conceived bilingual-bicultural education projects in the public schools are encouraging them to develop literacy and maintain fluency in their family languages to a greater extent than has been true in a long time or perhaps ever.

Enhancing the prestige of languages other than English can be approached in many ways. One of the most obvious is for the leaders of academia to press for the reinstatement of "foreign—or second—language" requirements for Anglos, and others, in qualifying for academic degrees. Another way of gaining added prestige for the many languages spoken by Americans of varied ethnic origins is to encourage the speakers of those languages to increase their knowledge and improve their command of their mother tongues, and, if they are not already literate in them, to become so.

Within bilingual classrooms, at least in the higher grades, at junior and senior high school levels, much greater use could be made of original source materials available in several languages, especially Spanish, for courses in history, social studies, art, music, and literature. Encouraging Spanish-speaking pupils to do simple research concerning early Puerto Rican and Mexican history by making use of original documents, either excerpts or full texts, which only those competent in Spanish could read, would be valuable ways of making students proud of their knowledge of languages. There is also an enormous body of contemporary literature in Spanish which native speakers of the language can take pleasure and pride in. And yet some colleges permit or encourage students in Spanish literature courses, even native speakers of the language, to read the literature in English translation rather than the Spanish original.

The relative prestige in the United States of languages other than English tends to rise as the percentage of educated, literate speakers of those languages does, and in proportion to the number who use an accepted (prestigious) form of the language. Lack of a sound knowledge of one's mother tongue, whether it be English or any other language, *is* a handicap, just as an inability to understand and use the lingua franca of any country also inevitably places residents or citizens of that country at a disadvantage. These two considerations are what bilingual education is all about. The urging of acceptance, or praise, of *any* kind of language because it is what someone speaks, because it is a means of communication, however inadequate, is doing a disservice to those pupils whose expectation is that the schools will help them gain mastery or competence in the languages they are learning. (A pleasure and delight in regional variations in accent and idiom is one thing, but the triteness and poverty of vocabulary and syntax and the lack of comprehensibility inherent in certain levels of non-standard language is another.)

In any case, those who believe that one way to achieve greater prestige for other languages is to downgrade the importance of English and to place less emphasis on the necessity for mastering it may well be damaging the cause of bilingual-bicultural education. (The increasing spread of public signs in Spanish and recent court decisions requiring that, for elections, information be available in Spanish for citizens with an inadequate knowledge of English, in order to ensure them equal voting rights, should not be construed as guarantees that the need for English will gradually lessen or disappear. The decisions have acknowledged that persons without a knowledge of English *are* at a disadvantage, and they constitute an attempt to rectify injustice deriving from a handicap. The handicap remains, however, in many other areas of life.)

Either bilingualism and biculturalism are feasible ways of life in the United States or they are not. One can't have it both ways. If they are, then bilingual education is useful and desirable. If they are not, then one might as well give up the idea of bilingual teaching and concentrate on one language. And given the circumstances, that language will logically be English—at least in the foreseeable future. Those who believe that a reversion to monolingualism is inevitable in the long run are opting, whether they intend it or not, for English. It would be unrealistic in view of the extent and status of English as a major world language to suggest that any other language is likely to take its place in the United States as a common means of communication among all the varied peoples who have contributed to its polyglot population and will undoubtedly furnish new elements in the future. The United States needs English, just as the Soviet Union needs Russian and the People's Republic of China needs its contemporary version of Mandarin, called *pu tung hua* (common, or standard, speech), which is based on a Peking dialect. (The standard language promoted by the former Nationalist government was referred to as *kuo-yo*, "national language," also based on a Peking dialect.)

Those who believe that bilingualism and biculturalism are valid concepts can further their development by working to increase the scope and improve the quality of bilingual education, and by making the bilingual programs in the schools serve as wide a range of ethnic groups as desire them, and can benefit from them, including the English-speaking. If enrollment is kept voluntary, no one will be forced to participate—and there will be some, both Anglos and non-English-speaking, who will prefer an all-English curriculum. But those who want to maintain facility in their mother tongue and become literate in it, while they are also being helped to learn English, should have that option.

The concept of bilingual-bicultural education for American-Indian children, though based in part on factors similar to those underlying the bilingual projects for pupils from other non-Anglo backgrounds, is in other respects different. Certain aspects are unique because of the Indian languages involved, the specific ways of thought and life of the descendants of the original occupants of the continent, and the history and relationship of native American Indians to the rest of the American society. The rationale for bilingual-bicultural education for Indian children is discussed in a chapter devoted specifically to the programs devised for them.

Whether or not one agrees with those who believe that in order to preserve the many different languages and cultural traits of the ethnically varied American people, a certain amount of propagandizing must be done and bilingual education associated with political activism, the undeniable fact remains of the acute, present need for bilingual-bicultural educational programs in public schools in many sections of the country and their potential value for all students, Anglo as well as non-Anglo.

Joshua Fishman, an authority on language loyalty—within ethnic groups and across political barriers—who has written extensively on the subject, expressed optimism about the future of mother tongues in an article published in *Materiales en Marcha* in December 1973.[2] He writes:

Yes, I do assume that most vernacular mother tongues are here to stay. Those that are protected by their own political establishments certainly are, and most of the others, that have no political power to back them, have learned or are learning to utilize modern social institutions and media on behalf of the sentimental, ideological, moral, esthetic, religious, or purely customary power with which they are associated.

For purposes of analysis, Fishman makes distinctions between "mother tongues" and "other tongues," non-political versus political power, and "intimacy" versus "status-distance" in language use and makes observations concerning political and societal realities, both intranational and international. (He is writing not only about the United States but the world in general.) As Fishman puts it:

> What is really of interest is not whether mankind will continue to speak and teach a huge array of MOTHER TONGUES for interaction with kith and kin and other intimates, and whether it will continue to speak and teach a rather small number of OTHER tongues for interaction with those who are physically and psychologically more removed, but, rather WHOM it will define as being in the one category or the other (and when), and WHICH other tongues will be involved.
>
> Of course, among the vernaculars without political power some will wax and others will wane, and still others (the ones that are most exposed to participatory social change guided by power structures related to other vernaculars) will vanish. However, new vernaculars are also being born out of pidgins round the world. All in all, therefore, I foresee only a small possible diminution in the total number of mother tongues by the year 2000 or by other foreseeable dates. Frisian—and Catalan—and Breton—and Basque and Yiddish-speaking mothers are likely to continue to feel and believe that their mother tongues are as good and as beautiful and as inimitable—at least for everyday use with their children, husbands, and grandmothers—as do mothers that speak Albanian, Afrikans [sic] or Hebrew. And the latter are likely to continue to believe that their mother tongues, for these same functions of intimacy, are every bit as good as French and English and Russian.

Suggesting the usefulness and need of a limited number of universally known languages, Fishman continues:

> Just as speakers of politically unprotected languages (not to mention speakers of politically threatened ones) must come to a *modus vivendi* with the political establishment that surrounds them, so must smaller political establishments recognize larger ones. Such recognition needs arise in connection with education, work, commerce, travel, military experience, and inter-group contact of

whatever kind, whether free or forced. There are, of course, societies whose bilingualism is fully indigenized and internalized—and these should be a lesson and a light to all of us—but, by and large, second language learning, whether societal or individual, involves a we-they distinction. The first question, therefore, is whose language is to be dominant in we-they interactions, and the second, and more interesting one, into which, if any, internal function should "their" language be admitted if IT turns out to be the dominant one for intergroup purposes? In this latter connection I foresee a long-term trend toward greater mutual toleration than would have seemed likely in 1900, when many nationalist movements were still at the white heat stage.

In regard to the increasing use of mother tongues in at least elementary education around the world, Fishman states:

More and more politically unestablished and unprotected vernaculars are being admitted into at least primary (or early primary) school functions in the western world, and I would expect this tendency to continue there and also to become more common, within the limits of feasibility, in other parts of the world with modernizing and consolidating minorities. The better known cases of Landsmal (Nynorsk), Frisian, Irish, Catalan, Lappish, Valdostian, and Romansh have their less well-known but equally numerous and revealing counterparts in Southern and Eastern Europe, Canada, the U.S.A., Latin America, and elsewhere. Indeed, I do not expect . . . the pressures for similar recognition for Basque, Breton, Occitan, and the like to disappear by the year 2000. Rather I expect them to be increasingly admitted into the elementary school of one type or another, in one form or another, very much as is and will be the case with vernacular forms of Arabic and of the more sizeable sedentary and concentrated African and Asian populations without political establishments that are primarily their own. *Often such recognition carries with it a modicum of further momentum into local governmental institutions and local mass media. However, it is really quite instructive to note the extent to which the latter half of the 20th century has witnessed the tapering off of secessionist movements and their satisfaction, instead, with a modicum of localized cultural autonomy.* [Italics added.] Of course, different parts of the world are at different stages in this accommodation process. While one part has cooled off, others are still boiling and steaming. Nevertheless, all in all, I would expect MORE vernaculars to be used/taught in the early elementary grades in the year 2000 than is the case today. Even Israel is timidly experimenting in this direction, and even with its Jewish population. *The result, however, will be that speakers of non-state languages will more often be taught two*

> languages at school rather than one—*the language of their intimacy and the language of their functional polity.* [Italics added.]

In speaking of the tendency—indeed the necessity—for countries whose languages do not have worldwide currency to teach their people some second language that does, Fishman discusses the factor of the waning of the worldwide influence of formerly dominant languages in the present period, referring specifically to French, and the possibility that it could conceivably happen to English—at some time in the future.

> Oddly enough, the same will be true [the necessity for learning a second, worldwide language] for almost all speakers of mother tongues that correspond to small and intermediate polities. These [people] are learning languages of more powerful regional and/or international intergroup contact and will continue to do so increasingly. . . . Some have themselves only recently established their political and cultural autonomy. It is hard for them to admit that ANOTHER language—however useful—should be made part and parcel of everyone's post-primary education when their own language has only so recently been admitted to academic respectability. For others, who recently basked in the sunlight of regional or international splendor, it is hard to admit that the fickle sun has shifted to others now and that they themselves must now do what they formerly glibly advised others to do: learn a language of wider currency and functional generality. Nevertheless, hard though it may be, I expect this trend to continue. France may be among the last to submit, for the pill is hardest to swallow in her case. Nevertheless, she will do it, as have Germany, Spain, Italy and Japan, and find her self-image untarnished in the end, for true culture will (in France) still and always be only French.

Fishman also writes at length about various aspects and prospects of English as the lingua franca of the world:

> Will I really come to an end without mentioning English, the linguistic *eminence grise*, at all? Will it continue to spread as a second language the world over, as a benevolent bonus or creeping cancer of modernity? *Perhaps, particularly since Russians and Chinese and Arabs (even "Francophone" Arabs) are increasingly inclined toward it, rather than toward each other's regionally dominant languages. Perhaps, because it is not dependent on either overt political or cultural control for its spread, but rather on less threatening commercial and technological expertise and efficiency.* [Italics added.] Nevertheless, *sic transit gloria mundi*. The mid-19th century could not foresee the end of French dominance as the international language of culture and diplomacy, but it came with the political and economic downgrading of certain centers and the

upgrading of others during the past century. English may enjoy a longer or shorter period of basking in the international sun. The fact that we cannot now foresee the end of its sway does not mean that it is greater or stronger or nobler than any of the other imperial languages of the past.

Fishman then brings up the often suggested disadvantage to Anglos of speaking a language of world dominance—their ignorance of other languages because they feel no need to learn any language but English.

In the meantime, during its heyday, the major negative impact of English is on the anglos themselves. Unlike linguistically less-favored populations, they have little need to learn other languages or to learn them well. . . . Surely they are paying a high price for the linguistic dominance that they have in the world of know-how and consumerism. The non-state peoples are grateful for minimal recognition of their mother tongues, but they often (and increasingly) learn both a national regional language and an international one as well. The small state, the intermediate state, and even large state peoples often (and increasingly) learn a wider regional or international language as well as their own. . . . Even corners of the anglo world have had to swallow their pride (e.g., in Canada, in the Philippines, in South Africa, in Puerto Rico). But the anglo heartland continues to speak only to God, and, as is well known in the U.S.A. and in Great Britain, God has always spoken in English when He was serious. However, if God were to become fickle and begin to speak Russian or Chinese in his more efficient undertakings, anglos too might begin to discover the broadening impact of bilingualism.

Coming, at the last, to a consideration of the philosophical rationale for linguistic and cultural distinctiveness, Fishman writes:

And finally, we come to consider the fraternity of mankind; . . . Are we not all becoming more alike? Do we not realize more fully with each passing decade the danger and folly of ethnocentrism? Does not both capitalist pragmatism and communist ideology require and lead to one language for us all? Perhaps, but not before the year 2000 and, if ever, not as a mother tongue, and therefore not as the vehicle of our deepest feelings, our most sensitive creativity, our most human humanity. The unity of mankind is a unity of fate, not a unity of face. It is a unity of ultimate interdependence, not of ultimate identity. It is true that modern technology and modern ideology lead everywhere in similar directions with respect to behavior and life styles. however, modernity is just one stripe in the cloak of many colors that every society wears. Other stripes are of treasured traditional, regional, local, and even class-derived vintage and, as a result, societal multilingualism will not merely linger on in backward corners of the globe, but it will defend and advance itself via modern methods and media (rather than merely giving in to such), and will do so within the very heartland of modernity per se.

The new ethnicity movements in the U.S.A. and similar movements already in existence (and others yet to come) in Great Britain, France, Spain, Germany, Italy and the Soviet Union, will help clarify the need of modern man for unique societal intimacy and intimate societal uniqueness: in his food and dress, in his music and poetry, in his art and artifacts, in his celebrating and mourning, in his dying and giving birth. Thus. . . with the continued cooling off of conflicted, exclusivistic, and ideologized ethnicity (nationalism) in most parts of the globe, it may become clearer even to intellectuals (who are always the last to understand reality since they are so convinced that it is merely their task to create it) that the fraternity of mankind requires a recognition and acceptance of mankind's diversity and the creative use thereof. Thus, it is the dialectic between uniformation and diversification which must be seen not only as the true foundation for sharply increased foreign language teaching by the year 2000 but additionally as the true foundation for much that is most challenging and creative in modern society (local, regional, and international) the world over.

To move the discussion of bilingual-bicultural education from the wide stage of the world to the narrower confines of the classroom, and from philosophical considerations to the mundane facts of life as they concern public school education, the rationale for the continuation and further development of bilingual teaching in the United States can be summarized in a few words. First, it is needed; and with immigration increasing rather than decreasing (as a result of the changes enacted in 1965 in the immigration laws), there is likely to be even greater need for it in the coming years. Secondly, it is helpful. Though it can by no means be guaranteed as the solution for all the problems of the pupils involved, it is proving of indisputable value. However sound or controversial social and pedagogical theories may be in the abstract, the real proof of educational recipes is what goes on in the classroom. And by and large, bilingual classrooms are happy, productive places. (This is not to suggest that everyone who is happy is necessarily learning something, or that one cannot learn if he is unhappy. Many a French and German pupil has proved the contrary, learning an impressive amount while being overburdened or unhappy in school. But the circumstances and reasons for the unhappiness are quite different from what we are considering here. And, if one can arrange educational situations and experiences so that children can learn and not be made unhappy in the process, that, too, is worth doing.)

Another factor which suggests that school systems had better investigate the potentialities of bilingual-bicultural education is that recent court decisions, and also findings of the United States Civil Rights Commission, are challenging school authorities to devise ways of providing equal educational opportunities for children from various ethnic minority groups who do not speak English. In a decision having reference to 1,800 Chinese pupils in San Francisco who were receiving no special help with their language problems (but also applicable to large numbers of Spanish-speaking students in the country), the U.S. Supreme Court ruled unanimously (in the *LAU V. Nichols* case) early in 1974 that schools receiving federal funds must provide such pupils with the same opportunities provided English-speaking children. The court ruling indicated that these pupils' opportunities would be equal to those of English-speaking pupils only if methods were used that enabled them to understand what they were being taught. In part the decision said: "There is no equality of treatment merely by providing students with the same facilities, text books, teachers and curriculum; for students who do not understand English are effectively foreclosed from any meaningful education."[3]

The U.S. Civil Rights Commission issued a report at about the same time, accusing the schools in the five Southwestern states where most of the 6 million or more Mexican Americans in the United States live, of largely ignoring the language and culture of the Chicano students. Only 70,000 of the 1.6 million Spanish-speaking pupils were receiving bilingual education, though they were greatly handicapped by their language problems. The Commission concluded that there was a need for more bilingual programs at least in the early grades for those pupils who spoke Spanish at home and did not understand English but were being taught exclusively in English at school.[4]

Another court case that may profoundly affect the attitudes of many schools boards toward bilingual education and that resulted in an immediate increase in bilingual programs in New York City was a class action suit brought jointly by Aspira of New York, Inc., and Aspira of America, Inc., two Puerto Rican organizations, against the Board of Education of New York City. They had charged the city school system with failing to meet the needs of Spanish-speaking pupils, thereby leading to extensive truancy and high drop-out figures among Puerto Rican pupils. The suit was settled by a consent decree, signed August 29, 1974, by U.S. District Court Judge Marvin Frankel. Under the terms of the decree, the Board of Education was required, and agreed, to devise a better method for identifying Spanish-speaking pupils and classifying them according to their ability to speak, read, write, and comprehend English and Spanish. This was to be done by October 1, 1974, and the board would be required to furnish an explanation to the court if they failed to accomplish this. By October 30 a list of pilot schools which would offer bilingual programs was to be drawn up by the Chancellor, and the programs were to be put into operation by February 1975. The decree mandated that by the opening of the following school year in September 1975, bilingual programs must be put into effect in all the schools in the city where children needed the special program. The consent decree emphasized that pupils served by the bilingual programs should spend maximum time with other children and not be segregated or isolated from them. The court retained jurisdiction and would rule on any disputes which might arise concerning the board's fulfilling of its obligations in the matter.[5]

Positive and productive aspects of bilingual projects, in addition to purely academic considerations, are commented on by teachers and students alike. The author was told by a principal of a school in Springfield, Massachusetts, with a heavy enrollment of Puerto Rican pupils that before the establishment of the bilingual project there, he would never have had time to talk to or escort a visitor around the school, since his entire day would have been devoted to handling "disciplinary problems." Such problems had now almost disappeared. Students of a New York City high school which one year had been plagued by violence and disruption attributed the peace of the following year partly to the introduction of bilingual studies.[6] There has been some variation in the degree of success of bilingual teaching in different localities and situations, but, by and large, teachers and students who have had the opportunity to participate in the projects are enthusiastic and confident that they are involved in a good educational experience.

No doubt increasing pressure will be exerted by various ethnic and linguistic segments of the American society for bilingual-bicultural education as an option for their children. And there will undoubtedly be legislation in response to those demands from constituents. Alan Cranston, Senator from California, late in 1973 introduced the Comprehensive Bilingual Education Amendments Act of 1973 (S. 2553) to improve bilingual programs and expand services into new areas. The bill, which was co-sponsored by Senators Kennedy of Massachusetts and Montoya of New Mexico, also proposed setting up a permanent Division of Bilingual Education in the U.S. Office of Education. S. 2553 was aimed at programs for elementary- and secondary-grade pupils. Senators Cranston and Montoya also co-sponsored a bill authored by Senator

Kennedy (S. 2552), the Bilingual Education Reform Act of 1973, which dealt primarily with higher education, teacher training, and vocational training. S. 2553 sustained for an additional four years the previously authorized figure of $135 million per year for bilingual education. Besides the fixed authorization ceiling, the bill also authorized Congress to appropriate additional funds that were deemed necessary. (Congress has never actually appropriated more than $35 million in any one year, though it has had authority to do so.) These bills, or portions of them, were incorporated into the final version of the Education Amendments of 1974, which became law as H.R. 69 in August of 1974.

Senator Cranston pointed out, in stating his reasons for introducing his bill (in *Materiales en Marcha*, December 1973), that there were at that time some 5 million children in schools throughout the country who needed bilingual education but were not getting it. In his own state alone it was estimated that there were 180,000 pupils of Spanish, Asian, or Indian descent in urgent need of help, with only about 25,000 receiving the necessary assistance.[7]

In whatever direction one looks, and from whatever point of view, it is not difficult to find reasons for establishing some type or degree of bilingual education in the public schools of the nation. The major and remaining questions are not, Why bilingual education but how, how much, at what levels, what types, and with what specific goals? One question that will, and ought continually to be asked is, How good are the programs and how can they be improved? There are no pat answers to any of these questions, since the problems involved are not easily solved. But the questions should be raised and answered—by the continuing development and adaptation of the general theory to the specifics of individual situations and differing circumstances if bilingual education is to gain full acceptance in all places where there is a need and a desire for it.

Notes

1. Elizabeth Willink, "Bilingual Education for Navajo Children," in Paul R. Turner (ed.), *Bilingualism in the Southwest*, University of Arizona Press, Tucson, 1973, part II, "American Indians, Assumptions and Methods."

2. Joshua Fishman, "Will Foreign Languages Still Be Taught in the Year 2000?"*Materiales en Marcha*, Materials Acquisition Project, ESEA, Title VII, San Diego City Schools, December 1973, pp. 12-15, 21.

3. *Time Magazine*, Feb. 4, 1974, p. 80.

4. *New York Times*, "Ideas and Trends," 10 February 1974.

5. *New York Times*, 30 August 1974, p. 1.

6. *New York Times*, "Academic Achievement Crowns a Peaceful Year at Morris High," by Pranay Gupte, 8 July 1973, p. 31.

7. Alan Cranston, "Comprehensive Bilingual Education Amendments Act of 1973," *Materiales en Marcha*, Materials Acquisition Project, ESEA, Title VII, San Diego City Schools, December 1973, p. 16.

Bilingualism and the Teaching of English in Puerto Rico

5 Since Puerto Rican pupils constitute a major segment of the largest language group involved in bilingual programs in the United States, the Spanish-speaking, it may be of interest to review what has happened over the years on the island itself in language use and language teaching.

Bilingualism and bilingual education in Puerto Rico have had a checkered history and exhibit certain complexities and paradoxes. The dominant language of the island, and therefore of the schools today, is Spanish, but English is taught as a subject in most, probably all, schools, public and private. In the public schools a daily English lesson, varying in length at different schools and grade levels, is scheduled as part of the regular curriculum from the first year of schooling on. How much English the pupils learn varies greatly, depending on many different considerations. As anyone who has ever visited the island or come in contact with Puerto Ricans in the continental United States is aware, some Puerto Ricans speak English well, others poorly or not at all. As a rule those who have a generally high level of education or who live in the more sophisticated metropolitan areas of the island where there is more contact with English-speaking people are more likely to know English than those from remote rural villages or from the poorest sections of the big cities. Other determining factors are often the socio-economic background of the family, the qualifications of the particular teacher of English involved, and perhaps most important, the amount of interest and motivation on the part of the student. In addition to the public school system, there are many good private schools, both non-denominational and parochial (Catholic) on the island. As in other parts of the United States, many families who can afford it send their children to private schools where more emphasis may be placed on the mastery of a second language or the curriculum taught in English.

Though Puerto Rico has, in theory, compulsory, free education for all children, there is no system for enforcing it. There are no truant (attendance) officers and no method of checking on pupils. If parents do not insist that their children go to school, no one forces them to go. So there are children who attend intermittently or stop after a few years, and undoubtedly some who never go to school at all and therefore don't learn English or any other part of the academic curriculum. There are variations in the degrees of competence of the teachers of English on the island; some may have a knowledge of the written language but an inadequate command of spoken English and a faulty pronunciation; others who have spent time teaching or studying in the continental United States or have had good English courses in Puerto Rico may speak fluently and accurately and be able to lead their students to proficiency in both spoken and written English.

One effect of the establishment of Spanish-English bilingual programs all over the United States has been an increase in contact and cooperation between schools and teachers in Puerto Rico and those on the mainland, which in the long run should result in the development of materials in both English and Spanish for the curriculum and in the upgrading of the English-language training of the teachers in the schools in Puerto Rico. Occasionally there has also been the disadvantageous side effect, for Puerto Rico, of losing at least temporarily some of its better teachers who have been recruited to assist in setting up bilingual programs for Puerto Rican pupils in mainland schools undersupplied with Spanish-speaking personnel. But these teachers often spend only one year on such an assignment, so the advantages and disadvantages will probably even themselves out eventually.

The teaching and the use of English over the years in Puerto Rico have had their ups and downs. Until 1898 Puerto Rico was a colony of Spain, and Spanish the language of the population. When, as the result of the treaty ending the Spanish-American War, the island became a territory of the United States, English naturally immediately assumed great importance. The United States War Department, which at first was in charge of everything on the island (including the schools), and later the civilian government recruited Americans, mostly young college graduates, to teach English in the schools of Puerto Rico. (The illiteracy rate—in Spanish—among the population when the island was ceded to the United States was 77.3 percent.[1]) Many idealistically motivated, or adventurous, young Americans, male and female, went off on something like a "peace corps" venture, making the trip by boat to San Juan and then by train and, in some cases, horse and buggy, to other cities and towns around the island to bring "American Education" to Puerto Rico. By and large they were hospitably received; most of them enjoyed their Puerto Rican experience, and a few of them stayed on and lived the rest of their lives on their adopted tropical island. Contemporary accounts indicate that many Puerto Ricans were not unhappy to be free of the yoke of Spain and welcomed the arrival of the Americans, though later a certain amount of disappointment set in when they found they were not going to be as free to govern themselves as they had hoped.

However extensive the good intentions of the Americans and the receptiveness of the Puerto Ricans may have been, the island's population was not transformed overnight into an English-speaking people. In the first place, there were never enough English-speaking teachers to provide proper instruction in all the schools, and those who were teaching did not for the most part possess the knowledge and techniques for the effective teaching of (English as) a foreign language commonly expected of teachers with such assignments today. Some of the American supervisors spoke Spanish, but most of the teachers on arrival did not, and some of them never learned much of the language. The relations seem to have been pleasant between the American teachers and the native population, and whatever success was achieved must be attributed more to the good will on both sides than to carefully planned language instruction.

General Henry, the American administrator, in the first official statement on education under American rule in Puerto Rico, referred to the possibility of recruiting teachers from the States to instruct schoolchildren in the new language being heard on the island.

> The system of school education should be looked into and it is my desire to ascertain how many teachers they (the municipalities) can pay who can teach the American or English language commencing with the younger children. It is believed that those who can speak English only can accomplish the purpose by object lessons. It is thought that American women for teaching can be obtained for $50 a month in gold, and they are well worth it. The young children are anxious to learn and now is the time for them to do so. If the alcaldes [mayors] will report to me how many teachers they can so employ, they will be brought from the United States and sent to these towns.[2]

One of the Americans who taught sixth-grade English, math and "bits and pieces of history and geography," and sixth-, seventh-, and eighth-grade English, in the town of Toa Baja in 1911 (and has spent all her life since then on the island), reminiscing in 1973 about her experiences there some sixty odd years ago, wrote:

> People I did see daily were the teachers. There was Doña Ana, teaching the fourth and fifth grades. Next came a man, in the second and third, a somewhat dour individual who seemingly knew not one word of English, or to have any desire to exchange

conversation with me. The smallest children were in the care of a sweet young married woman, with a personality well suited to her work, and a shy but reasonable command of English.

In my own room of between thirty and forty children, the sixth graders and I could do little but smile at each other (at first). The seventh graders, who had had a previous year under an "Americana" comprehended more and were interested. The eighth graders, now in a third year of English instruction, understood readily and were fairly fluent. All were interested and responsive. . . .

My preparation had been for high school Latin. Of grade subjects and methods I had nothing to fall back on but my own very dim recollections of grade school. . . . But we had a cheerful time together. The (today) scorned Law and Order prevailed always in my classroom, and I suspect it was the quiet discipline and peace that prevailed when Mister Piper (the district supervisor) visited us, that kept him from criticizing what I was doing, or perhaps mainly, what I was not doing.

At any rate, the War Department was running the show; they had selected us and placed us, Mr. Piper supervised us, and the good old American haphazard system ground its mistaken but somehow successful way through the years.[3]

On the subject of whether the curriculum was taught in Spanish or English after the American take-over in Puerto Rico, she explains:

Through the years there has been considerable variation and argument about the handling of English. . . . different administrations had different ideas. Possibly it is fair to say that the policy itself meant emphasis on English, but it was so absurd, with a multitude of teachers who spoke broken English or none at all. In the early days, I think it safe to say, the Department of Education did bring down college graduates who did good work in the schools, especially in teaching English, but on the whole the results have been rather pitiful. By the time of Commonwealth (1952) the consensus was that the children were not only not learning English, but were floundering in all other subjects not (taught) in their native tongue. There have never been enough teachers really able to handle English. . . .[4]

The same ex-teacher mentions, however, "Our daughter-in-law, herself a Puerto Rican, went to private schools in Ponce and speaks impeccable English."[5]

Writing for the *TESOL Newsletter* in April 1973, a general supervisor in the English Program of the Department of Education of Puerto Rico, Mrs. Viñas de Vasquez (who has since been named Director of the

English Program), described the six major changes in language policy in Puerto Rico between 1898 and 1947:

Up until 1898 Spanish had been the official language and the only language of Puerto Rico. That year marked the beginning of the teaching and learning of English in Puerto Rico. It also marked the beginning of the blending of two cultures, a situation which had met with considerable passive resistance, the majority of the Puerto Ricans being strongly traditional and resistant to change.

The first change was introduced by Dr. Martin Brumbaugh who became Commissioner of Education in 1900. The "Brumbaugh Policy" provided for the teaching of English and Spanish as subjects in the first grade. Spanish was to be used also as the medium of instruction in... grades 1–8 while English was to be the medium of instruction . . . in grades 9–12. Spanish was to be taught as . . . a special subject in the secondary grades (9–12).

Commissioner Roland Faulkner introduced the second major change in 1905. He aimed at the use of English as the medium of instruction in all grades of the public school system.

Commissioner Paul Miller introduced the third major change in 1916. Spanish became the language of instruction in grades 1–4, both English and Spanish in grade 5, English in the remaining grades, 6–12. The study of both English and Spanish as subjects continued in both the elementary and high schools.

Dr. José Padin introduced the fourth . . . change in 1934. He made Spanish the language of instruction at the elementary level (grades 1–8) and doubled the time devoted to English as a subject, from 45 to 90 minutes, in the seventh and eighth grades.

Dr. José Gallardo introduced the fifth . . . change in 1937. It involved a series of policies evolving from an effort to use both English and Spanish as the media of instruction. Some subjects were taught in Spanish and others were taught in English. The final development was instruction in the vernacular (Spanish) in the elementary school.

Commissioner Mariano Villaronga introduced the sixth major change in 1947. He made Spanish the medium of instruction at all levels of the public school system. In 1948 he initiated the English Program which is in effect today.

The matter which had caused Puerto Rican education so many setbacks was settled for good. The policy since 1947 has been to teach English as a subject and to use Spanish as the medium of instruction in all grades of the public school system beginning in the first grade.[6]

It might be considered one of the ironies of historical timing that during the greater part of the period when the educational system was concentrating on the teaching and learning of English, a knowledge of that language was not nearly so essential to the vast majority of the population as it is now, when fast, economical plane service encourages migration and makes travel back and forth between the Spanish-speaking island and the English-speaking mainland a common occurrence for many Puerto Rican families. This mobility of the Puerto Rican population makes a command of English desirable or a necessity not only, as in the past, for persons in positions of importance in political and business life but also for the large numbers of Puerto Rican citizens heading for the continental United States, seeking improvement in their economic situations. It is important now for the "little man" as well as the "big one" to know English.

It is true, of course, that before the island had achieved its Commonwealth status (Estado Libre Associado, literally Associated Free State), American officials were appointed to posts in Puerto Rico, and most of them did not speak Spanish. Puerto Ricans who wanted to converse with them had to use their language, English. Theodore Roosevelt, Jr., was reportedly the first American governor (1929–1932) who had even attempted to speak the language of the island's population, and, though he took lessons assiduously, he admitted to having referred to himself as "the mother of four children" and to the chief of the Bureau of Insular Affairs as "a tapeworm" *(solitaria)* instead of a bachelor *(soltero)* in his early encounters with the Spanish language.[7]

The Honorable Celeste Benítez de Rexach, who in 1973 was the Secretary of Education of the Commonwealth of Puerto Rico and as such a member of the Governor's Council, in an address to the opening session of the TESOL Convention in San Juan in May of that year, outlined the background and explained some of the reasons for the ambivalence in Puerto Ricans' attitudes toward the study and use of English in the schools and on the island. She pointed out that, at the end of the Spanish-American War, many Puerto Ricans admired the political system and the accomplishments of the nation to which their island had been ceded and that since they had been chafing under the control of Spain, their hopes and expectations for more freedom and equality as a territory of the United States outweighed the inconvenience of trying to get along with a people whose language was foreign and whose manner of life was so different from their own.

When conflicts developed because they were not given as much autonomy as they had hoped, many Puerto Ricans began to feel that they had exchanged the status of a colony of Spain for that of a colony of the United States. Much of the discontent, unfortunately, was focused on the language question and the policy of teaching English in the schools. The original emphasis on English, after the cession of the island to the United States, seemed to produce neither a command of Spanish nor of English but led rather to continued illiteracy in both languages for many pupils. As Mrs. Rexach phrased it:

A wave of nationalism swept across the Island, condemning the language policy as a sign of American imperialism and a menace to the identity of the Puerto Rican people. This polarized the situation—those in favor of continued association with the States just as blindly championed the sole use of English in the classroom.

It is not difficult to understand why the students became increasingly ambivalent, even hostile, to the learning of English. Official policy dictated that they study it and all about them they saw the need to speak English to get better paying jobs. And yet, at the same time, they felt that to study English, to speak it, was to deny their identity as Puerto Ricans.

The result of this early linguistic policy in Puerto Rico, with its emphasis on the "Americanization" of our people, was that the teaching of English in Puerto Rico became a political question. To a large extent, it still is.

For some independence advocates, learning English in school smacks of "colonialism" and is a tacit acceptance of American domination of our economic development and of our close political ties. For some statehood advocates, the mastery of English is a necessary step towards the cultural and political integration they believe essential for the advent of statehood.

It was only after the second World War that the Island government was granted full control of its school system. Some years later, in 1952, the people of the Island voted to become a free and associated state with the United States. Thus the Commonwealth of Puerto Rico was born. These two events, I believe, signal the beginning of a separate and unique period in the history of Puerto Rico.

We are now free to attempt to build a school system which best serves the needs of our society, best represents our culture and values.[8]

In carrying out the present policy of using Spanish as a medium of instruction for pupils in all grades but teaching English as a required subject from the first grade through all their years of schooling, Mrs. Rexach suggested that one of the first goals should be improving the quality of Spanish-language instruction, so that pupils would be led to a fuller and better knowledge, both written and spoken, of their native language. In setting this goal, Puerto Rican educators are following the same principles followed by the proponents of bilingual education in the United States. One of the basic tenets underlying the movement for bilingual teaching is that the more children learn about their first language and the better their verbal development, spoken and written is—in other words, the more they know about language in general—the better prepared they will be to learn a second language, any second language.

One of the hindrances to the effective teaching of English in Puerto Rico was the shortage of trained teachers competent to teach it, particularly in the smaller schools in rural areas. Puerto Rico is taking steps to remedy this situation and to departmentalize the teaching of English in the elementary grades. (It is already departmentalized at the upper-grade levels.) In the summer of 1969 the Department of Education began to recruit Puerto Rican high school graduates and beginning college students who are native or near-native speakers of English (those who have had most of their schooling in the United States or in private schools in Puerto Rico where English has been the medium of instruction) as candidates for training in a new "Bilingual Teachers Program." The plan calls for the trainees to teach English in the first three grades of the elementary schools and, at the same time, to take college courses leading to certification. Before being assigned to schools as provisional teachers, the trainees are given an intensive six-week course which includes methods of teaching English to Puerto Rican children, child psychology, and the analysis and use of materials assigned for the primary grades. The hope of the Department of Education is to train at least 2,000 special bilingual instructors to be assigned to all the elementary schools on the island. The teaching of English would then be departmentalized, with regular classroom teachers giving instruction in other subjects but all English classes to be taught by fully competent speakers of English especially trained in teaching English as a second language.

In the winter of 1974 this author stopped in at three schools in different towns in Puerto Rico (chosen at random simply because they were in the area where I happened to be) and requested permission to observe how English was being taught in these particular towns. As has always been my experience, I was courteously received and permitted to visit groups at various grade levels, fifth, seventh, eighth, ninth, and early elementary.

In two small towns in the southwest corner of the island, I talked with two of the new type of bilingual teacher-trainees and observed one at length, teaching English to first-, second-, and third-graders. In the first and second grades the work was oral. The teacher kept up a fast pace, changing activities frequently to keep the children on their toes and interested. They sang traditional songs, such as "Baa, Baa, Black Sheep," "Ten Little Indians," and "Old MacDonald Had a Farm"; they talked about colors and shapes by comparing the flags of Puerto Rico and the United States; they danced and played games in English; they practiced *left, right, up,* and *down* with physical body movement, standing, bending, stretching or pointing as they chanted, "Left to the window, right to the door, up to the ceiling, down to the floor." It was good second-language teaching for children, and from all appearances these children were enjoying their English lesson thoroughly. In the third grade the pupils were beginning to read in English, using a carefully programmed phonetic approach. The curriculum and materials are provided by the Department of Education of Puerto Rico and are standardized throughout the island.

The second bilingual teacher-trainee with whom I spoke in a neighboring village had attended school in the States through junior high school, and high school in Puerto Rico. She spoke correct, fluent, and unaccented English. She reported that her first-, second-, and third-grade pupils loved their English classes. Both of these bilingual teacher-trainees had gone through the required six-week intensive training course given by the Department of Education before starting their actual teaching work. In addition to teaching English to first-, second-, and third-graders in the schools to which they were assigned, they were taking courses at nearby universities for credits toward an A.B. degree.

According to statistics provided by the Department of Education in April of 1974, approximately 1,200 bilingual teacher positions had been filled by teacher-trainees who had taken the special six-week preparatory course and were enrolled in the auxiliary bilingual teacher-training program. At that time slightly over 60 percent of the schools on the island had one of the new type of bilingual instructors teaching English in the early grades. It is expected that more candidates will be recruited and that the program will be continued until there are 2,000 or more such bilingual teachers, enough to cover all the elementary schools on the island.

The costs of this teacher-training program have been paid partly by the Puerto Rico Department of Education and partly by federal monies from various titles of ESEA, Title I, Teachers' Corps, and Title V (before it was discontinued).

If this bilingual teacher training program can be continued, the quality of the English instruction in the elementary schools on the island should be greatly improved, with marked benefits for the pupils in their acquisition of a better command of oral English.

Of other formally organized bilingal projects financed under the provisions of the federal Education Act, such as those in operation in many parts of the United States, there are, or were in Puerto Rico during the 1972–73 school year, just two, both on the junior high school level, in the city of Bayamón. It may come as a surprise to those who are accustomed to attributing the educational difficulties of Puerto Rican pupils in cities of the continental United States to their inability to speak English, and therefore to fit in and function adequately in schools where everything is taught in English, to learn that for the Department of Education in Puerto Rico, a reverse problem exists. But there are Puerto Rican students who have difficulty in schools on the island, where the curriculum is taught in Spanish, because *English* is *their* dominant language. These are Puerto Rican children who have spent most of their school years in New York, Chicago, or other mainland cities, have attended schools where only English is used, and who, though they may understand Spanish and speak it with their parents or other relatives, have not learned to read and write it. When they reach adolescence, many such Puerto Rican young people are sent back to Puerto Rico to live with grandmothers, or uncles and aunts, because their parents, worried about drug use, crime, laxity of control, and other undesirable influences in Northern urban centers, feel that their sons and daughters will be safer back on their home island of Puerto Rico. In other cases, because of changes in the job market or for personal considerations, whole families will decide to return to Puerto Rico after some years of residence in the continental United States.

The two federally financed bilingual projects in Bayamón, a sprawling industrial city of 146,000 inhabitants 7 miles from San Juan, address themselves to the rather special educational needs of such English-speaking "returnees," though they include in the classes an equal number of Spanish-speaking or Spanish-dominant pupils who ask to be enrolled in the bilingual program. At the Papa Juan 23 Escuela Intermedia (Pope John the XXIII Junior High School), out of the 1,000 pupils enrolled in the morning session (2,000 students attend the school in all, on double session), 300 are grouped in a separate bilingual school made up of 10 classes of 30 students each. The curriculum is taught partly in Spanish and partly in English by 12 teachers who are all completely bilingual. This project has as one of its special assignments the development of materials suitable for such bilingual classes, and receives funds from Title I and Title III of ESEA. Some of the staff spend the mornings teaching at the school and the afternoons at the Curriculum Center of the University of Bayamón working on materials. The first director of this project, a Puerto Rican teacher and administrator who holds a master's degree from New York University, had spent the previous academic year (1971–72) in West Chester, Pennsylvania, setting up a bilingual program there.

Compounding the problems of running a "school within a school" is a scarcity of space—there are sometimes simply no classrooms available at Papa Juan 23 school for the bilingual groups unless other classes happen to be cancelled because of teacher absence or other reasons —and the fact that even though the bilingual school is housed in the newest of the school's cluster of buildings, finished in 1972, there is (or at least in the winter of 1972–73 was) no provision for electricity, so that tape recorders and other equipment requiring electric power cannot be used.

There is also resistance on the part of some pupils to learning, or at least to using, Spanish. If in learning English in schools on the mainland they have been made to feel ashamed of knowing Spanish or given the idea that it is an inferior language, when they return to the island some pupils will claim that they don't understand Spanish, or will say, scornfully, or proudly, "If my grandmother (or anyone else) speaks to me in Spanish, I answer in English." It is important that such students be led to realize that being bilingual, truly, competently bilingual, can be a great asset, not a liability.

Among the staff at the Pope John school (in spite of its clerical name, it is a public school) is one Catholic sister, originally from Minnesota and a resident of Puerto Rico for some 10 years, who had taught in the mountain town of Adjuntas before being sent to New York City by the Department of Education for special study in the field of bilingual education. On her return she was assigned to work in the newly established bilingual project at Papa Juan 23 Escuela. Another of the teachers is a young man who also spent a year in New York City, teaching in a public school. The University of Illinois at Champaign-Urbana has collaborated with the bilingual project in Bayamón, providing consultants and materials. In the 1973–74 school year two interns from the university were doing their practice teaching in the bilingual project at the Pope John school, one teaching science, the other algebra, both in English. The federal funding of the bilingual project at this school was to come to an end at the conclusion of the 1973–74 school year, but the program was to be continued, with the district assuming the financial responsibility.

At the José Padin Junior High School in Bayamón, 15 groups of 30 students each participate in a Title VII bilingual program. Of the group, half are English-dominant, with poor command of Spanish, and half are Spanish-dominant pupils who speak almost no English. Their enrollment in the bilingual classes is voluntary. One of the problems in Puerto Rico, as in the States, is finding qualified teachers for bilingual programs. The staff working in the bilingual program at José Padin school during the 1973–74 school year all had A.B. degrees and were bilingual, but most of them held only provisional certificates at that time. The services of a librarian are available to the students for two hours in the evening, and there are evening courses in both Spanish and English for parents. A sewing class is also offered. Special help from a Spanish-skills teacher is available to about 50 students at the school, who meet with this teacher in small groups during the day.

The José Padin school population is large, necessitating interlocking double sessions. The regular school program runs from 7:30 A.M. to 12:30 P.M. for the seventh and ninth grades. The eighth graders and the students in the bilingual program attend school from 12:30 to 5:30 P.M. The director of the bilingual project at José Padin school during the 1973–74 school year was a graduate of the Santurce public schools who had an A.B. degree from the University of Puerto Rico and an M.A. from New York University, and was working toward a doctorate in education from that university.

Puerto Rico is experiencing some problems having to do with tensions and conflicts between Puerto Ricans who were born on the island and have never left it and returnees from the States, "Neorriqueños" as they are being called. There seems to be a certain amount of cultural shock for each group on meeting the other. A project, financed with federal money under ESAA (Emergency School Aid Act), was begun in the 1973–74 school year to investigate the problem and try to find solutions for easing the return of Puerto Ricans who discover on returning to Puerto Rico that they do not know where they belong and do not really feel at home either on the island or in the States. A bicultural-bilingual project for high school students who had returned to Puerto Rico from mainland schools was set up in Carolina, Caguas, Toa Baja, Mayaguez, and Manatí. About 450 students were enrolled. The program was being extended in the 1974–75 school year to high schools in Ponce, Guaynabo, Fajardo, Arecibo, and Rio Piedras. The pupils followed the regular curriculum in mathematics and science but were given special courses in Puerto Rican culture, fine arts, and the Spanish language and were provided with tutoring services. The schools involved in this program also offered special counseling for the pupils and their parents to assist in resolving their special problems.

Another program geared to helping students of high school age who return from the States speaking more English than Spanish was being put into operation in the 1973–74 school year in five towns, Carolina, Caguas, Toa Baja, Mayaguez, and Manatí. This project, supported by Title I funds (under the Equal Opportunities provisions) calls for teaching the high school curriculum entirely in English and giving remedial work in Spanish to selected students whose first and dominant language is English. Surveys made by the Department of Education revealed that the impact on the schools of returnees from the United States was greatest in the above-mentioned five towns plus Bayamón

Norte (north) and Bayamón Sur (south). The program was to be extended to include Bayamón Sur in the 1974-75 school year. In most of the towns the problem was most severe in grades 7 through 12, though in Carolina it was noticeable even at the elementary level.

In several regular English classes at higher grade levels, which the author observed in two towns in the southwestern part of the island and at one school in the heart of San Juan, the teachers came from varied backgrounds. Some were men who had taken advantage of the GI bill to go back to school or on to college to prepare themselves for teaching. If they had not known English before enlisting, they had learned it in the Army. Others, both men and women, reported that they had attended Puerto Rican schools at the time when the curriculum had been taught in English. They had spoken Spanish at home and everywhere else but had heard and had worked in English during the entire school day and had acquired a good command of the language in this way. The system had evidently worked for them. When I asked why they thought the English curriculum had been dropped, they replied, "Politics." (They did not claim that the use of English as the medium of instruction had been successful in all places or for all persons, but they had presumably had well-qualified teachers in the city schools they had attended, had liked being taught in English, and had themselves become competent to teach in the language.)

At the higher grade levels the emphasis in the English classes the author visited was for the most part on reading and writing, with little attention paid to the oral aspects of the language. The teachers talked in English but they had little success in eliciting oral responses from the students, except in the case of those who were already fluent in English from some period of residence in the States. There were some exceptions to the rule of mostly written work. Pronunciation exercises on especially difficult sounds were practiced. At the junior high school visited in San Juan, one English teacher had a drama class—for selected, especially proficient students—which had put on a play in English earlier that year. At the same school there was also a language laboratory, equipped with some of the technical devices in common use today—film strips, reading machines, records, tape recorders, and the like. The teacher in charge of the laboratory, who was a reading specialist, had learned her English entirely in Puerto Rico but had attended brief training courses in the States. Students who were in need of special help were sent to this teacher in the language laboratory. The only problem seemed to be that there were far more students in the school needing help than could be served and accommodated by this teacher and the amount of space and equipment available.

Another teacher, whose English was excellent—she had come from the States—said she had to use a good deal of Spanish in giving explanations to her students since they often had difficulty understanding if she spoke only in English. In most of the classes at the higher grade levels that the author observed, the students were giving written answers to written questions about stories they were reading. There were also lessons in grammar and syntax, again written work—completing sentences by filling in blanks with correct words, prepositions, verb forms, or whatever was required. The resulting lack of fluency in speaking English and an inability to understand the spoken language is not unlike Anglo pupils' inability to speak or understand French or Spanish after several years of high school or college language classes, if they have been taught by the method formerly prevalent in the United States, which emphasized reading and writing but not speaking. In some of the language classes visited, ten or fifteen minutes of oral drill on the material being studied seemed called for, and might have made a great difference in the pupils' ability to handle spoken English.

In the junior high school in San Juan and in the elementary school in one of the towns visited, English was departmentalized with all English classes taught by special English teachers. In the smaller town the English lesson in a fifth grade was conducted by the regular classroom teacher, who taught all other subjects too. She spoke fluent, but accented, English and made occasional mistakes.

She had carefully prepared lesson plans and a coherent program for her English class, but she was evidently aware of some inadequacies in her own English and said she would very much like to spend a year in the United States to perfect her English. Of her 26 pupils, 7 had lived in the States, and they were the only ones from whom a visitor could elicit any oral responses in English. This school in the smaller town went through only the sixth grade. For seventh, eighth, and ninth grades, the pupils must travel to the neighboring larger town. For a high school education the students in both towns must go to Cabo Rojo, a city of about 36,000 some 20 miles distant. They are transported there daily by *público*, (a kind of taxi-bus common on the island) with the expenses paid by the Puerto Rican Department of Education.

In any school chosen at random on the island, it is a pretty good bet that one will find at least some pupils who have either been born in the continental United States or have lived there for some period of time. In this author's experiences in visiting classes in different places on several trips to Puerto Rico, this has been true. And the families who move back and forth between the island and the mainland are most likely to be from the less affluent and less privileged segment of the population (though not by any means necessarily the very poorest, since the decision to move may in itself be an indication of initiative and a determination to build a better life). But the really well-to-do and best-educated Puerto Ricans seldom choose to leave their island home except to travel for pleasure. They don't need to move to the United States to make a better living. It is, therefore, precisely the poorer Puerto Ricans—those who live in the remote rural areas or in the worst sections of the cities—who are most in need of learning English since they are the most likely to emigrate to the States at least for some period of time. If ever a place was "a natural" for bilingual education, both in needs and favoring circumstances, it is Puerto Rico.

Once the Department of Education has met its goal of providing all the elementary schools on the island with the new type of trained bilingual teachers, a good start will have been made toward improving the teaching of English in the early grades in Puerto Rico. If the schools can then build on this foundation by continuing to place more emphasis on fluency in spoken English, while students are developing further skills in reading and writing the language, there should be fewer problems for all concerned when these students are suddenly transplanted to schools on the mainland. If ways can be found to stimulate interest and encourage competence in the English language among the student population on the island, wherever they go in their subsequent academic or business careers they will reap the benefits of being bilingual.

The Department of Education of Puerto Rico makes no claim to having established bilingual education in its school system (with the exception of the special programs designed for English-speaking or English-dominant returnees). Indeed, the Department disclaims any intention or wish to promote bilingual education, as such, in its schools. The Director of the English Program stated the policy (in a letter to the author in the spring of 1974):

> You will want to keep in mind that the Puerto Rican public school system is not bilingual. Spanish is the only language of instruction and the only language spoken fluently by the majority of our people. English is taught as a required subject but is not a required second language, not forced on students against their own desire to learn and use it. As far as I know, there are no strong advocates for true bilingual education in Puerto Rico today; most educators, in fact, give primary emphasis to making Spanish language instruction even stronger.
>
> The Bilingual Teachers Program does not refer to bilingual education, either. . . . The purpose of that Program is to provide for the departmentalization of English instruction in the primary grades, thus relieving the already-overworked classroom teacher of the additional responsibility of teaching a second language.
>
> The new Teachers Corps program for 1974-75, if approved, will

concentrate on science and math, both to be taught in Spanish. Other Federal programs, such as Head Start, Career Education, and Follow Through, are conducted in Spanish and not intended as means of increasing bilingualism.

This attitude on the part of Puerto Rican educators is understandable in view of the history of education on the island and the confusion that resulted from the many changes in policies regarding language use in instruction in the schools, and also political pressures. Nevertheless, it seems logical to expect that improved teaching of English as a second language may result in a higher degree of bilingualism on the part of Puerto Rican students. Educators in mainland schools can perhaps be forgiven, in any case, for hoping that this will be the consequence. If present and future educational policies and instructional methods result in a better grounding for Puerto Rican pupils in English, as well as in Spanish, when they transfer to schools in the continental United States they will encounter fewer difficulties and present fewer problems in the school systems in the localities where they have come to live. At whatever age they come, it will be helpful to them to have a command of the lingua franca of the country.

There are problems. Money, of course, is one. Puerto Rico experienced its first teachers' strike in the 1973–74 school year, with the teachers demanding an increase in salaries. (And one-third of Puerto Rico's total budget in 1974 was already being spent on education.) Finding and training enough competent bilingual teachers is another. But if money is available for the training, it should be possible to find enough potential bilingual teachers among the large numbers of English-dominant but still Spanish-speaking Puerto Ricans who have lived in the continental United States for at least part of their lives.

Another factor that compounds the difficulty of improving the quality of education in Puerto Rico, as indeed in many other places, is population pressure, which overcrowds the schools and makes increasingly heavy demands on the resources of the island. There were 713,166 students in the Puerto Rican school system in August 1973. It is not uncommon for a teacher to have 50 or more students in his or her class, usually without sufficient desks or textbooks for all of them. Puerto Rico is moving to try to solve the problem of overcrowding by keeping the schools open all year. As the initial implementation of a new plan, in the fall of 1974 six junior and six senior high schools in representative communities began operating on a five-semester schedule, the so-called "quinmester plan." It was conceived as a pilot project; if it proves successful, the plan is to be adopted islandwide. (The quinmester schedule is in operation in some of the schools in Dade County, Florida, and has been found to have many advantages.)

The future of Title VII projects and other ESEA federally sponsored bilingual activities in the Puerto Rican school system depends, as it does in other parts of the United States, on what action Congress takes and how much money is made available for such programs in the years to come. It may be that the Commonwealth itself will have to be the major source of funding for bilingual education in Puerto Rico, as it may fall to the individual states and school districts all over the United States to set up and carry on bilingual projects in the schools.

Attitudes toward the teaching and learning of English in the island schools and, consequently, the prospects for bilingualism among the population will undoubtedly be more favorable if, as Mrs. Rexach pointed out in her address to the TESOL Convention, the language question can be separated from political issues and the desirability of knowing English be considered on its own merits rather than as an expression of relationship between Puerto Rico and the United States government. Expressing the position of the Department of Education of Puerto Rico, at that time, Mrs. Rexach stated:

> We are committed to the teaching of English as a second language here in Puerto Rico and I do not foresee nor do I intend to bring about any change in that policy. What I would like to see, though, is an awareness of the role that English will play in the future of this Island as a world community. This has nothing to do with statehood or independence. Regardless of its political status, Puerto Rico will continue to be a part of this world and, as such, we must do all we can to assure that our part is an active one.
>
> We can begin by separating English instruction from political ideology, from identification solely with the United States. English is taught the world over and, in the majority of nations, is the preferred foreign language. Let us view English then, as a "lingua franca," our link, economically, intellectually, socially, with the nations of the world.
>
> Recognizing our need to learn English because of its utility to us as an international language would have a significant effect on our educational policy. . . . Our students, and their teachers as well, would consider English instruction as a worthwhile goal for the Island, a step in the direction of full participation in world activities.
>
> Motivation would also be enhanced. For too long we have told our students that English would help them get a better job. This may be true, but it should not be the only, or even the main reason for learning English as a second language.
>
> There is an accruement to the learning of a foreign language which has been denied our students by our emphasis on economics and expediency. As I look back on my own efforts to learn a second language, and then some others, I recall how, during the process, I

97

became much more aware of language itself. Spanish became more real to me and more understandable. I discovered the worlds of other languages, the fact that people could manage quite well with a different world concept from mine.

These feelings are shared by almost everyone who learns a foreign language. It would seem to me that these are worthwhile growth experiences for all young people. I would like to see more of an effort made to motivate our students to learn a second language as an intellectual accomplishment, as a means of life-enrichment, and as an aid to identification.[9]

Mrs. Rexach also indicated that she would like to see greater diversity in the types of English courses offered in the schools in Puerto Rico, so that, beginning at least at the ninth-grade level, pupils might have a chance to choose between courses emphasizing literature and written assignments—designed for those intending to go on to college—and a program devoted to the practical application of language study, developing fluency and competence in English for everyday needs —work, travel, family, and social life.

In expressing her thoughts about the objectives of language study for pupils in Puerto Rico, the (then) Secretary of Education for the Island was echoing the hopes and aspirations of school administrators and teachers everywhere who are committed to the best ideals of their profession, those who try to look beyond the specifics of the hour's lesson and take the long-range view of the ultimate purpose of schooling—the intellectual development and the enrichment, to whatever extent possible, of the lives of their pupils.

The schools of Puerto Rico have a long way to go, as do many school systems on the mainland, if they are to accomplish their stated goals—to raise the level of education among *all* the students they are expected to serve. There are good elementary and secondary schools on the island, as well as universities and colleges of good standing. But much remains to be done to improve the overall picture. It seems logical to suggest that in trying to bring about that improvement, for pupils on the island of Puerto Rico as well as for Puerto Ricans attending schools in the continental United States, it is desirable, and perhaps essential, to study and learn to the best of their ability both Spanish and English, giving priority to the one or the other, according to the circumstances. Both languages are likely to be important to Puerto Ricans at some times and in many situations in their lives. Many Puerto Ricans are already bilingual. Because of its relationship with the United States through the accidents of history, Puerto Rico would seem to be particularly auspicious ground for bilingual education. Certainly more widespread development of bilingualism among the people of the island would be of enormous value to Puerto Ricans wherever they find themselves, at home or abroad.

Notes

1. Columbia Encyclopedia, 3d ed., 1963, "Puerto Rico." Also Robin McKown, *The Image of Puerto Rico*, McGraw-Hill, New York, 1973, p. 64. ("Eighty percent of the population were illiterate in 1898.")

2. Aida Negrón de Montilla, *Americanization in Puerto Rico and the Public School System, 1900-1930*, dissertation, New York University, Editorial Edil, Rio Piedras, printed in Spain, 1970, p. 10.

3. Anne Wall, "Reminiscences of Life in Puerto Rico," Bayamón, Puerto Rico, 1973, unpublished.

4. Ibid.

5. Ibid.

6. Paquita Viñas de Vasquez, "The Teaching of English in Puerto Rico," *TESOL Newsletter*, vol. VI, no. 3, American Language Institute, Georgetown University, Washington, D.C., April 1973.

7. Frances Parkinson Keyes, *All Flags Flying*, McGraw-Hill, New York, 1972, p. 640.

8. Celeste Benítez de Rexach, address delivered at the Seventh Annual Convention of TESOL, San Juan, Puerto Rico, May 10, 1973. Printed in Puerto Rico by the Printing Services Division of the Department of Education, Commonwealth of Puerto Rico, 705 Hoare Street, Santurce, Puerto Rico.

9. Ibid.

How Other Countries Deal with Their Language Minorities:
Bilingual Education in Other Parts of the World

The United States is not unique among nations in having a variety of languages and cultures represented in its population, and educational and political problems arising from that diversity. Canada, faced with a separatist movement on the part of some of its French-speaking citizens, is now trying to make amends for neglecting for so long their aspirations for maintaining their own cultural identity and for sharing more fully in the economic and political life of the country. Though both English and French are official languages in Canada,[1] there has always been more pressure on French-speaking people to learn English than on the English-speaking to learn French, and French-Canadians have often felt that they were being ignored by the Anglo majority. A royal Commission was set up in 1963 to study bilingualism and biculturalism in Canada, and as a result of its findings, steps were taken by the Canadian government to place more emphasis on French, making a command of the language a requirement for some federal positions. Many civil servants and other Canadians in positions of authority—including, if one can believe the newspaper reports, the Prime Minister's lady—suddenly found themselves working hard at the acquisition of a second language, which it would have been considerably easier to learn as children.

The Canadian Public Service Commission has set 1975 as the "target year for functional bilingualism," indicating at the same time that they consider the bilingualization of the Public Service as "one of the Commission's most challenging jobs." Their Language School is providing intensive courses in conversational French for selected public servants, with training classes in Ottawa, Quebec City, Montreal, and Toronto.[2]

The government's decision to upgrade the status of French has not won easy acceptance among Anglos, who have usually expected all

101

others to learn their language. In addition, since French-speaking Canadians are concentrated largely in the eastern provinces of Quebec and New Brunswick, the regulations requiring federal employees to have some knowledge of French are by no means popular among Canadians of other ethnic backgrounds, especially in the western provinces. Canadians of Ukrainian, German, or Italian descent see little reason for a requirement that a postmaster or other federal official should know French in order to be able to function in sections of the country where the percentage of French-speaking residents is lower than that of other non-Anglo Canadians. They would like to see more attention paid to their ethnic groups too. French-speaking Canadians, however, are the largest minority group, constituting 27 percent[3] of the total population, and no matter how many other ethnic minorities press for more recognition of their cultural and linguistic heritage, it seems likely that continuing emphasis will be placed on the French language and on the development of a greater degree of French-English bilingualism throughout the country.

The public educational system in Canada has been in the past, and, despite some modifications introduced in the course of the 1960s, still is, a largely segregated one, with the division based both on religion and language. Protestant children have attended English-language schools, and Catholic children, schools in which the instruction is in French. This religious classification has on occasion resulted in the placement, for example, of Italian children—whose parents wanted them taught in English—in Catholic schools where the medium of instruction was French. (Jewish children, since they were not Catholic, attended Protestant English-language schools.) As the result of vigorous resistance by some families to such assignments, a law was passed in 1969 allowing parents to decide whether to send their children to English- or French-language schools.[4] There is continuing controversy, however, on this subject, and French-speaking Quebecers resent and oppose the wishes of many new immigrants to send their children to English-language schools. They insist that French is the major language of Quebec and that newcomers should give priority to the learning of French rather than English. Many immigrants insist they prefer to have their children learn English. Whichever language they learn, the pupils will be, almost without exception, in segregated schools.[5]

Each of the ten provinces of Canada is responsible for the establishment and management of its schools. In spite of the attention given to the subject of bilingualism under the Trudeau administration, a careful reading of official statements and regulations regarding schools in the provinces of Quebec and New Brunswick, where the majority of French-speaking Canadians live, indicates that the emphasis is still on

French-speakers learning English rather than English pupils learning French. And in most cases French- and English-speaking children still attend separate schools run by separate school boards.

[Though] far-reaching change has characterized the organization and administration of education in the Province of Quebec since 1964, . . . two basic conditions which have their roots in 350 years of Canadian history remain unchanged: (1) Quebec has two parallel and distinct programs of education operating under a common Act, about five-sixths of the population following the program of the Roman Catholic section and the other sixth the Protestant; and (2) French is the language of instruction in nearly all of the Catholic schools. . . . Villages, towns, and cities are usually left as units for educational purposes. . . . Catholics and Protestants may each select a school board which operates independently.[6]

There have been notable innovations in recent years in the schools in Quebec, such as individualization of instruction, promotion by subject instead of grade, and the establishment of vocational schools and junior colleges for French-speaking students. This last development has opened up the possibility of education beyond the secondary level for French-Canadians other than those from the elite, moneyed class, who in the past were the only ones likely to have such opportunities. There are 4.9 million people in Quebec whose mother tongue is French, 788,000 whose native tongue is English, and some 371,000 who have some other first language.[7] Official descriptions of the Quebec educational system indicate that in the first six years of schooling, pupils will study "languages" and other specified subjects (but what the languages will be is not spelled out). In secondary schools (intended for pupils from about age 12 to 16), "the student's mother tongue and the second language . . . are required subjects."[8] Again it is supposed that for French-speaking pupils the second language would be English. (Whether for English-speaking students the required second language would be French is left unclear.)

In the province of New Brunswick, where, according to the 1971 census, about 34 percent of the population is French-speaking, the Schools Act (of 1967) required that:

In schools where the mother tongue of the pupils is English, the chief language of instruction shall be English and the second language French; where the mother tongue is French the chief language of instruction shall be French and the second language English. In schools where there are pupils whose mother tongue is

English and pupils whose mother tongue is French, classes shall be so arranged that the chief language of instruction shall be the mother tongue of the pupils, with instruction in French or English respectively as the second language, in accordance with the programme of studies.[9]

The schools in the last category are termed *bilingual schools*. In 1973, however, the Ministry of Education, in response to an inquiry from the author, described the language requirements for pupils in New Brunswick as follows: "The study of English as a second language is compulsory to French-speaking children from Grades 3 to 10 inclusive. . . . English-speaking students take French as a second language from Grades 5 to 10 inclusive. Some begin at Grade 3 level. This is optional."[10] This would seem to indicate that English-speaking children are not required to learn French.

The Ministry of Education for the province of Ontario (in which the capital, Ottawa, is located), informed the author that "instruction in all of Ontario's schools may be in French or English in accordance with parental wishes. In Ontario's elementary schools French is offered daily (20 to 80 minutes). In certain areas immersion programs are available. At the secondary level, no subject is compulsory. Out of 583,013 students (years 1 to 5) 213,869 studied French and another 27,226 studied Français (1972 figures—Secondary Education only)."[11] The different terms *French* and *Français* are sometimes used in Canada to make clear that pupils studying *French* are English-speaking, while those studying *Français* are native speakers of French. These statistics would indicate that in Ontario, for the school years given (1 to 5), less than half of the total number of pupils were studying the French language.

There has been an increase in emphasis on learning French and there have been greater opportunities for Anglo pupils to become proficient in the language, if they so choose. In the city of Ottawa, for example, an average of one 40-minute period of French per day is taught to pupils in grades 1 through 8. In other school districts in Ontario, French may be taught to all pupils beginning in the second or third grade. Some school boards make French a required subject; others do not. It is also possible in some schools in Ottawa for English-speaking students to be taught most of their subjects in French. These intensive immersion language programs are not compulsory, but pupils may apply for enrollment and all are eligible. Theoretically, all pupils in Ontario, no matter what their mother tongue, are now permitted to attend either French- or English-language schools. In practice, however, the French-language schools are attended mostly by French-speaking Canadians.[12]

In response to demands by other ethnic groups for some recognition of their mother tongues, a start was made under the Trudeau administration to provide money and materials for the teaching in public schools of such languages as Ukrainian, German, and Italian in areas with a heavy concentration of these ethnic groups. Among the minorities long neglected by Canadian authorities and greatly in need of educational services are the 240,000 Indians and the 16,000 Eskimos of the extreme north, though now, where Indian and Eskimo children make up the bulk of the school population, attempts are being made to use tribal languages as media of instruction.

Some interesting experiments in bilingual teaching have been carried out in the past decade or so in Quebec, usually under private initiative, such as those conducted by Wallace Lambert, a member of the faculty of McGill University and one of Canada's authorities on bilingual education. In a middle-class English-speaking community in a suburb of Quebec, Dr. Lambert, at the invitation of parents, developed a program using French as the medium of instruction for Anglo pupils. The reported success of the project has reinforced the belief of the proponents of bilingual education that there are no detrimental effects resulting from teaching children a second language and making use of that second language as a medium of instruction. This might be construed as an argument supporting the position that there is nothing wrong with insisting that all children, no matter what their mother tongue, should be made to learn and use only English in school instead of being permitted to develop their own language while learning English. But the implications are really rather different. The setting for Dr. Lambert's classes and the philosophy underlying the experiments were not such as to denigrate the pupil's home language or interrupt its development, as is sometimes the case when French-speaking children are required to learn or use English. The experimental classes served to emphasize the capacity of young children to learn languages. Outside of school the children were immersed in English, the major and favored language of the community. In any case, these projects, serving the purposes of research, are exceptions—small in scope—to the general practice in the Canadian school system of enrolling Anglo children in English-language schools and French-speaking pupils in schools where French is the medium of instruction.

Changes are taking place in the Canadian school system. English-speaking pupils in some instances do study part of their curriculum in French, and French-speaking pupils have greater opportunities to make use of their native language in pursuing their studies beyond the secondary level. (There have always been, of course, some Catholic universities in which French was the medium of instruction.) Whether the current emphasis on developing a greater degree of bilingualism among English-speaking Canadians will result in even more changes in the school system and increase the amount of bilingual teaching for both French- and English-speaking Canadians remains to be seen. But it would appear that Canada still has a long way to go before an educational system is developed which would be fully bilingual, in the sense that English- and French-speaking pupils would attend schools together as a matter of course, each group learning the other's language and being taught the curriculum both in their mother tongues and their second languages.

One of the few countries in the world to give equal standing to the two major languages of its population is South Africa, which has developed a high degree of bilingualism among its (white) citizens, requiring them to know both of the official national languages. All (white) pupils study both Afrikaans (a language based on, but different from, the seventeenth-century Dutch of the original settlers) and English; throughout the country, a majority of (white) South Africans, whether they are of British or of Dutch descent, speak Afrikaans and English almost equally well. The South African government has since 1948 pursued its goal of a fully bilingual (white) citizenry, largely through the medium of segregated schools, even for its white pupils. In a few instances English-speaking and Afrikaans-speaking children are still placed in what are called "parallel medium schools," where the two official languages are used as media of instruction. But for the most part, pupils attend a school in which their mother tongue is used in instruction and the other national language is taught intensively as a subject, beginning with the first year of schooling. Evidently, with few exceptions, the pupils become competently bilingual. The enrollment of the white pupils in separate schools is to a certain extent voluntary. If parents for some reason wish to send their children to a school where the curriculum is taught in the language that is not their mother tongue, they are permitted to do so, if the children can adjust and function successfully in that school. But if there is any doubt that the children will be able to learn in this situation, the parents are discouraged from enrolling them and encouraged to send them to their own native-language school.

There is evidence that South Africa lost ground a bit after the changeover from parallel medium to separate schools for English- and Afrikaans-speaking pupils. Bilingualism among the (white) population had risen steadily from 43 percent in 1918 to a high of 73 percent in 1951, according to census figures. But between 1951 and 1960 the percentage of whites able to speak both English and Afrikaans dropped to 66 percent. The English-speaking persons who could not speak Afrikaans remained constant at 15 percent between 1951 and 1960, but the Afrikaans section of the population, who had always been more bilingual than the English element, showed an increase in those who could not speak English from 11 percent to 18 percent.[13] Some observers from afar have stated their belief that the dominant political group, who are Afrikaans-speaking, view this as a desirable development, fearing that if people can speak English they will not want to speak Afrikaans. It seems to others, however, including the author, that South Africa is firmly committed to the policy of bilingualism for its white population.

There are also separate schools for Indian, Coloured, and Bantu pupils. In South Africa the term *Coloured* is used for persons of mixed ancestry.[14] For about 90 percent of them, the mother tongue is Afrikaans. The Bantus, numbering some 14 million,[15] are members of the black nations who, among them, speak ten different languages, Zulu, Xhosa, and Tswana being the major ones. In each case the native language of the pupils is used as the medium of instruction, with one of the official languages, English or Afrikaans, taught as a subject. Even at the university level, there is a division based on race and language. Of the eleven universities for white students, four are English, two make use of both English and Afrikaans, and the rest are Afrikaans—though all are open to enrollment to students from either group. There are three universities for Bantus,[16] one for Coloureds,[17] and one for Indians.[18] Though at present there are some Bantu students enrolled at white universities, the policy of the government is that eventually all non-white students will be accommodated at their own universities. This is intended to take place as soon as all courses of study are offered at the Indian, Coloured, and Bantu universities.[19]

South Africa's considerable accomplishments in developing a high degree of bilingualism in its society are indisputable, though all people opposed to the policy and philosophy of segregation, either of races or of ethnic-linguistic groups, will take exception to the means by which they have been achieved. The language-teaching methods would seem to be effective.[20] As for the literacy rate among the Bantu population, the Department of Bantu Education has estimated that it has risen from the 21.8 percent figure (in a UNESCO report) of 1952 to about 80 percent of the present population between the ages of seven and twenty, and to nearly 55 percent of the Bantu population as a whole.[21]

Among European countries, Belgium and Switzerland offer marked contrasts in their handling of diverse ethnic groups. Belgium has never resolved the hostility and conflicts between its Dutch-speaking Flemings and French-speaking Walloons. Brussels, the capital, is a bilingual city, with both Dutch- and French-language schools (not, however, bilingual schools). Otherwise the country is divided territorially, with Flemish-Dutch (Nederlands)[22] being the official language in the north, and French in the south. French-oriented citizens who consider French more important show little interest in learning Flemish, and there are frequent flare-ups of animosity between the two groups. When the five-and-a-half-century-old University of Louvain, which is in the Flemish section of Belgium, was in turmoil at the end of the 1960s, because of the bitter language conflict between Walloons and Flemings, the French-speaking faculties were being pressed to leave Louvain. The Belgian government, unable to resolve the differences between the two groups, made the decision to establish a new university town, Louvain-la-Neuve, southeast of Brussels to accommodate the French faculties. With the expectation of eventually accommodating about 18,000 students, the hope is to develop a full-fledged city of 50,000 inhabitants by the year 2000, with the university as the focal point.

Switzerland—long known for its successful handling of a three-language citizenry, French, Italian, and (Swiss) German—rules that in each canton the language of the majority is the official language, and every resident has to know it. But a Swiss citizen is entitled to use whichever language he prefers in federal matters. Pupils study the languages spoken in other cantons as well as their mother tongue, and many Swiss speak two or three languages. A fourth language, Romansch, with a vocabulary of Latin origin spoken by only 1 percent of the population, has also been declared a national language, and attempts are being made to keep it alive by using it in the early grades in schools in the *Grisons* and other sections where it is still heard. (Romansch, sometimes referred to as "Rhaeto-Romanic" and also called "Grishun" in the *Grisons*, is also spoken in a few areas in Italy—in Friuli and some valleys of the Alto Adige east and west of Bolzano, and in parts of the Dolomites.)

In order to communicate with their fellow Swiss, however, Romansch-speaking pupils must learn one of the other official languages. In the German-speaking parts of Switzerland, the written language is standard "high" German, but it is pronounced, in all oral communication among the Swiss, in a special way, unintelligible to other speakers of German, called "Schwuyzertütsch." All educated German-speaking Swiss, however, know the "high" German pronunciation and change to standard German immediately in talking with persons who do not understand the Swiss version of the language.

Linguistically divided populations exist in many other countries around the world and the resulting problems have been dealt with successfully in some places and with less happy results in others. When Ceylon (now called "Sri Lanka") chose Sinhalese as its official language, it left unresolved the linguistic problems of the Tamils. They make up about one quarter of the population and want their language acknowledged also. As frequently is the case, the different languages are spoken by people practicing different religions, the Sinhalese being Buddhist, the Tamils Hindu. The choice of Sinhalese as the only national language has created resentment and resulted in increasing tension between the two factions.

Similar conflicts have developed in Pakistan, where efforts to force the Bengalis to give up Urdu in favor of the official language, Sindhi, created language riots in the summer of 1972 resulting in the death of close to 50 persons. Madagascar also had problems when coastal tribes objected to the replacement in their schools of the native tongue, the Tamatave dialect, by the national Madagascar language.

India, the Soviet Union, and the People's Republic of China, all with extremely large populations who speak a great variety of languages, have problems which in many ways are more complex than those of European and North and South American countries. India, with twelve major languages and more than a thousand minor ones, had a serious problem to resolve after gaining independence from British rule. Wanting to assert its freedom from the domination of English, which had been imposed during the colonial era, India chose Hindi as its national language. But since only a third of its own people speak Hindi and few persons outside of India understand it, English was and still is needed for communication with the rest of the world, and indeed within the country itself. There are some Indians who share no common language but English, and it is not unheard of for a husband and wife who grew up and were educated in different parts of the country to find that English is their lingua franca.

Expressing government policy in 1967, Mrs. Gandhi said: "In the present-day world we cannot afford to live in isolation. Therefore there should be three languages, regional, national and international."[23] In practice this means that native languages are used as a means of early instruction for pupils who don't speak Hindi, Hindi is introduced later for these students, and English is taught as a foreign language. Universities are expected to provide facilities for study in both Hindi and English.

Many of the newly independent African nations face a situation not unlike India's. Some would like to do away with the languages of colonial domination, but the multiplicity of tribal tongues spoken throughout Africa makes some lingua franca a necessity. Though Swahili is being promoted for use in some localities (Kenya adopted Swahili as its national language in 1973 and it is widely spoken and understood in East and Central Africa), the use of English or French is still essential for worldwide contacts. Tribal languages are being used in teaching children in their first years in school, but for advanced education a more widely understood language must be learned. In countries which were formerly French colonies, it will be French; elsewhere probably English.

The Soviet Union has shown some variations over the years in its attitudes and practices regarding the different languages spoken by the many national minorities which it encompasses. On the whole it has accepted and supported the maintenance of regional languages, while emphasizing the importance of Russian as a medium of communication among all the different ethnic and linguistic groups which make up the Soviet Union. Prior to 1917 the majority of the inhabitants of the more remote parts of imperial Russia were illiterate; there existed, in fact, no written forms for some of the languages spoken in the non-Russian border regions. The literacy rate for the inhabitants of the Russian empire as a whole, according to the first All-Russia Census of 1897, was 21.1 percent but for Turkestan (today's Soviet Central Asian Republics) it ranged from 1 to 5 percent.[24] At the time of the Revolution it was estimated that about 70 percent of the total population was still illiterate.

With the aim of making it easier for the masses throughout the country to learn to read and write, after the Revolution the new government decided to simplify and standardize the orthography of the Russian language. Four letters of the Cyrillic alphabet which were considered unnecessary or redundant were dropped, cutting the number of vowels from eleven to nine and the total number of symbols from 35 to 31. There were two letters in the Cyrillic alphabet for the sound of *"ee"* (as in meet), two for *"e"* (as in met), two for *"f"* and a so-called "hard sign" (never pronounced), placed at the end of a word which would otherwise end in a consonant. The dropped letters were: i (ee), ѣ (e), ѳ (f), and the hard sign ъ. With the elimination of these extra letters the spelling of the Russian language became, with minor exceptions, completely phonetic, with one letter always representing the same sound (phoneme).

Linguistic scholars also assisted in revising ancient alphabets and in devising systems of writing for some of those languages spoken by people in remote areas which had previously existed only in oral form. Since the establishment of the Soviet system, at least forty nationalities have created written forms for their languages.[25] In the 1920s, schools offering instruction in the local languages were established all over the country. According to contemporary Soviet publications:

> Today such languages as Armenian, Azerbaijani and Georgian are used in every area of life in their respective republics. . . . The use of newly alphabetized languages (Abkhazian, Balkarian, Ingush and others) has expanded enormously. This applies especially to

Ukrainian, Byelorussian, Uzbek, Kazakh, . . . Kirghiz, Moldavian, . . . Tajik, . . . Tartar, and others.[26]

There are bilingual courses of study in both secondary and higher-level schools throughout the Soviet Union.

> For many years such courses have been given . . . in Abkazia, Adygei, Daghestan, Karachayevo-Circassia, Kabardino-Baklaria and North and South Ossetia, wherever it was deemed necessary by the local population. Bilingual courses of study are also in use, to one degree or another, in other non-Russian areas of the country.[27]

> At present, school instruction is being conducted in the Soviet Union in 56 different languages, and according to the laws applying to schools in the union republics, a pupil is free to choose the language in which he will receive his education.[28]

The Russian language remains, however, the major and official medium of communication for the many different peoples of the Soviet Union. It was the language of the group which led in the movement to overthrow the czars. It is the mother tongue of more than half of the inhabitants of the country. And it is taught to pupils throughout the Soviet Union. Government policy toward the Russian language can be gleaned from the following statement:

> Although school instruction at all levels, the publication of scientific and technical literature, and the training of scientific personnel are carried on in dozens of languages used by the peoples of our country, a fluent knowledge of Russian is still necessary, both for communication within the country, and for communication with other countries. Russian is one of the official languages of the United Nations. Besides, it is the country's most complete source of scientific and technical information on current development in all branches of knowledge. The growing cultural needs of Soviet people cannot be fully met unless the non-Russian inhabitants of our country know Russian. That is why a fluent knowledge of Russian, side by side with the mother tongue, has become common in our country.[29]

In addition to teaching Russian and the mother tongues of its many national groups, the Soviet Union has paid great attention to foreign languages, with marked success in developing fluency and competence in the major languages of the world on the part of students specializing in foreign-language study. Their language schools turn out graduates who speak French, German, Spanish, English (British or American as the case may be), like natives, idiomatically and with little or no discernible trace of Russian accent.

The Soviet Union, like most countries, still has some unsolved educational problems, such as a shortage of teachers in certain fields. More instructors in Russian language and literature for the non-Russian schools are needed (a parallel to the need in this country for training more and better ESL teachers). There is a lack of specialists in physics, mathematics, and foreign languages, especially for schools in rural areas.[30] This is true even though class size runs higher than in the United States, 35 to 40 pupils being considered a desirable number. As in the United States, very small schools, in which teachers may have to teach some subjects for which they are not qualified, are being phased out in favor of larger schools with departmentalized teaching (as regional schools are replacing American small-town high schools). "From both the economic and pedagogical points of view, small schools fail to meet the needs of today. . . . When planning the school network, efforts are made to avoid making small classes and to secure the standard class size (35-40 pupils)."[31]

In conformance with the laws permitting children to be taught in their mother tongue, in republics where several ethnic groups exist, more than one language may be used in teaching within the same school.

> The Constitution of the USSR guarantees children the right to be taught in their mother tongue and this right is exercised in practice where there are children of school age. That is why. . . the nationality composition of the population and the existing arrangement of schools, according to the languages in which children are taught, have to be taken into account. The Lithuanian SSR, for example, is inhabited by the Lithuanians, and also by other nationalities, Russians, Poles, etc. Children in Lithuania are taught in three languages—Lithuanian, Russian and Polish. In the republic there are schools with one language of instruction (Lithuanian, Russian or Polish) and those with two languages of instruction (Lithuanian and Russian, Russian and Polish, Lithuanian and Polish). . . . In each district and town, account is taken of the nationality composition of the population and of the existing network of schools from the point of view of the language in which instruction is given. This is done in order to organize better the education of children in their native language, both from the teaching and the economic point of view.[32]

Though it is not explicitly so stated in the above paragraph, one gathers from other statements that all non-Russian pupils at one time or another will have to study the Russian language, if they do not already speak it, since great emphasis is placed on the necessity for all persons to know Russian.

The People's Republic of China, with its population of roughly 800 million, the largest of any political entity in the world, is, not surprisingly, a multinational, multilingual, and multicultural society. Ninety-four percent of its people are of the Han nationality, but even they do not all speak the same dialect. In addition to the Han majority there are 54 minority groups, such as the Miaos of southern China, Tibetans, Mongols, and the Chuangs of the Kwangsi Autonomous Province, the largest of the minority nationalities. Ten of the minority groups have populations of more than a million persons; the Chuang population has risen from 7 to 10 million in the last decade;[33] others range in size from several hundred to several hundred thousand. Though proportionately small in the percentage they represent of the total population of China, the minority nationalities inhabit areas which constitute more than 50 percent of the land mass of the country.[34]

The government of the People's Republic of China has a dual language policy which recognizes the value to each minority of its own native tongue and at the same time emphasizes the importance of the language of the Han majority (in its "standard speech" form based on the dialect spoken in the Peking area, formerly referred to as "Mandarin"). This is considered the lingua franca of the country, which everyone should know. Great efforts are being made to teach this Han language to all the Chinese people, in order that, no matter what part of the vast country they come from, they will be able to talk to and understand each other, to communicate in one standard tongue.

As happens in other countries in the world, people in China who speak the standard language also often maintain fluency in regional dialects. It was reported in a newspaper account of a meeting in Peking between Mao Tse-tung and a boyhood friend, a naturalized American citizen, Dr. C. P. Li of Arlington, Virginia, that the two had talked to each other in the Hunan dialect—one not easily understood by people from other areas—which they had both used as children growing up in the same village in China.[35]

The mother tongues of the various ethnic minorities are now used as media of instruction in schools in the People's Republic of China; all areas of the country have their own publishing houses, and two produce films, making use of regional languages. But all pupils are also expected to learn the Han language. As part of the campaign to promote universal literacy, attempts are being made to simplify written Chinese. Since there are some 30,000 characters in the big dictionaries of the written language, learning to read and write Chinese is not easy. Government policy is to reduce the number of characters used in widely circulated printed matter, such as newspapers, to about 3,000. China now has 100 million children in school, and great progress has been made in raising the literacy rate among the population. It now stands at over 50 percent, up from the 10 percent figure of 1949 when the People's Republic was established.[36]

Written Chinese can be read by all literate speakers of the language, no matter what their dialect, since the characters have the same meaning for all (no matter how they are pronounced). But the spoken versions vary greatly and are, in fact, sometimes totally different. Since written Chinese makes use not of an alphabet with phonetic significance but of characters representing words or ideas (to some extent simplifications or reductions to an abstract form of originally pictorial ideographs), reading the symbols might be compared to the different ways an Englishman, a Frenchman, and a Spaniard would "pronounce" the picture of a horse. One would read "horse," the next "cheval," and the third "caballo." They would all recognize the picture but would not understand each other's "pronunciation" of the symbol.[37] The present policy of teaching all the inhabitants of China the same spoken language is aimed at providing all Chinese citizens with a means of oral communication with their fellow countrymen.

Work is also being done on devising a phonetic system of writing Chinese, using the letters of the Latin alphabet—transliterating the Han (Mandarin) pronunciation of the Chinese characters into the alphabet used in Western languages. A start was made on such a system of writing Chinese a good many years ago, and it is being carried forward by the present government as a means of helping children and grown-ups master the characters. It also helps the Chinese to become acquainted with the Latin alphabet and makes the Chinese language more accessible to foreigners. A sample transliteration and translation of Chinese characters (appearing as part of a language lesson in a contemporary English language magazine published by the People's Republic of China) reads as follows:

Běijing de Sì Jì

Peking's Four Seasons

Běijing   de   chūntiān   bǐjiào   nuǎnhe,   táohuār

Peking's   spring   relatively   warm,   peach   blossoms

kāi   le,   liǔshù   fā   yá   le.   Zài   gōngyuánlǐ

bloom,   willow trees   bud.   At parks in,

ýoulan de rén hěn duō.

strolling people quite many.

(Spring in Peking is rather warm, with peach blossoms in bloom and willow trees budding. There are many strollers in the parks.)[38]

A newspaper using an unusual character will often print the phonetic equivalent in Latin script in brackets next to it as an aid to readers. Quite a number of books are available with the phonetic-script equivalent of each character printed immediately beneath it. All children learn the phonetic script in school.[39]

China also pays great attention in its schools now to teaching foreign languages, through a system of intensive study, using the so-called "total immersion" method for those students specializing in such courses. The languages receiving greatest attention, in order of emphasis, are English, French, Russian, and Spanish.[40]

There seems little doubt that a diversity of languages can be both a valuable asset and also a potential source of conflict for a nation. It becomes apparent on looking into situations involving language minorities, language use, and language teaching in countries around the world that having one major, official language accepted and spoken by the majority of the population is a politically stabilizing factor, and usually socially and educationally advantageous. If the mother tongue of the majority in a country happens at the same time to be one of the widely known languages of the world, the inhabitants of such a country can consider themselves fortunate in already possessing a means of communication with people in many places on the globe and in not having to work to learn a universally understood language since they have been "born speaking one." The obverse and disadvantageous effect is that persons whose mother tongue is a major world language often have a tendency to believe that it is not only unnecessary for them to learn a second language but that it could be of no possible benefit to them to know one. They fail to realize that the loss is theirs if they never become acquainted with another language and culture; and they remain unaware of attitudes toward life, and ways of expression, different from their own. Some even develop a feeling that their mother tongue is better, per se, than all other less universally spoken languages, instead of realizing that each language has its own qualities, some richer or more subtle in one way, some in another.

Whatever the advantages of one major language for a nation, it is also apparent that in countries where different languages are spoken by different segments of the population, any attempts to denigrate the language of a minority and suppress its use are likely to result in resentment and in political and social divisions. Language is a much cherished expression of the distinctive culture of any ethnic or national group, and most persons do not want to relinquish this part of their particular heritage, whether it means to them losing the key to a literature, the ways of speech and thought of a Cervantes, a Molière, an Ibsen, or a Shakespeare, or, in a less literate milieu, simply forgetting the intimate family language of one's childhood.

There is a strong case to be made, of course, for the proposition that the class distinctions often accompanying ethnic and linguistic differences within given societies, rather than the ethnic and linguistic differences themselves, are frequently the source of conflicts usually attributed to linguistic and cultural differences. There are sometimes greater differences in attitudes, life-styles, manners and mores between different socio-economic groups within a nation than between relatively similar classes in different nations. (Cultural characteristics also often follow geographic or climatic lines, with northerners from several countries sharing certain resemblances, while southerners in those same countries may be more similar to each other than they are to their northern countrymen.) In Germany, for instance, where everyone has always spoken a common language, though with dialect variations, the marked class differences separating the aristocracy, the middle classes, and the peasant and laboring groups have provided fertile ground for unhealthy political developments. In each of the Scandinavian countries on the contrary, though class differences certainly exist, the social homogeneity of the population and the existence of a relatively large middle class in addition to the possession by all of a common language, have tended to contribute to stability.

Canada is also an example of a country where class differences, even among those who share a common language, create political divisions. The wealthier and more privileged French-speaking Canadians get along better with Anglos than do French-speaking citizens from a lower socio-economic group. And there are divisions between well-to-do French-speaking Canadians and poorer members of the same ethnic group. French Canadians have elected a prime minister and other federal officials from among their own ethnic-linguistic minority, but this fact does not appease the economically and socially less privileged among the French-speaking population. (The subject of class differences and their various manifestations in the United States does not fall properly within the scope of this book, but it will be touched upon briefly when it seems pertinent to particular situations in language learning and language teaching.)

Certain ethnic and linguistic segments of many nations' populations are representative of specific socio-economic groups. Sometimes this has resulted from the importation or immigration at some period in the nation's history of new ethnic groups to fill gaps in the labor force. It happened with the Tamils in Sri Lanka, who now find themselves a less privileged group; it was the experience of various national groups at different times during the development and expansion of the United States; it is happening today in Europe, where Turks, Greeks, southern Italians, Spaniards, and Portuguese are entering northern countries to perform labor and services which the nationals of those countries choose not to do themselves. These working visitors present educational problems associated with both language and socio-economic status when their children become part of the school population of the host countries. The major difference between these situations and similar ones in the past in the United States is that in European countries (with the exception of France), most of the "imported labor" is temporary, the workers are considered "foreigners" and for the most part do not remain to become citizens of the country where they are working, whereas in the United States those who have arrived as immigrants (or moved about as migrants) have stayed to become an integral part of the society in which they work.

The situation of language minorities in the United States is, of course, different from that of national minority groups in most other countries. The Soviet Union and the People's Republic of China, for instance, are made up of states which have been the homelands of their inhabitants for centuries. The peoples living in the component parts of the Soviet Union and also of China, have not emigrated from some foreign country to live in a new land of their choice. Their countries or states have joined, or have been incorporated into, the larger political entities. Within the United States only the Puerto Ricans and to a certain extent, and going farther back in history, the Mexican Americans (and going still farther back, the native American Indians) have had their homelands ceded to or forcibly taken by the United States. (French-speaking residents of Louisiana might make a similar claim, but their territory was Spanish before it was French, and the picture is more blurred by time and circumstance. There has been, however, a surprisingly strong attachment to French on the part of the Cajuns and also some of the descendants of Negro families who were French-speaking in an earlier era.) For members of all other ethnic and linguistic groups, the move to the United States has been voluntary and made with an awareness that they would be living in a country where their mother tongue was not spoken by the majority of the population. They have known that they would have to learn a second language to be able to communicate with people outside of their own group.

Even the situation of the Puerto Ricans and Mexican Americans, and their relationship to the larger society, do not really match that of, say, the Uzbeks or Kazakhs in the Soviet Union or members of minority nationalities in China. There is, as far as one can ascertain, not a freely undertaken large-scale movement of people from the outer provinces to the metropolitan centers, certainly nothing comparable to the extensive in- and out-migration which takes place between the island of Puerto Rico and the major cities on the mainland, or from the borderlands of Mexico up into the western heartland of the United States. But when a Puerto Rican leaves his island and moves to the United States mainland, he becomes a member of a language minority. At home in Puerto Rico Spanish is, and in spite of some early attempts to impose English, has, in fact, always been the dominant language of the island. (There are those who contest this, saying that the economic control is in the hands of English-speaking persons and that the better jobs require a knowledge of English, but this does not change the fact that the culture and first language of the majority in Puerto Rico, including the highest social and economic classes, is Spanish.) It is the "displaced" Spanish-speaking Puerto Rican in a Northern city where the majority speak English who finds himself in the minority, just as a Tartar or an Uzbek in the Moscow region would find that his language was not spoken by the majority there. If he did not already know Russian, he would find that it was imperative for him to learn it.

Whatever the reasons for a multiplicity of languages within a society, each nation has its own way of dealing with the educational situations arising from such linguistic diversity. In the United States, where the melting-pot theory obtained in the past, it is obvious now that members of many different ethnic minorities wish to maintain or regain a familiarity with their ancestral tongues, though few would deny that English, as the language of the majority and also as a major world language, is essential for communicating with their fellow citizens and for contacts with the rest of the world. It is undoubtedly easier for nations with a totalitarian system of government, of whatever political hue, to formulate educational policy for an entire population and to bring about changes in school systems, by fiat, than for countries like the United States or Canada, where schools are organized on a state and local basis. But in slow-moving and sometimes cumbersome ways, changes affecting ethnic minorities are taking place within the educational system of the United States.

The development of bilingual-bicultural programs in public schools represents one such major change in educational policy. Sparked originally by the federal action which provided guidelines and financial support, the movement is now spreading and growing in various areas in the United States, either under the mandate of state laws or the pressure of local demand. By the end of 1973 nine states had enacted legislation requiring or recommending bilingual teaching in certain situations; another dozen had such legislation under consideration; and five more indicated that they had pupils in their public schools who needed or could benefit from bilingual education. Among the states which had taken no action were ten which reported that they had few or no pupils whose mother tongue was not English and that, therefore, there was no need for bilingual teaching in their schools.

Among the state and locally supported bilingual programs are some designed as "transitional," that is, intended to provide pupils with instruction in their native language only until they can move into an all-English-language curriculum; others are aimed at the maintenance and fuller development of a pupil's mother tongue. Whatever the format and the immediate objectives, by the mid-1970s there was clear evidence of widespread feeling that bilingual-bicultural instruction was either a necessary transitional technique or a desirable permanent addition to public education in the United States.

Notes

1. Except in the Province of Quebec. On July 30, 1974, the provincial legislative body, the National Assembly, passed a law making French the only official language in the province. The Lieutenant Governor of the Province signed the bill into law on July 31, 1974. It is possible, however, that the question will face a court test. English-speaking opponents of the measure claim that the law is unconstitutional because the "British North America Act that in 1867 made Canada a separate political entity gave equality to French and English as the nation's official languages." (The New York Times, 1 August 1974, p. 5.)

2. Reference Paper No. 45 (revised September 1972), Information Division, Department of External Affairs, Ottawa, Canada, p. 17.

3. *Census 1971, Canada Yearbook*, 1972, app. 11, p. 1370.

4. Anthony Astrachan, "The Revolution on our Doorstep," *Saturday Review-World*, Sept. 25, 1973, p. 16.

5. If the new law enacted in July 1974 proclaiming French as the only official language in Quebec stands unchallenged, "all immigrant families whose first language is neither French nor English will have to enroll their children in French-language schools, and French-speaking families will not be free to place their children in English-language schools." (*The New York Times*, 1 August 1974, p. 5.)

6. *The Organization and Administration of Public Schools in Quebec*, 3d ed., Dominion Bureau of Statistics, Education Division, Ottawa, Canada, 1966, chap. VII, pp. 1, 10.

7. *Canada Yearbook, Census 1971*, 1972, app. 11, p. 1370.

8. 'L'Enseignment," *Profils du Québec*, Gouvernement du Québec, Ministère de l'Immigration, Direction de l'Information, Québec, 117, rue Saint André, Québec.

9. *Schools Act and Regulations*, (consolidated to 1972), Province of New Brunswick, Fredericton, New Brunswick, chap. 24, p. 49. Printed and published by authority of the Queen's Printer for the Province.

10. Personal letter from the Associate Chief Superintendent of Schools, Department of Education, Fredericton, New Brunswick, Oct. 1, 1973.

11. Personal letter from the Education Officer, Ministry of Education, Region 10, Ottawa Valley, Ottawa, Ontario, Sept. 10, 1973.

12. Personal letter from the Education officer, Ministry of Education, Region 10, Ottawa Valley, Ottawa, Ontario, Oct. 4, 1973.

13. E. G. Malherbe, "Commentaries/Session I," in L. G. Kelly (ed.) *Description and Measurement of Bilingualism*, published in association with the Canadian National Committee for UNESCO, University of Toronto Press, Toronto, 1969, p. 46.

14. The group referred to by South Africans as "Coloureds," most of whom live in the western Cape Province, numbered 2,018,533 in the 1970 census. They are identified in South African government publications as "a mixture of the remnants of the original Hottentots with other races and peoples. The only indigenous peoples with whom the early White settlers came into contact were the nomadic Hottentots and Bushmen. The Bushmen have remained a separate people. . . . The Hottentots were decimated by two epidemics of smallpox. . . . Those that remained have, over the years, interbred with other races and peoples and constitute the main body of the Coloured people today.
"The Cape Malays, a separate community among the Coloured, have for centuries retained their identity, their customs and their Muslim religion." From *This Is South Africa*, issued by the Department of Information, Pretoria, Republic of South Africa, Johannesburg, 1971, p. 7.

15. Ibid. (quoting the 1970 census), p. 7.

16. The Bantu universities are University College of the North in the northern Transvaal and the University College of Zululand, in Natal, the former serving students of the Sotho, Venda, and Tsonga groups, the latter Zulu students. The college (university) at Fort Hare is reserved for the Xhosa group. (From *This Is South Africa*, p. 85.)

17. The University of the Western Cape, established in 1961, had an enrollment of 975 students in 1971. Ibid., p. 87.

18. The University of Durban-Westville, with an enrollment in 1971 of 1,710. "In addition to the normal program of studies, the University at Durban offers courses in Sanskrit, Hindi, Telegu, Urdu and Persian, and a major in Oriental Studies leading to the A.B. degree." Ibid., p. 88.

19. Ibid., p. 55.

20. Figures compiled by E. G. Malherbe in 1967 indicated that among the Bantu, about 1.5 million spoke English, 2.5 million spoke Afrikaans, and about 1 million were trilingual, speaking both of the national languages in addition to their Bantu tongues. For the white population the figure for bilingualism was 66%, for the total population—white and non-white—the figure was 22%. Comparable figures for Canada at the same time were about 12% bilingual (speaking both French and English).

21. *South African Yearbook*, 1973, p. 83.

22. In November 1973, the Cultural Council of Flanders decreed that the word *Nederlands*, not *Vlaams*, be used in all official documents and in the schools to describe the language spoken by the Flemish, to emphasize that the language spoken in the Netherlands today is an offshoot of the earlier, Flemish, Dutch. Belgium and the Netherlands signed a treaty in 1946 to cooperate in Dutch language matters, compiling a dictionary which standardized spellings and indicated which words were from Flemish vocabularies and which from present-day Dutch. Work is also being done on a standard pronunciation guide. (This information is taken from "Special to the New York Times," 3 February 1974, p. 14, by Paul Kemezis, "The People of Flanders Achieve Status in Language—The Dutch They Speak.")

23. Quoted in Theodore Andersson and Mildred Boyer, *Bilingual Schooling in the United States*, vol. I, Southwest Educational Development Laboratory, Austin, Texas, 1970, p. 32.

24. Yuri Desheriyev, "National Languages and Interlingual Communication," *Soviet Life*, no. 8 (203), August 1973, p. 18.

25. V. Zhamin, *Education in the USSR: Its Economy and Structure*, Novosti, Moscow, 1973, p. 11.

26. Yuri Desheriyev, op. cit., p. 18.

27. Ibid., p. 19.

28. V. Zhamin, op. cit., p. 14.

29. Yuri Desheriyev, op. cit., p. 19.

30. V. Zhamin, op. cit., p. 43.

31. Ibid., p. 56.

32. Ibid., p. 60.

33. *New York Times*, 28 October 1973.

34. "About National Minorities in China" (no author given), *China Reconstructs*, vol. XXI, no. 12, pp. 6-7.

35. *New York Times*, 9 September 1973, p. 8.

36. The above statements regarding language policies in the People's Republic of China are based on an oral report given at the San Diego Multilingual Conference, April 1973, by Mr. Jack Chen, then consultant to the New York State Department of Education, Albany, New York. Mr. Chen, son of a Chinese father, was raised in the West Indies and later (from 1950 to 1971) lived and worked as a journalist in the People's Republic of China. His

father was foreign minister of China during the Wuhan Revolutionary Government of 1927 and later a member of the Nanking Central Government. Additional details were provided by Dr. John B. Tsu, of Seton Hall University, and Mr. John MacDonald of Exeter, N.H.

37. This attempt to describe written Chinese is a drastic simplification, to which any Chinese scholar versed in the language may justifiably take exception. It is intended only to suggest the situation which exists among Chinese people of different areas who can communicate in writing but not in speaking, unless they have learned the Han language.

38. "Language Corner," *China Reconstructs*, op. cit., p. 41.

39. Information furnished by Mr. Jack Chen. See note 36.

40. Information furnished by Mr. Jack Chen. See note 36.

State-Mandated
Bilingual-Bicultural Education

7 When in the fall of 1971 House Bill 3575, "An Act Providing for the Establishment and Implementation of Programs in Transitional Bilingual Education," was passed by the Legislature of the Commonwealth of Massachusetts, that state became the first in the nation to have on its books a law mandating bilingual education for pupils in its public schools. The Massachusetts bilingual law was not only the first such state law in the country; it was also more stringent in its provisions than any passed since then by other states. It calls for each school district to take a yearly census of school-age children in the district "with limited English-speaking ability," to classify the children "according to the language of which they possess a primary speaking ability," and it requires the state to offer a program of up to three years of transitional bilingual education to such children whenever at the beginning of a school year there are 20 or more within the district who speak a common language other than English. The bill states that the Commonwealth will provide financial assistance to compensate for the additional cost of such programs, though a limitation was set of $2.5 million for the first year, $3.5 million per year for the second and third years, and $6 million per year for the fourth and subsequent years of programs in transitional bilingual education. No time lag was permitted in the implementation of the law, as has been the case in some other states. Transitional bilingual programs were to be established in the year following the enactment of the legislation.

Because payment by the state for the additional costs of bilingual classes is being made only at the end of each fiscal year, when towns and school districts file reimbursement forms for programs carried on during the previous school year, statistics on the first year of operation of the bilingual law were slow in coming in and definitive final figures could not be ascertained at the time of this writing. Tentative statistics given out August 1, 1973, by the Bureau of Transitional Bilingual Education of the Commonwealth of Massachusetts indicated that during the 1972-73 school year at least 7,816 students in 31 towns and cities had been served by the state-mandated transitional bilingual programs: 4,597 Spanish-speaking, 2,054 Portuguese, 485 Italian, 167 Greek, 213

French, and 300 Chinese. Eighty-one percent of the pupils were in elementary school, nineteen percent in secondary. The number of teachers involved in the programs was 439, of whom 306 were listed as bilingual and 133 as teachers of English as a second language.

It was estimated that in the 1973-74 school year, some 50 towns and cities in the state might be qualified or required to offer transitional bilingual programs. Though many of the locations where state-mandated programs took place were clustered around the greater Boston area, they were also to be found widely spread throughout the Commonwealth, from Cape Cod and other coastal sections to cities and towns in the western part of the state. A list, originally published in June 1973 but updated for the author in November of that year, showed that the following cities were providing transitional bilingual classes for pupils enrolled in their public schools:

ATTLEBORO (*Portuguese and Spanish*)
BRIDGEWATER (*Portuguese*)
BROCKTON (*Portuguese and Spanish*)
CAMBRIDGE (*Portuguese, Spanish, Greek, Italian, and French*)
CHELSEA (*Spanish*)
CHICOPEE *Spanish*)
CLINTON (*Spanish*)
EVERETT (*Italian*)
FALL RIVER (*Portuguese and Spanish*)
DARTMOUTH (*Portuguese*)
FALMOUTH (*Portuguese*)
FITCHBURG (*Spanish*)
FRAMINGHAM (*Spanish and nine diverse language groups*)
GLOUCESTER (*Italian*)
HAVERHILL (*Spanish and Greek*)
HOLYOKE (*Spanish*)
HUDSON (*Portuguese*)
LAWRENCE (*Spanish, Portuguese, and French*)
LEOMINSTER (*Spanish*)
LOWELL (*Spanish and Portuguese*)
LUDLOW (*Portuguese*)
LYNN (*Greek and Spanish*)
MALDEN (*Italian*)

MEDFORD (*Italian*)
METHUEN (*Spanish*)
MILFORD (*Portuguese*)
NEW BEDFORD (*Portuguese and Spanish*)
NEWTON (*Italian*)
PEABODY (*Spanish and Portuguese*)
REVERE (*Italian*)
SALEM (*Spanish*)
SCITUATE (*Portuguese*)
SOMERVILLE (*Portuguese and Italian*)
SOUTHBRIDGE (*Spanish*)
SPRINGFIELD (*Spanish, Portuguese, and Italian*)
STOUGHTON (*Portuguese*)
TAUNTON (*Portuguese*)
WALTHAM (*Spanish, Italian, and French*)
WATERTOWN (*Armenian*)
WESTFIELD (*Spanish*)
WOBURN (*Spanish*)
WORCESTER (*Spanish and Greek*)
and BOSTON, which had transitional bilingual classes in *Chinese, Greek, Haitian French, Italian, Portuguese, and Spanish.*

There had been, and still were in 1974, federally financed Title VII bilingual projects in at least seven of the cities which were setting up transitional bilingual classes: Boston, Chelsea, Holyoke, Lawrence, and Springfield for Spanish-speaking pupils; and Fall River and New Bedford for Portuguese.

A certain amount of controversy is going on at present among those in the forefront of the bilingual education movement concerning the relative merits and desirability of "transitional" versus "maintenance" bilingual programs. The former are aimed at helping students, usually new arrivals in a school system, over the difficult language hurdle and making it possible for them to keep up in their academic work while they are learning enough English to be able to function successfully in regular English language classes; the latter have as their goal encouraging pupils from various ethnic groups to perfect and maintain their knowledge of their mother tongue while also mastering English—in other words, developing truly and competently literate bilinguals. Whatever the final outcome of the controversy over transitional versus maintenance programs (and they are by no means mutually exclusive), as the director of the Massachusetts Bureau of Transitional Bilingual Education pointed out at a conference of language teachers where the subject had been raised, educators have to be realistic, and school systems must do whatever is possible to help students in the particular circumstances prevailing at any given time. The transitional bilingual programs mandated by state law in Massachusetts are addressing themselves to a very real and pressing need. What has been accomplished in the first year or two of their operation is real and noteworthy. One need only step into a few of the bilingual classrooms to appreciate what it means to a newly arrived student who understands little or no English to have access to a teacher who speaks his language.

In the Haverhill High School, for instance, in 1973, world history, world geography, accounting, and clerical practices were being taught in Spanish for pupils who would find it difficult or impossible to follow such courses in English. The director of the Haverhill bilingual program, who taught some of the Spanish-language high school courses, was a Boston-born Anglo who spent his undergraduate years at the University of Puerto Rico in Rio Piedras and is therefore familiar with the home island of his students, as well as being fluent in Spanish. Haverhill also has kindergarten classes conducted in two languages for Spanish-speaking pupils and some ungraded classes for pupils of mixed ages and grade levels who need instruction in subject matter in Spanish while they are learning more English. The Spanish-speaking staff included one teacher born in Spain, one Mexican-born but Texas-raised, and others of Puerto Rican origin.

Haverhill has always had a large Greek colony (and at least one mayor of Greek background). For newly arrived Greek pupils, it provided a Greek-speaking teacher in the 1973-74 school year, a man who had formerly taught high school in Greece. He was an enthusiastic teacher of the Greek language, and, going beyond the priorities of the law, was trying to corral children of Greek families who didn't understand the language to give them some instruction in their ancestral tongue. In the fall of 1973 Haverhill was in its second year of operating bilingual classes under the provisions of the state law, but the school system had been aware of the problem earlier and had been carrying on some bilingual teaching even before the law was enacted.

The city of Lawrence has an extensive program of bilingual education established to fulfill the requirements of the Massachusetts Bilingual Act: in the 1973-74 school year, 20 classes for Spanish-speaking, two for Portuguese, and three for (Canadian) French. Lawrence had had 10 Title VII federally financed bilingual classes (for Spanish-speaking junior and senior high school pupils) before the enactment of the state legislation. The Spanish-speaking population of the city represents 11 different countries of origin, the major groups being Puerto Rican (50 percent), Dominican (15 percent), Cuban (10 percent), and Ecuadorian (10 percent). Haverhill and Lawrence, as mill towns, have had a long history of attracting "foreign labor," immigrants from Canada and Europe, to work in their textile plants and shoe shops. The two and three-story red brick factory buildings, evidence of more prosperous days, still line the river banks, some empty, some occupied. Though industry is no longer booming, there continues to be, as there has always been, a steady influx of new residents from Europe, from the Near East, and now, from Puerto Rico, who don't speak English on arrival.

Another Massachusetts city, Lowell, in the fall of 1973 had placed about 300 students in bilingual classes, some of them Portuguese, but the majority Puerto Ricans. The origins of Lowell's Puerto Rican population can be traced, at least in part, to a period when migrant agricultural labor was needed in nearby areas. Though there is no longer a demand for migrant field workers, Puerto Ricans continue to come to this Northern city because they have heard of it from other natives of their island, or have relatives living in the area. Many of the bilingual classes are housed in one school, with pupils brought there by bus from various sections of the city, but there is bilingual teaching going on in other school buildings, too. In the 1973-74 school year, of the twenty-one teachers involved in the bilingual program, eight were Spanish-speaking, three were Portuguese, and the balance were ESL specialists, two of whom were assigned as "follow-up" teachers to go along with students when they left the bilingual program and moved into junior or

senior high school. There was wide variation in the levels of academic
work going on in the bilingual classes in the 1973-74 school year, ranging
from a sixth-grade biology class taught in Portuguese, to kindergarten
and first-grade classes conducted in Spanish and English. One class
notable for the care and patience exhibited by the teachers was a group
of mentally retarded children who were being taught rudimentary concepts in both Spanish and English by bilingual teachers. (Massachusetts
is one among several states which require that mentally retarded
children shall be enrolled in regular schools and included as much as
possible in school activities with other pupils.)

As one travels throughout Massachusetts one sees school systems
working to put into practice the mandate of the state bilingual act,
grappling with the problems which it presents and attempting to find
solutions for them. This is not to say that there have been no objections
to the idea of bilingual education, especially when forced on local school
boards from above. There has been a certain amount of resistance at
many different levels, from superintendents and principals on down the
hierarchy, and from leaders in the Anglo community to some members
of the ethnic groups whom the bilingual programs are being designed to
serve. One superintendent was so firmly opposed to the idea that he
proposed introducing a bill into the legislature himself to rescind the
state bilingual act.

Some ESL and regular classroom teachers worry about the future of
their positions, and also may feel resentful if they consider that they were
doing a good job before the introduction of bilingual classes. Anglo
members of a community can be both fearful and disapproving if they
have not been made aware of the special needs of the pupils, informed in
advance about the purposes of the program, and prepared for the
introduction of something new into the traditional school system, which
they may believe served them and their children very well. Administrators and directors have sometimes felt hampered and frustrated by the
rigid requirements of the state law, which they feel is being enforced too
inflexibly, too soon, and with not enough leeway given to those on the
spot responsible for the functioning of the programs. Comments have
been heard to the effect that the people who wrote the law ought to
spend a year out in a school district trying to put it into practice, that
perhaps then they would understand the need for more flexibility in
interpreting the provisions and permitting local administrators to make
decisions based on the immediate situation. (The other side of the coin is
that, to the state administrators, it may sometimes seem that local school
boards, in determining how many of its pupils have a "limited command" of English, are influenced in their judgments of what constitutes
a "limited command" by their own wishes in the matter. The state

Bureau of Bilingual Education is trying to work out better guidelines to answer such questions.)

It has been difficult in many cases to find enough qualified teachers to teach specific subjects in languages other than English, especially at the more advanced levels. And one hears occasionally of both students and teachers who think that a greater proportion of the time should be devoted to instruction in English for a particular class or group than the state guidelines permit. Complaints are also sometimes made by the staff of the bilingual programs that their pupils are the stepchildren of the school system and that if there is a dearth of classrooms, it is always the bilingual classes that are shunted to the library or the boiler room or the broom closet.

There can also be instances of a lack of understanding, if not animosity, between different ethnic and linguistic groups within a bilingual program, a kind of pecking order based on variations in socio-economic and class status. An awkward situation can arise if bilingual pupils from different sectors of a program are automatically linked together because they all happen to be enrolled in the program of bilingual education. A group of well-cared-for and particularly well-groomed children in one bilingual class may be astonished and resentful to have the school nurse examine them for head lice, because children in a different language section of the bilingual program, who had lived in particularly wretched conditions in their place of origin, had shown evidence of having them. But these are matters of the simple tact which is necessary in handling delicate personal situations, in school and out, and have basically nothing to do with the concerns of bilingual education. By and large, consideration and affection are evident in the handling of the pupils in bilingual classes wherever one finds them in the country.

By the end of 1973, some five years after the first federally financed bilingual projects were established, eight other states besides Massachusetts, as widely divergent geographically and culturally as Alaska, Arizona, Colorado, Illinois, Louisiana, Maine, New Mexico, and Texas, had enacted some kind of legislation either requiring or recommending or supporting bilingual-bicultural education, under certain provisions, in their public schools. In nine more, Connecticut, Florida, Michigan, New Jersey, New York, Oregon, Rhode Island, Washington, and Wisconsin, similar bills were being introduced or were under consideration. Even without the mandate of law, in many towns and cities in these latter states bilingual programs had been set up under state or local aegis, in addition to those already in operation under federal sponsorship.

Among the states which had taken no legislative action relating to bilingual education were eleven which reported having few or no children in their schools whose mother tongue was not English: Alabama, Arkansas, Delaware, Hawaii, Kentucky, Minnesota, Mississippi, North Carolina, North Dakota, Tennessee, and West Virginia. (North Carolina, in making this statement, excepted the Cherokee Indians living on the reservation in the northwestern part of the state.)

It may come as a surprise to some, in view of the multiple ethnic backgrounds of the people now living in the Hawaiian Islands, that the Department of Education of that state claims English as the mother tongue of practically all of its students. But, in spite of exclamations of disapproval from some linguistic activists who feel that a diversity of languages should be promoted in Hawaii, it is a fact that Hawaiians by and large are English-speaking and that they also take pride in the successful amalgamation of diverse peoples into the unique group which they represent, today's Hawaiians. It is true that some descendants of the original Polynesian inhabitants of the islands greatly regret having lost their old language. It is now spoken widely on only one of the islands, Lanai. In most other places, Hawaiian children speak English when they reach school age, and it is reasonable for the school system to use English as the medium of instruction for all children, no matter what their original ethnic background may be. The only Title VII bilingual project ever started in Hawaii, one using and teaching Japanese, was discontinued in 1970.

A situation may be developing in Hawaii which in the future will call for either bilingual education programs or intensified work in ESL. In the early 1970s Filipinos were moving into the islands in large numbers, and there was also a noticeable increase in Samoans. Some pupils in Hawaii, even though they speak no other language, nonetheless have a limited command of English on entering school and need help in developing language skills, oral as well as written. Hawaii has done an excellent job of developing a language-arts program, known as the Hawaii English program. The author, who dropped in unannounced at a school chosen at random in a town on the island of Maui, observed it in operation. Kindergarten and first-grade pupils, in self-directed activity, were using materials developed for the Hawaii English program to teach themselves the correct usage of prepositions, plurals, and other aspects of syntax in which they were deficient.

Other states which by 1973 had enacted no legislation relating to bilingual education but which reported in response to inquiry that there were pupils in their schools with an inadequate knowledge of English who would benefit from bilingual teaching were Delaware, Idaho, Kansas, Maryland, Nebraska, Nevada, South Dakota, Utah, and

Wyoming. Idaho and Utah have each had one federally sponsored (Title VII) bilingual project, and Utah presented proposals requesting funds for two additional projects but had received no response by the end of 1973. Nebraska has Spanish-speaking pupils in its schools, as well as Indian children who speak tribal languages, who might profit from being taught in their mother tongues. Maryland reported a growing interest among its Hispanic community in bilingual education. Nevada explained that because the total number, though not the proportion, of its pupils whose mother tongue was not English was small in comparison to more populous states, it had not been able to compete for the limited amount of federal money available for bilingual projects. The 1970 census indicated that there were about 10,000 Spanish-speaking students in the state, but the state had taken no action regarding bilingual teaching for them. South Dakota, with many Indian children among its school population, has had one Title VII project for Oglala Sioux, at the Loneman Day School. Prior to 1971 the use of any language but English as a medium of instruction had been prohibited by law. In 1971 legislation was enacted to lift this restriction, but it did not require bilingual teaching.

In other states which by 1973 had passed no laws mandating or recommending bilingual teaching, a variety of situations prevailed. New Hampshire, which had had the first federally sponsored French-English bilingual project in the country, was supporting the concept of bilingual education by paying the salary of the director of bilingual projects and that of his secretary. It had enacted no legislation regarding bilingual teaching, except for rescinding a law which had prohibited the use of any language but English in public schools. In the interests of New Hampshire's many French-speaking residents, persons active in the state's bilingual affairs have organized a council to further cultural relations with Quebec. California, though it had by 1973 enacted no overall state law regarding bilingual teaching, had passed individual bills providing for the establishment of specific bilingual-bicultural projects, two for Chinese pupils in San Francisco among them. In Georgia, an ESOL (English to Speakers of other Languages) program was in operation in the Atlanta schools, and it was predicted that with the prospect of a growing Spanish-speaking population, bilingual education was a possible expectation for the future. Iowa was providing some bilingual teachers and aides as well as ESL instruction for its migrant pupils. Montana, with three Title VII projects for Indian children in reservation schools, had taken no action to provide bilingual teaching elsewhere. Ohio was providing special summer and fall educational programs for migrant Spanish-speaking pupils in some 30 locations (in addition to the Title VII bilingual project in Lorain).

Oklahoma's only bilingual education was being carried on in its three Title VII projects for Cherokee, Seminole, and Choctaw Indian pupils. The state itself had taken no action in the field. Vermont, which accepted federal funds for a program involving pupils of French-Canadian extraction, evinced no interest in developing bilingual education through the State Department of Education. Virginia is providing ESL instruction for pupils who don't speak English and believes this is the most effective means of serving the needs of such pupils in its schools.

In the states which have enacted laws requiring or recommending bilingual teaching, there are wide differences in the number and size of the projects and in the languages involved. Alaska is developing materials and is training staff to teach Eskimo pupils in the Yupik (Eskimo) language, and Indian children in a variety of Athabascan dialects. While the total number of pupils is small, what Alaska is attempting to do is impressive, since the Eskimo and Indian villages are widely scattered and difficult of access and since materials must be devised in languages which do not have a body of written literature to draw from. State-run programs in Arizona, Colorado, New Mexico, and Texas, which are extensive in number and size, are directed mainly toward Spanish-speaking Mexican-American children, while Maine and Louisiana are concerned with pupils whose ancestral language is French. California, with its ethnically more varied population, must consider bilingual education for Chinese, Portuguese, and some speakers of tribal Indian tongues, but its major objective, of course, is to develop materials, train staff, and devise programs and techniques which will offer better educational opportunities for its Spanish-speaking Mexican-American pupils who make up the majority of all those in the state whose mother tongue is not English.

A survey conducted by the author in the course of 1973 elicited the following more detailed information regarding bilingual-education regulations, policies, and practices in all fifty states.[1]

Alabama had no bilingual teaching. There are few or no pupils who do not speak English.

Alaska had bilingual programs operating in 17 Yupik Eskimo village schools, 11 Athabascan Indian village schools, 3 Inupiat Eskimo schools (with 7 more projected), and 1 Aleut school.

In the fourth year of the Title VII federal projects, the state was assuming more than half the costs, providing $233,300 as against $187,000 of federal funds.

Senate Bill 422 provided $200,000 out of state general funds for a study to implement bilingual programs in seven Inupiat villages, with an additional $200,000 to be used for a native language center at the University of Alaska at Fairbanks. In one town, Bethel, which is less isolated, the children do speak English on entering school; therefore, literacy in English is the first priority in the bilingual project there.

Among the problems being encountered were a lessening of community interest when the novelty of the bilingual program wore off and demands by some community people for payment for participation.

Arizona had enacted state legislation regarding the desirability of bilingual education in Arizona schools. The bill was undergoing revision at the time of this writing. Approximately 96,000 children in the state are Spanish-speaking, 22,000 speak Indian languages—representing 17 different tribes. Approximately 5 percent of pupils who speak a language other than English were enrolled in bilingual programs in the 1972-73 school year. The number of pupils enrolled in bilingual classes was expected to rise when the new 1973-74 state bilingual program was put into operation. All the bilingual classes were at the elementary level, except for one at Phoenix High School.

Arkansas had no bilingual legislation or programs and had few or no children in the schools who do not speak English.

California: *Materiales en Marcha* for March 1973 provided the following information:

Assembly Bill 2284, introduced by Pete Chacon and signed by the governor, appropriated $5 million to school districts for the establishment and maintenance of bilingual programs. It is a one-time allocation of funds and a nominal amount considering the need, but can be seen as an acknowledgement of bilingual education as part of the curriculum for public schools. The state also took the responsibility for making recommendations for Bilingual Teachers' Credentials, recognizing the need for qualified bilingual teachers.

Mr. Chacon also planned to re-introduce Assembly Bill 2285, which the governor had vetoed in 1972, *requiring* schools with a student population of 15 percent not fluent in English to hire a person fluent in the language of the children to establish communication with the parents.

In the July 1974 issue of *Materiales en Marcha* it was reported that Governor Reagan in signing the largest budget in California history had cut the $8 million allocated by the state legislature for bilingual education to $4 million and had eliminated $145,000 which had been authorized for bilingual teacher training. According to Assemblyman Chacon, the remaining $4 million represented a 10 to 12 percent reduction in the funding of bilingual programs compared to the previous year's funding level.

Colorado: House Bill 1224 was introduced in 1973 making it *mandatory* to provide bilingual education in districts with 100 pupils under the age of twelve or with 25 percent of pupils in grade levels K through 4 who have limited English language skills. Amendments making it *voluntary* for school districts to establish bilingual programs were on the House floor at the time of this writing. $2.2 million was the suggested appropriation. If the bill were to be enacted, approximately 9,500 pupils would be added to the 2,500 already involved in the Title VII bilingual education projects in the state. In addition to those in the Title VII projects, another 600 pupils were already being served by locally funded programs, and 5,000 were in ESL, Head Start, and Migrant Education (Title I, Title III, and other compensatory) projects.

There were in the state 100 elementary schools with 50 to 100 percent Spanish-surnamed pupils, 100 elementary schools with 20 to 50 percent Spanish-surnamed, and thousands of pupils in Title I compensatory projects because of language conflict.

The languages involved in present bilingual programs are Spanish, Ute, and Navajo. Spanish-surnamed pupils in Colorado numbered 80,000 or 13.7 percent; Indian pupils numbered 2,500 or 0.4 percent. The State Department of Education estimates that one out of every four elementary school children speaks enough of another language to make bilingual education necessary—approximately 50,000 pupils.

Connecticut: Legislation introduced in 1973 to *require* school districts to offer bilingual programs and to provide state aid was "boxed" in the Appropriations Committee at the time of this writing.

The State Department of Education had taken no "official position" regarding bilingual teaching; the consultant for Foreign Languages, ESOL, and bilingual education in the department stated that his aim was to encourage the maintenance of bilingual programs in all towns with 4 percent or higher enrollment of Spanish-surnamed pupils but that he expected that the expansion of bilingual programs might be slow unless some financial aid was offered to local school districts. Approximately 10 percent of Spanish-surnamed pupils were being served by bilingual programs in the 1972-73 school year.

In October 1973, bilingual programs were operating in 11 Connecticut cities: Hartford, New Haven, Bridgeport, New Britain, New London, Meriden, Windham, Waterbury, Stamford, Norwalk, and Guilford, varying in size from 200 to 300 pupils in New London to 1,000 in Bridgeport. The cities with the largest Hispanic enrollment are Hartford and Bridgeport (over 20 percent), and New Haven (11 to 12 percent). The bilingual programs in Connecticut cities are financed in a variety of ways, federal

Titles I and VII. Model Cities, and state and local moneys. Bridgeport offers some transitional ungraded bilingual classes for pupils in grades 3 through 5, 6 through 8, and also offers bilingual history and science classes at the high school level. New Haven, which has the oldest of the state's bilingual programs, has a "fairly well developed program" in one high school. Waterbury has added Portuguese and Italian bilingual classes to its previously all-Spanish bilingual program.[2]

The University of Hartford conducts a special bilingual Teacher Corps program in the Hartford schools.

Delaware had no bilingual projects and no legislation relating to bilingual teaching, though it did have some pupils who might benefit from it.

Florida had not yet enacted a state bilingual law, though such legislation was under discussion. There are enough students in its schools who do not speak English to warrant such legislation. Florida was the first state to have extensive bilingual programs, those established in 1962 for Cuban refugees in the Miami area. These have been expanded to provide bilingual teaching in most of the schools in Dade County (the Miami school district). There has also been a federal project for Miccosukee Indians, using their tribal tongue. Since the language of the Miccosukee Indians had not been written previously, much of the initial effort in this program has been directed toward devising a written form of the language.[3]

Georgia had no bilingual programs in operation in 1973 and no legislation concerning bilingual teaching. There are about 12,000 Spanish-speaking persons in the state but no statistics on the number of Spanish-speaking pupils. There is an ESOL program in the Atlanta schools. It is expected that Georgia's Spanish-speaking population will grow and that, therefore, bilingual education may be feasible in the future.

Hawaii had no bilingual programs and no legislation regarding bilingual teaching. The State Department of Education indicated that there were not enough children in their schools who do not speak English to make bilingual education necessary.

Idaho had no bilingual law nor was the state considering one, though there are pupils concentrated in one or two places, such as Nampa and Caldwell, who might benefit from bilingual programs. Under ESAA Idaho had a program in Nampa aimed at desegregation. There was one Title VII project in Caldwell for Spanish-speaking Mexican-American students. (These were federal, not state, projects.)

Illinois passed a bill on September 10,1973, *mandating* bilingual education *by 1976*, in schools with 20 or more students of the same language background who have a limited command of English. Sixty schools in Chicago and another thirty-five downstate had bilingual programs paid for out of state funds (in addition to the Title VII projects operating in nine Chicago schools). In October of 1973 it was estimated that about 16,000 out of 100,000 pupils with limited fluency in English were enrolled in bilingual programs.

Indiana had no bilingual legislation and no funding for bilingual education.

Iowa had no state bilingual law and none under consideration. For migrant pupils it was conducting an ESL program. A federal grant for a Teacher Corps Program related to bilingual education had been given to a professor at the University of Iowa.

Kansas has no bilingual law and none under consideration, though there are some children in its schools who have a limited command of English.

Kentucky has no bilingual law and has none under consideration, having few or no children whose mother tongue is not English.

Louisiana in 1968 enacted several laws to further the preservation and utilization of the French language in the state. Though not mandating bilingual teaching or bilingual classes as such, Act 408, House Bill 437, required that by the 1972-73 school year, all public elementary schools must offer five years of instruction in the French language, high schools must offer at least three years, and in addition, the programs must include the culture and history of the French populations of Louisiana and other French-speaking areas of America. (Parents can request that their children be exempted from these classes.) Section 2 of the same Act provided that educational television operated under the auspices of any public institution "shall be bilingual in character, paying due regard to the proportion of French-speaking listeners within the broadcast area."

Act 409, House Bill 438, authorized the establishment by the Governor of a Council for the Development of French in Louisiana (CODOFIL), to consist of no more that 50 members, "empowered to do any and all things necessary to accomplish the development, utilization and preservation of the French language as found in the State of Louisiana for the cultural, economic and tourist benefit of the State."

Act 257, Senate Bill 374, required institutions under the control of the State Board of Education, which offered teacher certification programs in the teaching of high school French, similarly to offer teacher certification programs in the instruction of elementary-school French.

Act 458, House Bill 650, authorized the establishment of a non-profit French-language television corporation to be known as *Télévision-Louisiane*, empowered "to establish, manage and operate a broadcasting facility at and in conjunction with the University of Southwestern Louisiana at Lafayette, which operation shall be conducted primarily in the French language."

Act 256, Senate Bill 371, "to further the preservation and utilization of the French language by removing discrimination against French without in any way detracting from the present status of the English language," amended the statutes to provide that "all legal notices may be published in French, in addition to English."

The state legislature and the State Department of Education provided $1,000,000 for the second year (1972-73) of the French-language programs in the elementary schools. In November of 1973, the program was in existence in 26 of the 64 parishes (counties) and employed 170 French associate teachers from France and Quebec, in 1,080 schools, teaching approximately 30,000 children.

These French-language classes were in addition to the federal bilingual projects, of which there were one Title VII project for Spanish-speaking children in the New Orleans area, three Title VII projects for French-speaking children, and four ESAA Bilingual-Bicultural Programs for French-speaking children, black and white. Since the federal programs were bringing about $1 million into Louisiana, the state was matching federal spending for bilingual and second language teaching in its schools.

Maine had enacted legislation permitting and supporting bilingual education for pupils with a limited command of English, and reimbursed school districts in part for the costs of such teaching. (The costs of bilingual programs are figured into the total expenditures for education in a district and as such they are reimbursed by the state.) In one of the "unorganized territories" in the north, Sinclair, which has a largely French-speaking population, the State Department of Education is itself providing bilingual teaching. (The unorganized territories are areas so sparsely populated that the localities are unable to provide for public education.)

The Maine Bilingual Act signed by the Governor April 20, 1973, reads as follows:

Subject to the annual approval of the commissioner, the school committee or school directors of any administrative district having a high concentration of such children (those with a limited command of English) may provide early childhood programs involving bilingual education techniques designed to provide these children during not more that five years of the education of each child with educational experiences which will enhance their learning and potential. Bilingual instructors shall be subject to section 59 requiring certification of teachers by the State Board of Education, in both course content and language of instruction.

Maryland had enacted no legislation concerning bilingual education, but there was a Governor's Commission on the Concerns of the Spanish-speaking which was studying the possibility of such legislation. Pupils are classified by surname in data gathered by the State Department of Education rather than as speakers of a language other than English. However, approximately 1,420 students at the elementary and secondary level in seven school systems in Maryland had been identified as needing instruction in ESOL. All were receiving some special help or attention, but none were enrolled in bilingual programs. The major groups are Orientals (Korean, Japanese, Chinese), Latin Americans (Cubans and Puerto Ricans), Greeks, and Yugoslavs. The foreign population in Maryland is relatively small but growing steadily and becoming increasingly heterogeneous, a fact which makes the implementing of bilingual programs more difficult. There is interest in bilingual programs, however, particularly in the Hispanic community.

The College of Education of the University of Maryland, College Park, offers graduate courses for teachers in bilingual education.

Massachusetts, as stated earlier in the chapter, was the first state to enact a law requiring schools to provide bilingual teaching in districts which have more than 20 pupils of the same language background who do not speak English.

Michigan had not enacted a bilingual education law but was considering such legislation. It has enough pupils in its schools who do not speak English to warrant such action. If a law is passed recommending bilingual education, school districts would be reimbursed in full for the additional costs of such programs.

Minnesota had no bilingual programs and furnished no information regarding the makeup of its school population. In the early 1970s, however, the Legislature passed a law relating to bilingual-bicultural teacher training and provided close to $1 million for it.

Mississippi had not enacted legislation relating to bilingual education, is not considering such legislation, and does not have many children in its schools who do not speak English.

Missouri had not enacted legislation relating to bilingual education, is not considering such legislation, and does not have enough pupils who do not speak English to warrant bilingual teaching.

Montana had enacted no legislation relating to bilingual education and had none under consideration. It had three federally funded Title VII bilingual projects for Indian pupils in public schools on three Indian reservations.

Nebraska had not enacted legislation relating to bilingual education and had none under consideration. There are some Spanish-speaking pupils, and Indian children in both public schools and reservation schools, who might benefit from being taught in their mother tongues, but no state-run bilingual programs were in existence.

Nevada had not enacted legislation relating to bilingual education and had none under consideration, though there are enough pupils in its schools to warrant bilingual teaching. The fastest-growing minority group in the state is the Spanish-speaking. There are conflicting data on the number of such students, the civil rights survey indicating approximately 6,000, the 1970 census closer to 10,000, mostly located in the Clark County-Las Vegas area. There are scattered pockets in the state where a tribal Indian language is dominant, but most of the approximately 3,000 Indian pupils in the state speak English as their first language.

New Hampshire had not enacted a state bilingual law but had amended the law requiring the use of "English only" as the medium of instruction in the classroom, to permit the development of experimental bilingual programs approved by the State Department of Education.

A group of persons involved in bilingual affairs in the state has organized a Council for the Development of French in New England (CODOFINE), patterned on the Louisiana Council (CODOFIL).

The objective of CODOFINE is to:

organize, implement and/or coordinate the educational and cultural activities and programs in the New England area relative to:

1. The development of the French language and Francophone culture on every level and in every appropriate field of endeavor.

2. The development of French bilingual educational programs and opportunities on every level and for anyone in the New England area who wants them.

3. The development of cultural contacts, activities, and

exchanges between the New England area and other Francophone areas in the world.

4. The identification of personal and social needs of the New England area Francophone population on all levels and the corresponding development of educational and cultural programs to meet those needs.

The chairman of the New Hampshire State Board of Education, who is himself bilingual, speaking in French at a meeting at the University of New Hampshire in Durham, reported that the State Board of Education had voted unanimously on September 19, 1973, to support bilingual education and the work of CODOFINE.[4]

CODOFINE is incorporated under the laws of New Hampshire. The president in 1974 was Robert Paris and the address was Notre Dame College, 2321 Elm Street, Manchester, N. H. 03101.

New Jersey was in May of 1973 considering legislation relating to bilingual education, the bill being patterned after that of Massachusetts. The State Department of Education indicated that it believed bilingual programs were needed, feasible, and desirable. The New Jersey Bilingual Coalition had been formed to try to expedite the passage of the proposed legislation. Though the department was unable to predict whether the bill would be passed, it indicated its belief that if the legislation were enacted, New Jersey's bilingual programs would be good, since the state was prepared for them with both personnel and curriculum.

New Jersey has had federally financed bilingual projects in nine cities, all basically for Puerto Rican children except for one in Union City for Cubans. There are some 85,000 Puerto Rican children in New Jersey schools. (These statistics are derived, however, from classification of "Spanish-surnamed" pupils, not by language dominance.) In addition, there are approximately 8,500 Cuban children in the schools. According to the 1970 census New Jersey has over 300,000 mother-tongue speakers of Italian, as well as 61 other language groups, one-half of which are represented by a thousand or more speakers. In the 1973–74 school year there were bilingual classes only for Spanish-speaking.

An article in the *New York Times* (1 September 1974, p. 40) by George Vecsey, containing summaries of the education picture at the opening of the school year in several states, reported that a likely development in New Jersey would be a "statewide bilingual program enabling foreign students to be taught in their native language until, gradually, they learn English." The article also stated that at least 39 communities in the state already had such programs and that Montclair had opened three learning centers for 92 students speaking 13 languages.

New Mexico in 1973 enacted a law called the "Bilingual Multicultural Act," the purpose of which is to ensure equal educational opportunity for students in New Mexico. It calls for the
establishment of bilingual-multicultural education programs in
the public schools, at the discretion of local education agencies,
and provides also for reimbursement by the state for the additional
costs of such bilingual programs. Though bilingual teaching was
not made mandatory, the State Board of Education issued a statement of policy supporting bilingual-multicultural education as a
process to improve education for all children, on the premise that
"every individual has a right to retain and expand his identity, his
culture, and his language, and to participate in various cultural
forms and values."

The ethnic composition of the school population in New Mexico
was listed as: Spanish-surnamed, 40.7 percent; native Americans
(Indians), 7.7 percent; blacks 2.2 percent; Orientals, 0.2 percent;
and others (Anglo-Americans), 49.2 percent. The Board of
Education's statement of policy suggested that this population
"offers the opportunity for all students to make cultural pluralism
a reality for the state."

It was stated that the bilingual programs should be located in
regular public schools and should not have the effect of segregating
students by ethnic group. It was also stated that it was important
that bilingual-multicultural programs "include specific objectives
for developing complete functionality in English for all students so
that they will be proficient in the national language."

In order to be eligible for state financial support, each program
must provide for the educational needs of linguistically and culturally different students, including Native American (Indian)
children and other students who wish to participate, in grades K
through 6, with priority to be given to programs in K through 3;
use two languages as mediums of instruction for any part or all the
curriculum of the grade level or levels within the program; use
teachers who have specialized in elementary education and who
have received special training in bilingual education; and
emphasize the history and cultures associated with the students'
mother tongues.

New York: a bill was introduced in the Senate in 1973 by Senators
Garcia and Giuffreda, which would make bilingual education
mandatory in school districts with 25 or more pupils whose
dominant language was other than English. The bill was read and
committed to the Committee on Education. No definitive action
had been taken on it at the time of this writing. The State
Department of Education had in August 1972 issued a statement
of policy in regard to bilingual education calling for the "total
involvement of our educational system to help non-English

speakers become, along with all other pupils, all that they are capable of becoming." In 1969 the State Department of Education had established an Office of Bilingual Education "for the purpose of meeting the educational needs of children who have English language difficulty. This office coordinates the efforts of other instructional units in promoting, developing and evaluating bilingual and English as a Second Language materials and programs throughout the state."

Though there was no overall state bilingual law in operation mandating bilingual teaching for all pupils with an inadequate command of English, the state was supporting the concept and providing funds for some bilingual programs. For the 1973-74 school year, $929,000 was being expended in New York City, under Chapter 20 of New York State Laws, for bilingual programs serving 1,779 students, of whom some 1,400 were Spanish-dominant. In addition, New York City was spending $4,050,000 of tax-levy funds (Program 30, Module 5) for bilingual programs serving 6,381 pupils, 4,783 of whom were Spanish-speaking. Other language groups included in the bilingual programs were French, Italian, Greek, Chinese, and 70 pupils representing six other foreign languages.

The percentage of children being served by bilingual programs in the 1973-74 school year was still relatively low. The Position Paper on Bilingual Education issued by the Department of Education in August 1972 indicated that there were some 300,000 pupils in New York State classified as non-English-speaking, with 117,489 Spanish-dominant in New York City, and an additional 42,716 who spoke Chinese, Italian, French, Greek, German, Arabic, and Portuguese. Many of the non-English-speaking pupils were concentrated in five large cities, New York, Buffalo, Rochester, Syracuse, and Yonkers; but Brentwood, Long Island, was mentioned as the second-largest Puerto Rican community in New York State, and Port Washington as having students who spoke 22 different languages. Other statistics in the 1972 Position Paper showed that Puerto Rican pupils made up 22.8 percent of the New York City school population (259,879) with more than one-third of them (94,800) described by the 1970 school census as non-English-speaking. Of these, approximately 25,000 were receiving instruction in English as a second language, and some 6,000 were enrolled in completely bilingual-bicultural programs.

The Position Paper stressed that the state bilingual program "affirms the importance of English and at the same time recognizes that the native language and culture of a child can play a major role in his education." It expresses the belief also that "there is no experiential substitute for the successful learning experiences gained by non-English-speaking children who are permitted and encouraged to learn in their dominant language."

North Carolina had no bilingual programs except for Cherokee Indians on the Cherokee Reservation. There are few pupils in the state who do not speak English as their mother tongue. No legislation regarding bilingual education is contemplated, though the Department of Education states that if there were a need, it would establish such programs.

North Dakota had no bilingual law, had no bilingual programs, and had no pupils in the schools who did not speak English.

Ohio had no legislation relating to bilingual education and no state-run bilingual programs, though it had 33 special Migrant Education Programs which were seasonal and in session only for short periods of time in the fall and summer. There was one Title VII federal bilingual project in Lorain, and two federally financed (Title I) ESL programs in Cleveland and Toledo.

Oklahoma had not enacted legislation requiring local school districts to offer bilingual education, but the State Department of Education offered supervisory services and help with the special federal projects financed under Title VII (three projects for Indian pupils in eastern Oklahoma), and Title I (for children of Mexican-American migrant workers in the southwestern border area of the state). Oklahoma has an Indian Education Division of the State Department of Education. The goal of the Department of Education is to help the Indian children "become coordinate bilinguals so that they may keep identity with their native language and culture, but also be able to compete and achieve an identity with the English-speaking society in which they must live and work."

Oregon had not passed a bilingual law but was considering such legislation, since there are children in its schools who speak languages other than English, including some Indian tribal tongues.

Pennsylvania had had since the spring of 1972 a mandate from the Secretary of Education regarding the education of children whose dominant language is not English. There had been no legislation by the General Assembly (by December 1973) but the State Board of Education had adopted an amendment to the state regulations relating to curriculum requirements (applicable to the situation of children who spoke a language other than English). In Pennsylvania the mandate of a member of the Governor's cabinet has the strength of legislation. The mandate permits a school district to employ either bilingual teaching or ESL programs in educating pupils whose dominant language is not English, but is specific in demanding that school districts insure equal educational opportunity for every child. And the Guidelines promulgated by the State Department of Education contain the statement, set in capital letters for emphasis: "It is the feeling of the Pennsylvania Department of Education that the *bilingual* approach is not only preferable, but also more closely in line with the rationale of the program and the department's commitment to the multicultural and multilingual American."

Explaining the rationale for the mandate, the Guidelines state: "This mandate hinges on the growing awareness that this Commonwealth has the responsibility to educate each person in the language he speaks best as well as a moral and legal commitment to the realization that America is a multilingual and multicultural society."

The Guidelines spell out carefully and in detail a variety of possible educational methods for children whose dominant language is not English: full bilingual programs beginning in kindergarten and continuing through the grades, and modified bilingual programs both for kindergarten and early grades and for intermediate and upper grades, some with emphasis on English, some with emphasis on the native language. ESL programs range from those involving total immersion, suggested as preferable for lower grades, to a variety of arrangements for different proportions of the school day devoted to ESL and to learning parts of the curriculum in the native language.

The mandate also calls for using bilingual personnel, when necessary, as administrators, counselors, school psychologists, nurses, doctors, dentists, attendance officers, and in a number of other positions relating to liaison between school and community.

The Commonwealth of Pennsylvania does not provide specific funds for bilingual classes but, like all states, pays part of the costs of public education and would therefore reimburse school districts in part for the costs of these special programs. The Guidelines also suggest that school districts apply for and make use of all pertinent federal grants.

The Guidelines were to be revised after an evaluation of the first year of operation.

Rhode Island had not in December 1973 enacted legislation relating to bilingual education, and no state funds were being provided for bilingual programs. It was expected, however, that a bill would be introduced in the next year.

South Carolina had enacted no legislation relating to bilingual education, and has none under consideration, since the state has few or no children whose first language is not English.

South Dakota had not enacted legislation relating to bilingual education, but in 1971 the legislature amended the law to permit the use of a language other than English in teaching children who could not use English. The Pine Ridge Reservation, where there was a Title VII project for Lakota Sioux, using their tribal language, is probably the only area in South Dakota where there are a considerable number of children who do not speak English. There are not sufficient numbers of other minority groups to justify a bilingual program in the schools.

Tennessee had not enacted legislation relating to bilingual education and had no bilingual programs operating in its schools, since there are relatively few pupils whose first language is not English. The figures (1973-74) of the school population in the state were listed as 279 Indian, 519 Spanish, 725 Oriental, 191,020 Negro, and 696,961 all others, out of a total of 889,504.

Texas enacted a bilingual law (Senate Bill 121), signed by the governor May 28, 1973, to provide for the establishment of bilingual education programs in public schools and to furnish supplemental financial assistance to help local school districts meet the extra costs of such programs. The Texas Bilingual Act requires the governing board of each school district to determine not later than the first of March each year the number of school-age children of limited English-speaking ability in the district and to classify them according to the language in which they possess a primary speaking ability. Beginning in the 1974-75 school year each district with 20 or more children of limited English-speaking ability in the same language classification in the same grade level must provide bilingual instruction commencing in the first grade and increasing the program by one grade each year thereafter up to the sixth grade. All subjects required by law must be taught in the child's first language and in English. The children must be taught to speak, read, and write both English and their first language, and also the culture and history associated with their native language as well as the history and culture of the United States. The bill also requires that the Central Educational Agency conduct bilingual education training institutes for developing adequate bilingual personnel for staffing the programs. As in the case of Massachusetts, children with limited command of English must be given at least three years of bilingual education.

Texas, with its heavy concentration of Spanish-speaking Mexican-American pupils has been in the forefront in developing techniques and materials for bilingual education and has had bilingual programs in many of its school systems, paid for out of local, state, or federal funds. In 1972 Texas had 35 ESEA Title VII projects in operation. ESAA grants approved in June 1973 amounted to $3,562,143 for projects in 16 cities.

The number of children participating in bilingual projects in the 1972-73 school year (from 40 projects reporting) was 30,500, of whom 23,537 were Spanish-dominant and 6,963 English-dominant. The passage of the mandatory bilingual act will ensure that within a few years, the number of pupils being served by bilingual programs will increase substantially.

Utah had not enacted legislation relating to bilingual education and had none under consideration. There is a need for bilingual teaching in three or four districts but without federal funding, the opportunities for establishing such programs seem remote. Utah has one Title VII bilingual project for Navajo children in the San Juan district. The Intermountain Indian School in Brigham City filed an application in March 1973 for a Title VII project to teach vocational subjects in Navajo, but received no response. The Ogden City School district filed an application for Title VII funds to establish bilingual programs, but received no response.

There were ESL classes in five schools in the Carbon school district. The Utah State Board of Education did not have full statistics on children in its schools who are speakers of languages other than English. There are some children who speak Spanish, Greek, Ute Indian, and Navajo Indian. Its ethnic breakdown of the school population for fiscal year 1973 showed some Indian children in all but one school district, the largest number, 1,550, in San Juan, and Spanish-surnamed in all but six districts, with heaviest concentrations in Salt Lake City (2,796), Ogden and Granite (some 1,700 each), and Davis and Jordan (each with over 1,000). There were bilingual classes for children in grades K, 1, and 2 in the Guadalupe center of the Catholic Church in Salt Lake City, but no other bilingual programs in the state except for the federal project in the San Juan district.

Vermont had not enacted legislation relating to bilingual education and had none under consideration. The one bilingual project in the state, for pupils of French-Canadian ancestry, is federally financed and directed (Title VII).

Virginia had, in 1973, enacted no legislation relating to bilingual education and none was under consideration. There were ESL, but not bilingual, programs for students from various language backgrounds, the majority being Spanish-speaking. At present ESL classes are considered the most effective means of serving the needs of pupils in the state who speak languages other than English. In 1973 there were ESL programs in Alexandria, Arlington, and Fairfax. There were also some federal programs designed for children of migrant workers in Accomack and Northampton counties.

Washington had not enacted legislation requiring bilingual education though the subject had been discussed. A joint resolution had been presented to the legislature which would require a study of bilingual needs. Every fall the schools submit statistics to the Superintendent of Public Instruction about the number of pupils of four minority groups, black (Negro), Asian (Oriental), American Indian (Native American), and Spanish-surnamed (Latin American). The totals and percentages in the report of October 1972 were Negro, 21,308 (2.7 percent); Oriental, 11,721 (1.5 percent); American Indian, 13,126 (1.7 percent); and Spanish-surnamed, 16,087 (2 percent). The total school population for that year was listed as 790,805.

There were two Title VII projects operating in the state, both for Spanish-speaking Mexican Americans, in Ephrata and Yakima. About 500 other students are receiving ESL instruction, but there are no other bilingual programs as such. According to the Supervisor of Foreign Language Programs, "The prospects are good, however, for the expansion of bilingual programs because the state legislature has provided some $700,000 per year for rural emphasis, most of which will be bilingual." The office of the superintendent of instruction was in the process of preparing guidelines for the procedures under this program.

West Virginia had no bilingual programs and no legislation relating to bilingual education, presumably because there are few or no pupils in the state whose first language is not English.

Wisconsin had by the fall of 1973 enacted no legislation relating to bilingual education, though several bills had come before the legislature. The State Department of Education had taken no particular stand on the issue, but a newly established "Special Educational Needs" unit in the department was about to come to grips with the question. There were two bilingual projects operating in the state, in Milwaukee (Title VII) and Waukesha. Data on the number of Spanish-speaking pupils in the public schools were collected in the 1971-72 school year, the total for the state in that year being 9,785: 4,352 in Milwaukee, 1,478 in Racine, 625 in Waukesha, and 580 in Kenosha. These figures represented small percentages of the total school populations in these cities, 3.3 percent for Milwaukee, 4.7 percent for Racine, 4.8 percent for Waukesha, and 2.6 percent for Kenosha. The three districts having more than 10 percent Spanish-speaking, Almond, Darien, and Norway-Raymond, were small systems, and the total number of Spanish-speaking pupils was small. In other school systems throughout the state the percentages of Spanish-speaking children were low.

Wyoming had not enacted legislation relating to bilingual education and had none under consideration, though there are enough children in the public schools who do not speak English to warrant bilingual instruction. There are Indian children in both public and reservation schools who speak tribal languages, but they usually speak English too, on entering school.

Notes

1. All the following material, unless otherwise indicated, including quotations and statistics, has been taken from personal letters to the author from the offices of state departments of education, or from questionnaires filled out and returned to the author by persons in authority in those offices, or from printed material relating to bilingual education supplied to the author by state departments of education.

2. *Connecticut Education*, Connecticut State Board of Education, Hartford, October 1973.

3. For additional information about the Miccosukee project, see Chapter 8 of this book.

4. *Concord Monitor*, Concord, New Hampshire, September 25, 1973. Also confirmed by the minutes of the New Hampshire State Board of Education meeting, September 19, 1973.

Bilingual-Bicultural Education for Native American Indians

8 The history of Indian education is far too complex to be gone into in detail here. Some Indian children have attended Catholic or Protestant mission schools; others have received their education in schools run by the Bureau of Indian Affairs (BIA), a federal agency within the Department of the Interior. Indian pupils have attended public schools in towns and cities off the reservation, either returning home each night or living in dormitories in those towns, provided and supervised by the BIA. The BIA schools on the reservations have been of various types, day schools, boarding schools, or a mixture of the two, to accommodate children from the immediate vicinity and those living too far away to come and go daily. The BIA has also established off-reservation boarding schools, sometimes at great distance from the pupils' homes. Some Indian pupils have even attended schools run by their own tribes—a long time ago, in Indian Territory. And now, finally, once again some of the schools on reservations are being supervised by Indian school boards made up of locally elected members of the tribe.

The financing of Indian schools has also been extremely complicated. Indian education has been paid for out of tribal funds (in the early days in Indian Territory), by religious organizations, by federal appropriations to the BIA through the Department of the Interior, by state governments, by private charitable contributions and foundation grants, and by "Johnson O'Malley" money (this legislation was aimed at supplementing the budgets of public schools attended by many Indian pupils who lived on non-taxable reservation lands). Most recently, since the mid-1960s, more federal money has been made available for Indian education under the various provisions of federal education acts.

It is, of course, inaccurate and misleading to group all Indians together and speak of them as one people. The term *Indian*, as used in the United States, encompasses innumerable peoples as different from one another in language and culture as the Scandinavians are from the Italians.[1] The choice of the word *Indian* to identify the original inhabitants of the continent was ridiculous to start with, based as it was on the misapprehension among European navigators and explorers that the newly discovered islands of the Caribbean and the North American continent were part of the fabled Indies of the East. But the term was used and it stuck, and "Indian" became the overall name for the original inhabitants of what is now the United States, as well as those living in other parts of the Western hemisphere. (Some Indians today choose to call themselves "Native Americans" as an alternative.)

As for the names of individual tribes or bands of Indians those, too, were often what other people, sometimes white men, sometimes other Indians, called them. It is not difficult to guess that the names "Nez Percé," or "Gros Ventres" should be attributed to the French. But even a name of Indian origin like "Navajo" is not what this tribe called themselves. In English today they do refer to themselves as "the Navajo Nation," but in their own language, they are Diné (the people). "Navajo" comes from a word in the Tewa language meaning "cultivated fields." The Navajos were originally one with the Apaches. "Apache" again is a Tewa word signifying "strangers" or "enemies." After their contact with Pueblo Indians, the Navajos learned agricultural and weaving skills, acquired livestock (introduced into the Southwest by the Spanish), and settled down. They thus became "enemies (or strangers) of the cultivated fields," "Apache de Navahu" (the *de*, of course coming from Spanish), and in time they were known as the "Navajo," Apaches who had become agriculturists or herders.[2]

The schooling which the many different Indian tribes received over the years, whether under the aegis of the missionary or the employee of the BIA, or in public schools, has been varied, to say the least. The results have also varied from examples of unqualified success to unmitigated disaster. Policies have fluctuated, good and bad administrators have come and gone, and well-meaning or hostile representatives of federal and state governments have brought their influence to bear. Whatever the fluctuations within programs and variations among institutions, two factors have usually remained constant. The Indians, as "wards of the government," have had little to say about what kind of education their children would receive, and the instruction in schools for Indians was in English, whether the pupils spoke it or not. A third factor, present in the majority of schools much of the time, was the stated aim of "acculturation," making the Indian over in the white man's image.

Even this aim, however, when furthered by an Indian tribe itself, was not necessarily accepted or praised by the "establishment" in power at the time. When the "Five Civilized Tribes,"[3] were running their own schools in Indian Territory, before the ultimate implementation of the provisions of the Dawes Act resulted in bringing the communal way of life to an end, John Benedict, the newly appointed superintendent who investigated the schools at the turn of the century listed, as a criticism, that the pupils were learning Latin and concentrating on purely intellectual pursuits instead of learning trades.[4]

Whatever the vagaries of Indian education over the years, the passage of federal education legislation and more specifically the Bilingual Act of 1967 changed significantly the direction of Indian education in the United States, by emphasizing the importance of respecting both the language and the culture of the child, whatever his ethnic origin, and the use, when feasible, of the pupil's mother tongue in some way in the educational process.

Among the federally financed bilingual-bicultural projects put into operation in the late sixties and early seventies, after the signing of the Bilingual Act of 1967, were a number for Native American Indian pupils. There were programs making use of the Navajo language in Arizona; Cherokee, Choctaw, and Seminole in Oklahoma; Lakota (Sioux) in South Dakota; North Cheyenne, Cree, and Crow in Montana; Zuñi, Navajo, and Acoma (a type of Keresan) in New Mexico; Navajo in Utah; Miccosukee (a language derived from Muskogean) in Florida; and Passamaquoddy (an Algonquian tongue) in Maine. Some Eskimos in Alaska were also being taught in Yupik. There were bilingual classes using Chamorro for natives on Guam, and Palau for pupils on Saipan in the Marianas (Trust Territory of the Pacific).

The varied Indian bilingual projects were based on many of the same considerations that led to the establishment of bilingual programs for children from other ethnic minorities: that it was proper and desirable for them to maintain facility in their mother tongue even though, and while, they were learning English: that they would benefit greatly if their mother tongue was used as a medium of instruction in school, at least in the early years; that their own cultural heritage should be taken into account in the development of curriculum and the setting of educational goals; and that the values of their particular heritage should be respected and taught in the schools they attended.

There were and are, of course, many aspects of the situations and circumstances affecting Indian pupils which differentiate the concept of bilingual-bicultural education for them from bilingual teaching for children from other cultural and linguistic backgrounds. In the first place, no claim can be made that their language will ever be of use in communicating with anyone outside of their tribal enclaves. Also there are myriad Indian tongues and dialects, some spoken by only a few hundred persons, such as Miccosukee and Acoma. There was, to be sure, the much publicized advantage to the Army during the war of having Navajo marines who could transmit secret messages by speaking to each other in Navajo, a "code" which the enemy was unable to break. But that was a rather special situation. In general the secret aspect of Indian languages has limited application (aside from permitting Indians to withhold a knowledge of their most sacred rituals from those outside the tribe). American speakers of Spanish, Italian, French, or other languages, if they travel beyond the borders of the United States, will find their mother tongues spoken in other parts of the world. But developing a better command of a tribal tongue will not serve Indians except on their reservations or among their own people.

As for becoming literate in one's mother tongue, an important goal in most bilingual education programs, learning to read and write American-Indian languages presents very particular and unusual problems. None of the Indian languages spoken on the North American continent had a written form at the time of the white man's arrival, and many of them still do not. They have been transmitted orally from generation to generation, with consequent mutations and variations. One of the first things which must be done in many of the Indian bilingual projects is to devise ways of transcribing the spoken language, choosing among variant forms, developing an orthography acceptable to all, compiling dictionaries and grammars, and getting down on paper (or, in some cases, temporarily on tapes for later transcription) tribal legends, history, songs, and rituals which might otherwise be lost. A major exception among the Indian languages is Navajo, which has a standardized orthography worked out several decades ago.[5] Another exception is Cherokee. A remarkable member of the tribe, Sequoya, who was born in Tennessee about 1760, early in the nineteenth century developed a system suitable for writing Cherokee. Sequoya, who grew up in the tribe, was the son of a white man and a Cherokee woman of mixed ancestry, the daughter of a chief in Echota, Georgia. He devised a syllabary for transcribing Cherokee which in 1821 he submitted to the chief men of the nation, for their approval. Within a short time most members of the tribe had learned to read and write their language. The first periodical printed in any Indian language was the *Cherokee Phoenix*, a weekly newspaper in English and Cherokee, published at New Echota, Georgia, the capital of the Cherokee nation from 1828 to 1835. In 1844 the *Cherokee Advocate*, another weekly, half in English, half in Cherokee, started publication in Tahlequah, Indian Territory (now Oklahoma), under the auspices of the Cherokee Nation (one of the Five Civilized Tribes), and was published, with some interruptions, for many years.[6]

It is also true that some of the early Catholic missionaries and Protestant ministers tried their hands at translating the Bible into the languages of their parishioners. Father Sébastien Rasles (sometimes Râle), a Jesuit priest who lived for many years with Abenaki (Algonquian) Indians at Norridgewock, Maine, in the late seventeenth and early eighteenth centuries, worked on a dictionary of their language. He fell victim to the bitter conflict between the British and the French and their competition for Indian loyalties, being killed at the age of sixty-seven on August 23, 1724, by a raiding party sent out from Boston to eliminate him and his Francophile Indians. His Algonquian dictionary had been stolen in an earlier raid but not destroyed. It is now preserved in the library of Harvard University.[7]

John Eliot, a Protestant minister living in Roxbury, Massachusetts, in the seventeenth century also invited some local (Natick) Indians to live in his house and teach him their language. With their help he made a translation of the Bible between 1661 and 1663, a copy of which is also in the Harvard Library. But for the most part the work done on Indian languages in the early years of contact between men of the church and various Indian tribes hardly suffices as a useful transcription and codification of the languages as spoken today. When it comes to classroom needs, for beginning readers or for textbooks in various subjects, it is, of course, necessary to write completely new materials in the American Indian languages of pupils in the bilingual programs.

One of the Title VII Bilingual projects in New England is on the Passamaquoddy Reservation, "down East" in Maine. The Passamaquoddy Indians, numbering about 1,000 according to the 1970 Tribal Census, 513 present (on reservation), and 495 absent (off reservation) are more closely related to the 2,000 or so Malecites living across the St. Croix River in Canada than they are to the other, perhaps better known tribe of Maine Indians, the Penobscots, though they are all of the same Algonquian linguistic stock. The Passamaquoddies' forest land, adjacent to Route 1 in the vicinity of Princeton, Maine, called "Indian Township," consists of some 18,000 acres of productive timberland. The resident members of the tribe live on two reservations about 50 miles apart, one at Peter Dana Point on a lake near Princeton, the other near the mouth of the St. Croix River at Pleasant Point, not far from Perry. A few also live at a spot along the river between the two reservations referred to as "the Strip." There is a grade school at the Pleasant Point Reservation but no high school. Pupils from this area have sometimes attended one of the nearby high schools, at Calais or Eastport. Children who live at the Strip are brought by bus to the grade school at Dana Point. Since there is no high school at Dana Point either, students go by bus to Woodland High School, about 15 miles away, or attend one of the many half-private half-public boarding academies located throughout the northeastern part of the state. Many Maine communities have not been able to provide high school facilities for their older pupils, and it has long been the practice of the state to contribute to the support of these "private" academies which accept students for whom no local public high school is available. (The report is that Indian students tend to get along better at the boarding academies than in the local town high schools, because they encounter less prejudice against them in the former.)

The Passamaquoddies, like the Penobscots and Malecites, are Catholic, and until the introduction of the bilingual program the school attended by the children at Dana Point was staffed exclusively by the Sisters of Mercy. A sign pointing the way to the reservation reads St. Anne's Mission, founded 1604. There is a resident priest, a church, and living quarters for the teaching sisters. Though the school is now run by the Passamaquoddy Tribal Council and provides a bilingual project, the Sisters of Mercy, at the request of the Indians, still furnish teachers to work in the English-language part of the curriculum. (Those old Jesuit priests did their work well. If there is a Jesuit heaven, they must be viewing with satisfaction, as a well-earned reward for the hardships and sufferings they endured, the apparently lasting conversion of the Indians among whom they lived and whose desperately uncomfortable and hazardous lives they shared.)[8]

In the new school building on the Dana Point Reservation there are classrooms, offices, a kitchen, and a large all-purpose room equipped with long tables for serving breakfast and lunch.This building is the home of the Title VII bilingual project, which involves children from age four through the sixth grade. The old school structure now houses only the seventh and eighth grades. Six members of the Passamaquoddy tribe are working in the bilingual program, four as teachers, two as aides, and others are involved in food preparation and general maintenance. The director of the bilingual project is himself a Passamaquoddy, a graduate of one of the local high schools, who has studied at Harvard. (This author, as a native of the state, can vouch for his thoroughgoing, authentic Maine accent in English; whether that unmistakable coloring shows through in Passamaquoddy it would be interesting to know.)

The Passamaquoddies have maintained their native language solely through oral use. There had been no written form of the language in use before the inception of the bilingual project at the school. Most children who live on the reservation speak only Passamaquoddy when they reach school age, and they have found themselves learning English and trying to master the usual beginning school curriculum simultaneously. The bilingual project, which originally began its work with first-grade pupils, now has a special Early Childhood Education program for children from four to six years of age. Eighty children in all were enrolled in bilingual classes in the 1973-74 school year, the fourth year of the project's operation. They are being helped to preserve their knowledge of their tribal tongue, learning to read and write it as well as English.

Materials have been prepared and printed in the Indian language for use in the classes. Literacy classes in both Passamaquoddy and English are also conducted for parents at the school. And even the priest, who had not spoken the language of his parishioners, is being taught some Passamaquoddy by the bilingual personnel. Since there has been a close association between the Catholic church and the Passamaquoddy tribe for some 300 years and since their Catholic faith is an important element in the lives of many of the Indians, the bilingual project at Dana Point has involved itself in the activities and ritual of the church, introducing some of the native language into the Mass, translating some prayers into Passamaquoddy, and teaching them to the priest. The pupils from the school have also presented pageants and programs in the church at Christmas and on other special festival days.

In developing a written form of the language the bilingual project has had the assistance of a linguistic specialist from M.I.T. Though some of the early missionaries' work on the Algonquian language, such as Father Rasles' dictionary, can be of use as reference material, most of it has only limited application in transcribing the modern everyday language. The director of the project maintains contact with some of the six Malecite communities in New Brunswick, Canada, in connection with cultural aspects of their related tribes. He has also found it useful to compare notes concerning common problems and concerns, with other Title VII bilingual projects of similar size, such as the one for Chippewa and Cree Indians on the Rocky Boy Reservation in Montana.

The only craft work for which the Passamaquoddy Indians used to be known in Maine was basketry. In the early decades of this century some of the residents of the Pleasant Point Reservation used to make a summer encampment on the banks of the Kennebunk River at Kennebunkport and travel through the resort colonies along the coast, selling their handiwork to the summer visitors, fragrant sweet-grass sewing baskets and a variety of larger baskets woven of split-ash strips. Only a few of the older members of the tribe do basket work any more. What they make is sold in private (or tribally owned) shops near the reservations. (There would hardly be space available any longer for an encampment in the middle of the high-priced real estate of the Maine coastal communities.) Some attempts are being made at the school to encourage pupils to learn the craft of their elders, but there is not a great deal of interest in it.

The Maine Indians, like a few other small groups living in the Northeast, but unlike most of the Western tribes, have no formal treaty relationship with the United States government, for the simple reason that the federal government did not exist when they met and were either exterminated by or came to an accommodation with the white interlopers in their territories. Many of the Indians who were living in what is now New England were killed; others drifted up into Canada. Any agreements which were made between the Indians who were left and the white man's government were contracted with the colonies, now states. So it is the state of Maine which bears the responsibility for the Indians living within its borders, having accepted this responsibility from Massachusetts when Maine separated from the Commonwealth of Massachusetts. Because of this fact, none of the federal money normally channeled through the Bureau of Indian Affairs or other federal agencies has in the past been available to Maine Indians. Now exceptions to and adjustments of the rigid rules excluding them from participating in federally financed projects are being made, and Maine Indians are benefiting from the federal concern for the well-being of various poor minority groups, including Indians. In addition to educational projects, some new housing has been put up on the reservations and other improvements carried out, paid for with federal money.

The state of Maine, however, has its own Department of Indian Affairs, established in 1965, and a Passamaquoddy from the Dana Point Reservation was appointed as commissioner. The Indian tribes have for many years had a representative at the Maine Legislature, empowered, however, to participate only in the discussion of matters concerning the tribes, and having no vote. Many questions remain to be solved, such as the settlement of land claims and demands by the Indians for more control over the cutting and marketing of their timber resources. The State Department of Education assumes the overall responsibility for the supervision of schools on the reservations and the education of Indian children attending schools both on and off reservation. On the staff of the Maine State Department of Education is an "Indian Educator," whose office is located near the Passamaquoddy Reservation and whose function is to assist in upgrading the quality of educational services for Indian pupils. Things are looking up since the days when Indian education came under the jurisdiction of the Fish and Game Department. Undoubtedly one of the most hopeful developments for Maine Indians is the involvement of the tribal council in the management of its schools, and the establishment of bilingual instruction for pupils on the Passamaquoddy Reservation.

At the other end of the East Coast, some 30 miles inland from Miami on the Tamiami Trail, is another Title VII bilingual project, this one being carried on by the Miccosukee Indians. The Miccosukee are a small group, numbering about 450 in all, roughly 250 registered members of the tribe and another 200 living in scattered clusters along the road which runs through the Everglades. This band of Indians belongs to the Hitchiti-speaking branch of the Muskogean linguistic family. They had probably established an independent status as early as 1778, when the name, spelled as "Mikasukee," appears.[9] The present Miccosukees are descendants of those Indians who fled into the Florida swamps rather than submit to forced removal to Indian Territory, the "solution" which had been conceived as a way of gaining posession for covetous white settlers of the rich land in the Southeast occupied by Indians.

The Miccosukees are described by those who know them as "fiercely individual and independent," and also as harboring deep ambiguous feelings regarding the white man, stemming from their ancestors' harrowing experiences of being hunted down in the swamplands like animals (along with runaway slaves). The soldiers sent out to round up the Indians for the long march into the country west of the Mississippi set aside for them (as it was stated then, "forever") finally had to admit defeat, and the Miccosukees and others remained in Florida. But adult Miccosukees report that in their parents' day, obstreperous children were warned that if they were too noisy, "The soldiers will hear you and come get you." This threat of a soldier bogeyman, used as a disciplinary technique, was enough to quiet the noisiest child and to quell incipient mischief.

Anyone who has driven along the Tamiami Trail, now marked Florida Route 41, from Miami to Naples, will have seen the several Indian Village signs, identifying the homes of the Miccosukees, some simple frame houses, some more traditional open-sided thatched-roof structures which can serve as shelter in the mild prevailing climate. It is an otherwise undeveloped area of water, hammocks of solid land, and swamp, inhabited by fish, water birds, and alligators. In 1962 a BIA school was established for the Miccosukees at a location about thirty-five miles inland from Miami. Before that, children of these Indians who wanted to go to school had to travel by bus to the Miami-Dade County schools. But most Miccosukee parents were not inclined to send their children to be educated in the distrusted white man's way, and many of them did not attend school at all. In 1971 the Miccosukee tribe contracted with the BIA to run the school themselves, and it is now under the overall direction of the tribal council. (The Miccosukees have also contracted to direct their own health and welfare programs, the first Indian tribe to take over the management of all of these services from the BIA, under such a contract arrangement.)

The new school building, located on the old Tamiami Trail, a bit back from the present auto route, is a handsome stone and wood structure. In the same complex there is also the tribal office. The school building has classrooms, a kitchen, school offices, and technical facilities, such as a copying machine, projectors, and tape recorders, which are part of the expected equipment of contemporary educational institutions. But even more important than buildings or equipment is the fact that there are members of the Miccosukee tribe working in the school, teaching the children in the Miccosukee language.

In the Head Start building down the road—a temporary location pending the final construction work on a new building already under way—Miccosukee women are caring for the youngest members of the community, and participating in the activities aimed at preparing them for their later school experiences. It is perhaps especially important for a group like the Miccosukees, whose mistrust has led them to ignore educational possibilities for their children, to be able to feel that they are setting the direction and establishing the goals for the education of members of their tribal community.

Most of the Indian women seen in the school, whether working in the classrooms, the kitchen, the Head Start program, doing clerical chores in the offices, or writing and illustrating Miccosukee texts for use in the classroom, wear the boldly beautiful skirts which are the traditional style of dress of their tribe. Bands of brightly colored patchwork and rickrack decorate the skirts, each one different and original. There is no traditional, set pattern; each woman works out her own individual design. In a display case in the entrance hall are examples of Miccosukee beadwork, dolls, and baskets, and on the shelves of a cupboard are unfinished baskets and dolls and patchwork strips being made by the pupils, who are learning at school the traditional crafts of their tribe.

Several federal grants provide money for different programs in the school and community. The Title VII bilingual project, begun in the 1972-73 school year, in 1973-74 involved 42 pupils ranging from first through sixth grade, grouped in two ungraded classrooms. Some of the children live nearby; others are brought by bus from as far as 15 miles away. At present the school goes only through the sixth grade, but it is hoped that eventually classes will be provided for all grade levels through a secondary program.

The director of the bilingual program is a white man who has taught in schools in Miami and other areas and has had wide experience in the field of education. Undoubtedly in time, here, as in other bilingual projects, the white Anglo project director will work himself out of a job, as more Miccosukees become trained and skilled in overseeing and managing their own school system. A local woman member of the Miccosukee tribe is the language specialist for the project. A trained linguist, associated with the Summer Institute of Linguistics, has been called upon to contribute his expertise to a study of the Miccosukee language (spoken by no other group except the Seminole tribe of Florida) and to help in devising a written form for it. The Miccosukees refer to their language as "Eelaponke" meaning "our language" to distinguish it from the different dialect spoken by other Seminoles (the Cow Creek-Muscokee group) living more to the north, which the Miccosukees call "Cheeshaponke," "their language."

The Miccosukees have a strong instinct for holding themselves apart, at times tending to look with disfavor even on marriage between members of their tribe and non-Indians. Until a decade or so ago, the Miccosukee language had not been studied by linguists, and some members of the community would still prefer to have their language remain unknown to outsiders, wishing to keep knowledge of the tribe and their ways to themselves. But most of the Miccosukees favor the bilingual project in the school and approve the work which is being done in preparing written materials and teaching the pupils to become literate in their mother tongue.

The Acomita Day School at San Fidel, New Mexico, midway between Albuquerque and Gallup, serves children of the Acoma (Á-co-ma) Pueblo. Rising above the flat semi-desert landscape some 20 miles distant from the school is the legendary ancient home of the Acomas, the "enchanted mesa," an uninhabited high rock formation whose sides are sheer unscalable cliffs. According to legend, at a time far in the past, some of the mesa walls broke off during a storm taking with them the only pathway up to the top. Those members who were on the mesa at the time were trapped with no means of descent and perished. The remaining Acomas established a new pueblo on another mesa nearby, which is now popularly known as the "sky city," and reputed to be the oldest inhabited settlement in the United States. Acoma was mentioned as early as 1539 by Fray Marcos de Niza, under the name Acus—a corruption of the Zuñi name for it—and it was visited in 1540 by members of Coronado's army.[10] A first church, built by a Spanish missionary priest sent to Acoma in 1629, was replaced in 1699 by the massive adobe structure which now crowns one edge of the mesa and commands the eye from all parts of the pueblo in the sky. Only a few families still live in the old village on the mesa; most members of the tribe, and the majority of the children at the Acomita Day School, reside in the fertile valley farmland surrounding the school.

The Pueblo Indians, those "corn growers" of the Southwest, among whom the Acomas were counted, were of four different linguistic stocks, Kiowa-Tanoan (several pueblos, among them Taos), Zuñi, Shoshonean (the Hopis), and Keresan (Ke-rée-san).[11] Keresan, spoken by a number of pueblos including Acoma, Laguna, Santo Domingo, Cochiti, San Felipe, and Santa Ana, has been classed by some linguists with the great Siouan-Iroquoian group.[12] The language developed and spoken by the Acoma Pueblo is a distinct type of Keresan, specific to their group and not understood by the residents of other Keresan-speaking pueblos. The

Acoma Indians are a relatively small tribe, their population being counted as 2,420, of which 1,689 are resident.[13] One hears the Acoma language spoken by the Indians still living up on the mesa, but most of the families residing in the valley below have a need for English, are surrounded by it, and speak less of their old tongue. On the school playground English is the language the children use with each other. It is in the classroom that they are learning the language of their ancestors.

Because the Acoma's language is spoken by a small number of persons and is in danger of being lost unless steps are taken to preserve it, one of the aims of the bilingual project at the Acomita Day School is to get the language down in writing and to teach it to the pupils at the school. The staff are working to develop an orthography, collecting dictionary entries, and writing a primer. They are also making recordings of folk tales and videotapes of older members of the tribe relating stories.

The bilingual program originally involved only the kindergarten and first-grade groups, but all 230 children at the school benefit from the various bilingual-bicultural activities carried on by the staff. The director is an English-speaking educator; the community coordinator for the project is a member of the Acoma tribe, who previously worked at a school on the Navajo Reservation. Among other duties, he teaches dances to the children and supervises sports and recreation. One can sense the rapport between him and the children, as they call out or run to him on the playground, using his first name.

The Acomas were skilled potters and one still sees examples of their work, full size and in miniature, in the village on the mesa. But most of the Acoma families are involved in agricultural pursuits or other types of work in the modern economy. The Acomita Day School is under the supervision of the Southern Pueblos Agency of the BIA. When the parents were first asked whether they wanted their children to participate in a bilingual-bicultural project at the school, aimed at preserving the Acoma language and culture, only two families hesitated. When they were assured that their children's English would not be neglected, they too gave their consent. Like the Miccosukees, some of the Acoma Indians feel strongly about keeping knowledge of their religious rituals within their own community and therefore had some hesitation about helping outsiders write down their language. To be seen at the school is a statement signed by tribal authorities: "Although we fully support all of the above [the bilingual program in the school], we will continue to reserve the right to privacy in regards to all religious rituals of the Acoma tribe."

A few other Keresan-speaking children are involved in a bilingual education project jointly with Spanish-speaking Mexican-American pupils. The Grants, New Mexico, municipal school system includes some Keresan pupils in its Title VII bilingual program, with the BIA cooperating in disseminating Keresan materials for the Cubero Elementary School.

There are other Title VII bilingual projects operating in towns which have both Spanish-speaking and Indian children attending their schools. One hundred miles or so north of San Francisco, the Ukiah Unified School District in California, combines Mexican-American and Pomo Indian pupils in a bilingual-bicultural project involving more than two hundred students from kindergarten through sixth grade in five schools. The staff is working on developing texts in both Spanish and the Pomo Indian language. Attention is paid to the historical and cultural roots of both groups and participation by the community has been encouraged. Pomo is one of the many Indian languages which were being spoken by Indians in California before the white man's arrival. It has been said that there were at least twenty-one different linguistic families identifiable in Indian California, with some 135 regional dialects.[14] Many of the Indian groups have died out, as have their languages. But there are still innumerable tiny reservations in the state and a large number of different Indian groups, living both on and off reservations, some of whom still speak their original tongues.

Another joint Mexican-American and Indian project is being carried on in Cortez, Colorado, for two groups of Indian pupils, Ute and Navajo, and Spanish-speaking children. Cortez is just north of the New Mexico border, near the "Four Corners" area where Arizona, Utah, Colorado, and New Mexico meet. Cortez is a few miles from the Ute Mountain Indian Reservation, the border of which touches the Navajo Reservation. There are both Ute and Navajo children attending Cortez public schools, as well as Spanish-speaking Mexican Americans and some Anglos. The two Indian languages are totally different, the Ute belonging to the Shoshonean division of the Uto-Aztecan linguistic family,[15] while Navajo is an Athabascan tongue. The bilingual project — identified by the acronym SUN for *Spanish-Ute-Navajo*—operates in five schools which are under the jurisdiction of the Southwest Board of Cooperative Services, based in Cortez. Navajo pupils are concentrated in the village schools of Rico and Egnar, where Navajo workers have been attracted to hillside mines. Navajo teaching aides and materials have been introduced here. Of the 68 pupils in the country school of Egnar, 44 percent are Navajo. Navajo teacher aides have brought fry bread, rug weaving, and coyote tales into the classroom, and the white children are learning to play in Navajo.[16]

Two Cortez elementary schools have Ute programs, while similar programs for Spanish-speaking pupils are in operation in Cortez and the village schools of Dolores and Mancos. In all, 372 students in 17 classes, ranging from kindergarten through sixth grade, were involved in project SUN in the 1972-73 school year. A monthly newsletter, "Sunbeam," was being published, and a lay advisory committee was meeting regularly. Eighteen percent of the students in Cortez are Indian, and the drop-out rate for Utes has been high. Hopes have been expressed that the bilingual-bicultural program will bring about a change in this pattern, since the project fosters a positive self-concept for the students of all the different cultures.

The Gallup-McKinley County Schools in New Mexico are also involved in a Title VII project for Indian pupils of two very different cultures, Zuñi and Navajo. There are bilingual classes in four schools which come under the jurisdiction of this public school system, Church Rock, Tse Bonito, and Thoreau (about 20 miles west of Gallup) and Zuñi (39 miles south of Gallup on the Zuñi Reservation). Compared with the Navajos the Zuñi are a small tribe, the population numbering 5,180, 4,200 of them resident, and their reservation consisting of 407,000 acres. The Zuñis are not related linguistically to any other group in the United States, and their language is spoken only by the Zuñis. The Zuñis are thought to be a blending in prehistoric times of at least two different cultures. It is also believed that they absorbed members of various other groups at a later time, including some Tlascalan Indians from Central Mexico who accompanied Coronado's expedition into Zuñi territory in the mid-sixteenth century. They have maintained a distinctive cultural life and are considered generally a progressive tribe. They produce less pottery than formerly but are well known for their skill and art in jewelry making. Some 900 silversmiths and stonecutters work at least part time at their crafts.[17] The goal of the Title VII programs for Zuñis and Navajos is gradually to introduce English as a second language to those students who do not speak it on entering school, while helping the students maintain their first language and their own cultural characteristics. The intent also is to develop understanding and respect for Anglo, Zuñi, and Navajo cultures alike. A staff of bilingual-bicultural team leaders, teachers, and paraprofessionals are being trained who can communicate with the children in their native language and help them develop a positive self-image, while leading them to competence in English and an understanding of Anglo society.

Of all the Indian tribes in the United States, the Navajo Nation, as this group refers to itself, is, of course, the largest, in population and in the size of its reservation. According to the 1970 census, there were some 135,000 Navajos, most of them living on or close to the reservation. The Navajo reservation, which lies mostly in northeastern Arizona but extends across state lines, north into Utah and east into New Mexico, contains some 16 million acres (about 25,000 square miles) with another 2 million acres of public land adjacent to it also used by Navajos. This is an area almost as large as the states of New Hampshire, Vermont, Connecticut, and Rhode Island put together. The vast extent of the lands they occupy and the kind of lives the Navajos have traditionally lived—that of sheepherders—have been important factors in determining the kind of schooling the Navajos have had, in their educational history under the auspices of the Bureau of Indian Affairs.

Most Navajos do not live in towns or villages—there are few on the reservation—but in widely scattered family enclaves. A large amount of grazing land is required for each herd of sheep (it has been estimated that one sheep needs thirty acres of the kind of grazing land available on the reservation); Navajo families have lived out on range land with their sheep and other livestock, widely separated from each other. Most children if they wanted to attend school had to be brought by bus to day schools, sometimes a considerable distance. Unpaved roads on the reservation are often impassable after heavy rains or snowstorms, and attendance at day schools has been irregular because of this. The alternative was for children to leave their families at an early age to go to boarding schools on or off the reservation, or live in BIA dormitories and attend public schools in neighboring towns. Eight border towns in which students live in dormitories and attend the local schools are Flagstaff, Holbrook, and Snowflake, Arizona; Gallup, Ramah, Aztec, and Farmington, New Mexico; and Richfield, Utah. (In the spring of 1974 there was talk of discontinuing the Holbrook dormitory.) In theory children living at boarding schools on the reservation may go home on weekends, but traveling conditions, especially in winter, are often so bad that arranging visits home is not always feasible. At the boarding schools, pupils have usually been supervised by English-speaking persons and have attended classes conducted in English, a language most of them do not know when reaching school age.

When Navajo children went away to boarding school their problems were compounded by the language barrier, and being separated from their families and the environment in which they felt comfortable. Closeness of family ties is one of the predominant factors in Navajo culture. Their first exposure to school was often a traumatic experience for Navajo children. The Bureau of Indian Affairs has sometimes tried to bridge the communication gap by employing Navajo aides to interpret in classrooms, and to assist in guidance work and in similar areas. But teaching the pupils to read and write the language they spoke—Navajo—was not commonly part of the curriculum, though it was done in a few instances. And the concept of using the pupils' mother tongue as a medium of instruction (for the various subjects in the usual school curriculum) did not make its appearance until late in the 1960s.

Among the bilingual programs for Navajo pupils are two Title VII projects in schools on the reservation in Arizona, the Rough Rock Demonstration School and the Rock Point Community School. Both of these schools are supervised by locally elected Navajo school boards who derive their authority to manage the schools from a Tribal Council resolution. They receive most of their funds and the use of government buildings through a "contract" with the BIA. There is another Title VII project, involving two schools, Sanostee and Toadlena, across the state line in New Mexico, but still within the borders of the reservation. This is under the jurisdiction of the Navajo Area Office of the Bureau of Indian Affairs. This bilingual program involves 164 students in kindergarten through second grade and places major emphasis on the training and career development of Navajo teachers and aides.

Rock Point lies in the northeastern corner of Arizona, roughly 20 miles, as the crow flies, south of the Utah border and some 30 miles west of New Mexico, though state lines don't mean much on the Navajo Reservation and are largely disregarded. For an unwinged creature, the distances are somewhat longer and the approach a bit more roundabout, though Rock Point is on, or just a brief turn off, a paved all-weather road, Route 63. This north-south highway runs down past Round Rock and Many Farms to Chinle and the Canyon de Chelly (locally pronounced "Shay.") The Rock Point Community School is a self-contained campus, with dormitories, classroom buildings, kitchen and dining rooms, housing for the staff, and a newly constructed, well-appointed tribal meeting room, built in the traditional hexagonal shape of the Navajo hogan.

The locally elected Navajo school board, which manages the school under a contract with the BIA, consisted in the 1973-74 school year of six male members of the tribe, only one of whom had attended school and learned English. The others have a very limited knowledge of English. They meet a full day once a week to interview prospective dormitory "mothers" and other applicants for positions and to discuss the affairs of the school. The board has the responsibility for hiring the director and staff and overseeing the operation of the school. When they have dealings with persons who do not speak Navajo—such as the present author—an interpreter, a person from the community who speaks both Navajo and English, solves the problem of communication. He also keeps the minutes and other records and performs many liaison services.

Present at their meetings and a party to their discussions is the director of the school, an Anglo, whose Ph.D. dissertation at the University of New Mexico was in the field of Navajo orthography. Other Anglos on the staff also speak some Navajo. The director of the Title VII bilingual project, though still a relatively young man, gained his knowledge of the language in an earlier career as a missionary. Another member of the staff, an Anglo, has the title of teacher coordinator. He also performs services similar to those of a guidance counselor. Before coming to Rock Point he had taught in a high school in the San Juan district of Utah which had a number of Navajo pupils. He acts to coordinate academic activities. He also functions as a "troubleshooter" for the non-Navajo teachers, handling attendance and discipline problems. In the matter of discipline and truancy, he says that he doesn't try to force pupils but prefers, rather, to explain situations in order to help them understand that the choices are theirs, and to make them realize the advantages of staying in school and the behavior expected of them if they wish to stay.

Some of the children attending Rock Point live in the dormitories; others are brought in daily by bus. In the 1973-74 school year some 250 pupils in kindergarten through third grade were enrolled in the Title VII bilingual program. Working at the school were nine Navajo classroom teachers, one substitute, two interns, three Navajo-language specialists, a teacher of Navajo social studies, a teacher of science-in-Navajo, and a teacher of Navajo literacy, in all, fifteen people teaching children in Navajo. All are taking courses toward degrees. There are several Navajos with degrees working as English-language teachers and in training roles in the Title VII program.

A Navajo woman, a language specialist, who holds an M.A. degree in bilingual education, is responsible for developing and coordinating a coherent Navajo-language curriculum. She also acts as a Navajo-teacher trainer, sometimes teaching the children herself, as a way of instructing other teachers. There are only five college-educated Navajos on the staff. It has been estimated that the reservation needs at least 2,000 Navajo-speaking teachers and has no more than 200. One of the solutions for schools like Rock Point and Rough Rock is to train teachers from within the community. Both schools are attempting to do this, each in its own way.

In all, there are 350 pupils at the school. All participate in activities or components of the bilingual program. Eight classrooms (the lower grades) are set up as coordinate bilingual classrooms. Here one can observe teaching taking place in Navajo at one end of the room and in English at the other. In another two classrooms at a higher grade level, a Navajo-language teacher comes in to teach Navajo literacy. In the rooms of the upper six classes, social studies and science are taught in Navajo. For those children who do not speak Navajo at home (a small proportion of the pupils), Navajo as a second language is taught in small group sessions.

An observer at the school will see the youngest children being taught concepts and subject matter in Navajo and beginning also to learn English from English language teachers. In the kindergarten and lower grades, children may be listening to a Navajo teacher telling them Navajo tales, as a way of improving their oral comprehension. In one room, children sitting on the floor put together the cut-out pieces of a wooden puzzle, with a Navajo letter symbol on one side and a picture on the other, matching the written symbol with the initial sound of the Navajo word represented by the picture—the kind of learning game useful to beginning readers in any language.

A Navajo social studies teacher, working with older students, uses various techniques to draw them into discussions if they are shy or hesitant about expressing their ideas. He encourages them to draw and paint pictures of their houses and families, their horses or trucks, their sheep and cattle, and the landscape, as a means of getting them to talk about Navajo ways of life. Sometimes he deliberately makes a mistake in describing something, and is pleased when they rise to the bait and challenge him. At some stage, younger children will learn both Navajo and English names for family relationships. There are differences in concept and terminology which have to be made clear, such as that "first cousins" in English are considered "brothers" and "sisters" in Navajo when they are a mother's sister's children, not however, when they are a mother's brother's offspring, or a father's nieces and nephews. (Navajo clan relationships are rather complicated and difficult to explain.) Differences in manners and attitudes in the Anglo and Navajo worlds will be acknowledged in some discussion. One example might be that though it is considered impolite by Navajos to stare at people or look them straight in the eye when talking to them, in Anglo society the opposite is true, and they are expected to look at the person to whom they are talking. The English expression "shifty-eyed" is in itself an indication of how Anglos interpret a refusal to look at them.

To an uncomprehending Anglo ear, spoken Navajo sounds somewhat stern and harsh, perhaps because of the many glottal stops, initial, medial, and final. One can imagine that it is impressive, and well suited to discipline when uttered firmly, and that a child told in Navajo to do something, would do it on the double. Written Navajo also looks complicated to the uninitiated. The accepted orthography makes use of some letters of the English alphabet, with adaptations and additions. A slashed l, (ł) is used for a sound not found in English, and a double vowel (ii, for instance, an idea taken from the Finnish) indicates length. Since Navajo is a tonal language, accent marks are used to show a high tone, combinations of high and low tones to indicate rising or falling tone, an apostrophe to mark a glottal stop, and a hook under a vowel to indicate a nasalized vowel. To speakers of Navajo, it is presumably no more difficult than learning to read and write English or any other language. In fact, since Navajo is more phonetic, some consider it easier.

All pupils are taught English from kindergarten on, first to speak and understand the spoken language, then to read and write it. The ESL specialist herself learned English not as a first, or even a second, but as a third language, since she spent some childhood years in Indonesia and spoke Dutch and Indonesian. She taught in BIA schools before the inception of the bilingual programs and gained knowledge and expertise in teaching English to Navajo pupils. Her Ph.D. dissertation at the University of Arizona was on a comparison of methods of teaching English to Navajo children. At Rock Point she not only teaches English to the pupils but also trains other teachers in ESL techniques. She was in 1974 conducting a course for Northern Arizona University in the teaching of elementary reading, and had previously taught courses in elementary-school mathematics for the University of New Mexico.

Since there is no high school at Rock Point, for schooling after the grades at the community school, students must go to the public high school at Chinle, a day school 50 miles away, or to the BIA high school at Many Farms, a boarding school 35 miles away. For those who want to and are able to continue their studies beyond high school, there will be the choice of going away to colleges or universities in the Anglo world or attending one of the colleges on the reservation, at Ganado or Tsaile. Children who are firmly rooted in their own culture and who have a sense of their own worth are more likely to develop to the full extent of their capacities. The years pupils spend in their community-run school, and the bilingual-bicultural approach to education prevailing there, will give them a good start on whatever path they choose to follow in the future.

The use of the Navajo language as a medium of instruction at Rough Rock pre-dates the passage of the Title VII (bilingual) legislation. In 1966 the school made use of some Title I funds to develop a bilingual approach to teaching the pupils from the Rough Rock area. A grant from the Carnegie Foundation also has helped support a Curriculum Center, which prepares materials in both English and Navajo suitable for the education of Navajo children.

Rough Rock lies in the heart of Navajo country, 17 miles west, on an unpaved road, of Route 63, the paved north-south highway which goes from the southern edge of the Navajo Reservation almost to the Utah border. The physical plant of the Rough Rock Demonstration School consists of a modern compound of dormitories, classroom buildings, kitchen and dining room, water tower and power plant, the Curriculum Center building, and residential quarters for the staff. A mile or so away, adjacent to the trading post, is the old Rough Rock high school, two small buildings which were still being used in the 1973-74 school year pending the completion of a planned new high school. Rising impressively behind Rough Rock is the enormous Black Mesa, sacred to the Navajo people. It is accessible via an extremely steep and frequently washed-out road, navigable by pick-up truck or jeep in good weather, on foot or on horseback in bad. On top of this mesa, 1,500 feet above the plain below, another school is in the process of development, the Kitsillie elementary school, to be operated as a bilingual school in collaboration with Rough Rock. The Kitsillie school commenced operation in the summer of 1974, the plan being to hold classes when good weather permitted access to Black Mesa, and to close for vacations in winter when roads become impassable. The 425 students attending the Rough Rock school live mostly within a 10 mile radius of the compound, about two-thirds of them brought in daily by bus, the other third living in the dormitories. (The dormitories also house some students of high school age.) The supervisors of the dormitories are Navajo-speaking members of the tribe, hired by the Navajo school board. This locally elected board (in the 1973-74 school year) was made up of seven men, only four of whom spoke English and whose formal years of schooling totaled about ten. They had hired the Navajo director, Navajo principals, and a teaching staff, half of whom are Navajo. The director of the Title VII project is an Anglo woman whose doctoral thesis (at the Univeristy of Arizona) concerned educational problems related to cultural differences in Anglo and Indian children.

At Rough Rock the children, all of whom speak Navajo, are taught to read and write their language which is also used as a beginning medium of instruction in various subjects. They also receive intensive work in English as a Second Language, taught by specialists in the field. (In the 1973-74 school year, one of the ESL instructors at the school was a former member of the Peace Corps who had taught English for two years in Africa.)

A programmed list of carefully worked out and standardized objectives for developing a command of spoken English has been compiled and reproduced as a guide for the teachers. A computerized system for checking the progress of pupils has also been developed. The director and staff of the Rough Rock bilingual project have devoted a good deal of attention to the preparation of materials.

Navajo aides are used in various capacities. A visitor may come upon a grandmotherly figure, dressed in the traditional velvet blouse and tiered skirt of the Navajo women, putting materials away and making order in a classroom, or combing and arranging the hair of one of the younger children. Or she may be escorting a line of pupils, towels over their shoulders, on their way along the corridor to the shower room. For many of the children who live with their families and not in the dormitories, home is a hogan with no running water or toilet and limited bathing facilities, so the pupils take their showers at school. On occasion the smell of mutton stew and fry bread is wafted along the corridor from a room where the traditional food is being prepared by teachers or aides, for sale to other staff members, to earn money for some special project.

The Rough Rock Demonstration School, which has been well publicized, receives support for its many different programs and activities from a variety of sources, including federal and private agencies, and foundations. *Reading Is Fundamental*, a non-profit organization established to encourage reading, has given books to the pupils; the Save the Children Federation has contributed money to pay for individual photographs to be taken of the pupils at school and for supplies, such as bales of hay, to be sold at low cost to families on the reservation, with the proceeds to be used for barn repairs and articles for the local co-op. The Bureau for Education of the Handicapped of the U.S. Office of Education provided funds in 1974 for a new project, the making of videotapes to be shown to parents of handicapped children to demonstrate how such children can be helped not only at school but also at home by the parents. The system is portable, operating from the battery of the truck which transports it. Thus the videotapes can be shown to families living far out on the reservation in hogans with no electricity.

The director of the Rough Rock School (in the 1973-74 school year) was a Navajo woman who holds an A.B. degree in elementary education from a college in Indiana. Before assuming the position of director, she had held various positions at the school since 1968—as teacher, Navajo language specialist, director of the Curriculum Center, elementary school principal, and deputy director of the school. In addition to the Title VII bilingual program, Rough Rock has a Title I project, for which a full-time director was appointed in 1974. (The purpose of the Title I money is specifically to alleviate learning deficiencies.) The former director of the school moved on to head up the newly formed Navajo Tribal Office (or Division) of Education, which has offices in Window Rock, and headquarters located at the College of Ganado, both on the reservation.

As is the case with other Title VII bilingual projects throughout the country, the bilingual program at Rough Rock functions within the overall structure of the Demonstration School. Both the school and the bilingual project have occasionally run into difficulties of the kind not uncommon to new ventures, being criticized for sins of omission or commission, or being plagued with delays in the acceptance of proposals and the signing of contracts. Such complaints and delays are not unusual in the overall picture of bilingual education. Undoubtedly the future course of bilingual education at Rough Rock, and other Indian schools, will follow to some extent the direction taken by the bilingual education movement in the country at large. How much federal money is made available for special projects directed toward the needs of minority groups will be an important factor. Additionally, the future of bilingual education for Indian children will depend on attitudes prevailing both within the BIA and among tribal leaders, regarding the needs, rights, and privileges of native American Indians within the American society,

Attitudes within the BIA are changing. In a report concerning bilingual education in schools under the jurisdiction of the BIA, compiled by the Language Arts Branch of the Indian Education Resource Center of the BIA in Albuquerque, New Mexico, in the 1973-74 school year, a brief review was given of the status of bilingual education in the 201 schools within 10 of the Bureau's administrative areas. The information included the number of schools in each area already operating as bilingual schools, the number of bilingual programs in the planning stage, the number of additional schools needing bilingual teaching, and the number in which, in the opinion of the Language Arts Branch, there was no need for bilingual teaching.

The Portland (Oregon) and Billings (Montana) Areas, each with just one school, were not considered in need of a bilingual program. The Muskogee and Anadarko Areas in Oklahoma, the former with two schools, the latter with five, were also judged not in need of bilingual teaching. The other areas were analyzed as follows: Of the 33 schools in the Aberdeen (South Dakota) Area, 5 already were bilingual, 13 were preparing bilingual programs, 11 more needed such programs, and only 4 did not. In the Juneau (Alaska) Area, there were 55 schools, of which 7 had bilingual programs, 13 were preparing for bilingual teaching, 33 more were deemed to need a bilingual program, while only 2 did not. Of 10 schools in the Eastern Agencies, 1 school was bilingual, 7 had requested bilingual programs, 1 more needed bilingual teaching, and 1 did not. The Albuquerque (New Mexico) Area, with 13 schools, had 5 bilingual schools, 1 more preparing such a program, 5 more in need of bilingual programs, and 2 considered not in need of bilingual programs. In the Phoenix (Arizona) Area, of 22 schools, 5 were preparing bilingual programs, 14 more needed them, and only 3 did not. The Navajo Area, with 59 BIA schools, more than in any other area, had 10 schools with bilingual programs, 2 were in the course of preparing programs, and all the other 47 schools were deemed in need of bilingual teaching.

The Center for Applied Linguistics in Arlington, Virginia, which, at the request of the BIA has sponsored conferences dealing with Indian education, in March 1973, published a list of recommendations of action which the BIA should take to improve school programs. Among the suggestions were:

Community control should be adopted as the guiding principle in all plans and actions relating to Indian education.

Parents and community groups should be involved in the decision-making and curricular processes of school operation.

Final decisions about the implementation of language policies should be made by the Indian tribes as directed by Indian parents, not by the BIA or other external authority.

Within the above stricture, the language of the home should be the language of beginning instruction and special attention should be given to developing the English language skills of all children.

Where children enter school speaking only the ancestral language, that should be the language of beginning instruction; where children enter school fluent in both the ancestral language and Standard English, the local Indian educational authority should decide the role that each language should play in the child's school life.

Alternatives to boarding schools should be studied, and in the interim, steps should be taken to permit students closer contact with their families and members of their communities.

Instruction in English as a second language should be offered from the time the child enters school.

In addition to being used as the beginning language of instruction, where appropriate, ancestral languages should be taught at high levels as well, including secondary and college. It should be mandatory for teachers and supervisory personnel involved in bilingual kindergarten or Head Start programs to be fluent in the Indian language being used for instruction.

Additional funds should be provided and personnel prepared for the development of instructional materials appropriate for Indian children, especially in regard to ancestral languages and cultures.

Where children enter school speaking only Standard English, the Standard English curriculum of the area should be adapted to meet the cultural needs of the children.[18]

According to the 1970 census the Indian population is growing four times as fast as the population as a whole. The figures show a rise from 523,591 in 1960 to 792,730 in 1970 and a doubling of their population since 1950. The major reason for the rise is probably improvements in health care over the past fifteen years or so, which have cut the infant mortality rate in half and added four years to the life expectancy of adults. (The Indians are still not the fastest-growing ethnic group in the United States. That falls to the Filipinos, whose population rose 95 percent in the sixties.)[9] The increase in Indian population, especially when compared to the figures of many years ago, would seem to indicate that the Indians were prospering. Other statistics, however, show that they are the poorest minority group in the country. A Census Bureau (statistical) report issued in July of 1973, as well as a study made by the Civil Rights Commission in May of the same year, showed that the Indians had lower median incomes than any other group in the country and lagged behind in most other factors regarded as socio-economic measurements. The only optimistic note in the Census Bureau report related to education. According to its figures, 95 percent of all Indian children between the ages of seven and thirteen and more than half of all Indians between three and thirty-four were attending schools in 1970. The number of those attending college doubled between 1960 and 1970. (The total number in college still remained very low when compared with the general population.) The statistics for Indians on the Navajo Reservation, however, were not so favorable. The median number of school years completed there was 4.1 as compared with a national median for Indians (and blacks) of 9.8 and an overall national median of 12.1. Only 17 percent of persons 25 and over on the Navajo Reservation had finished high school. (Nationally one-third of all Indians had completed high school—up from less than one-fifth in 1960.) For the total population in the United States, the figure for those who had completed high school was 52.3 percent.[20]

It is hoped and believed by many that community (local and tribal) control of their schools, and bilingual schooling for Indians will have a salutary effect on the attendance and drop-out rates for Indian pupils. A statement by Peter MacDonald, Navajo Tribal Chairman in 1974, has been placed conspicuously inside the entrance to the Ramah, New Mexico, tribally run high school as a reminder to students of their potential capacities: "Every time I hear someone say how good we Navajos are with our hands, I want to ask why doesn't someone give us a chance to show what we can do with our heads."

There are colleges now, recently established, on the Navajo Reservation at Ganado and Tsaile, and more Navajo students are attending colleges in the Southwest and in other parts of the United States. But, as Calvin Trillin has written, "The first large group of Navajos to attend college happens to be in college at a time when adaptation and assimilation are no longer universally accepted goals, and the young

Navajos tend to see their education not as a way of rejecting their culture but as a way of defending it."[21]

"Navajo Education," a monthly newspaper of the Diné Bì Oltà Association (the Navajo Tribal Education Association), carries the following statement in a box at its masthead: "The association is dedicated toward upgrading the educational systems on the Navajo Reservation. The association supports the concept of bilingual, bicultural education as a means toward such improvement."

There was a good deal of movement between 1960 and 1970 of Indians to urban areas, but in 1970 at least half of the Indians in the United States still lived on reservations.[22] They are living not just as clusters in the midst of a larger Anglo community, such as the Spanish-language *barrios*, the Chinatowns, the Little Italys, or the "other-side-of-the-track" residential areas for newly arrived immigrants or less-favored minority citizens, but in their own unique society. An editorial, entitled "Our Purposes," in an early issue of the *Navajo Education* newspaper expressed the views of the Navajo Education Association, but it might be said to speak for many other tribes too:

Education is one of the largest businesses of any kind in the Navajo Nation. There are schools operated by the Bureau of Indian Affairs, there are public schools under the authority of the states of Arizona, New Mexico, and Utah, there are schools supported by churches and there are community schools with the control in the hands of local leaders. There is one church-supported college and one tribal-supported college.

In many communities, the only other business or source of employment besides the trading post or gas station is the local school. In addition to being places of employment and institutions where our children supposedly learn the skills that will help them throughout life, schools also comprise training grounds for emerging community leaders and they can serve as community centers in locations that need a place to focus the collective energies of the people.

Schools are extremely important in Navajo life in modern times. This newspaper is about those schools. No other publication has existed on the reservation which is dedicated toward disseminating information about education and we felt it was time to make a concentrated effort.

There are many educational philosophies and all have their advantages and disadvantages. There are many schools and all have their problems and their successes. In this paper we hope to provide information about many facets of education, about many types of schools and about various and perhaps conflicting ideas.

As believers in a free press, we will try to present as much information as possible and present it fairly, so readers can make up their own minds.

Our own ideas on education are rather basic. We believe in bilingual, bicultural education because it seems that children who have their first way of life secure can take on a second way of life and be the richer for having both. We believe that community schools controlled by local people will eventually prove to be more effective in educating our children than other types of schools. We believe that schools will be better for Navajo children when they are staffed with a majority of Navajo teachers who are conscientious and qualified. We repudiate all racist views, believing that Navajo and Anglo cultures are neither better nor worse than each other, but that they are different and that each is valuable.[23]

Notes

1. *New York Times*, 5 June 1973, Report of a commencement address at Wells College by Ladonna Harris, Comanche Indian and wife of former Senator Fred Harris of Oklahoma.

2. Ruth M. Underhill, *Red Man's America: A History of Indians in the United States*, rev. ed., pp. 203, 226, 241. (Paperback Edition.) The University of Chicago Press, Chicago, 1971.

3. The Five Civilized Tribes were the Cherokees, Choctaws, Chickasaws, Creeks, and Seminoles. They had lived in the Southeast before their "removal" to Indian Territory (now Oklahoma) after passage of the Indian Removal Act of 1830 under the presidency of Andrew Jackson.

4. Angie Debo, *And Still the Waters Run: The Betrayal of the Five Civilized Tribes*, rev. ed. Princeton University Press, Princeton, N.J., 1972.

5. Dr. Washington Matthews, a Fort Defiance surgeon, in the 1880s did valuable work in transcribing the language and collecting materials for a grammar and dictionary. Missionary Fathers at St. Michaels in Arizona about 1910 produced a dictionary and English-Navajo catechism. Father Berard Haile, a Franciscan priest, made many contributions to the study of the Navajo language, among them *A Manual of Navajo Grammar*, published in 1926. From 1929 to 1939 he worked with Edward Sapir, a Yale University linguist, whose observations about the tonal aspects of Navajo were important in making accurate transcriptions. In the 1930s the BIA brought together experts to work on the language. Dr. John Harrington, a Smithsonian Institution linguist, developed the alphabet which is the basis for the one used today. In 1940 William Morgan, Sr., and Robert Young devised the first practical orthography, incorporating Sapir's discovery in the 1920s of "pitch inflection" in Athabascan languages. Their book *The Navajo Language*, originally published by the then United States Indian Service in 1943, has since been republished by the Deseret Book Company, Flagstaff, Arizona, most recently in 1967. The currently accepted orthography is often referred to as "the Young and Morgan orthography." (This résumé is a condensation of "A Brief History of Navajo Literacy," by Penny Murphy, in Curriculum Bulletin No. 10, *Indian Education*, "Analytical Bibliography of Navajo Reading Materials," Office of Education Programs, United States Bureau of Indian Affairs, 1970, pp. 4-14.) The Office's address is 1951 Constitution Avenue NW,

Washington, D.C. (Additional information was provided by Dr. Wayne Holm, Director, Rock Point Community School, Chinle, Arizona.)

6. Frederick Webb Hodge (ed.), *Handbook of American Indians*, Smithsonian Institution, Bureau of American Ethnology, GPO, Washington, Bulletin 30, part II, 1912, p. 232.

7. "Maine Indians: A Brief Survey," prepared by the (Maine) State Department of Indian Affairs, February 1971, p. 8.

8. See listings in the bibliography referring specifically to the life of Sébastien Rasles (sometimes Râle) listed under Rasles, Francis, Schuyler, and Sprague, and those referring to various editions of the "Jesuit Relations" listed under Kenton, Kip, Parkman, and Thwaites.

The *Jesuit Relations* were yearly reports sent back to France by the Jesuit missionaries. The *Relations* were published annually from 1632 to 1673 by Cramoisy of Paris, at the behest of the Father Provincial of Paris. Publication ceased in 1673; the *Relations* continued to be sent but remained in manuscript until 1861. In 1858 the Cramoisy series was re-issued by the Canadian government. A few years later Parkman retold the story in his *Jesuits of North America*. In 1894 Burrows Brothers Company of Cleveland undertook to republish not only the original Cramoisy issues, with translations, but practically all the *Relations*, as edited by various persons. Seven hundred and fifty sets of 73 volumes each, with page-by-page presentations of the original French, Latin, and Italian texts, were published. Various persons have worked to edit and make selections from this voluminous material, notably Edna Kenton, and Reuben Gold Thwaites.

9. John R. Swanton (ed.), *Indian Tribes of North America*, Bulletin 145, Smithsonian Institution, Bureau of American Ethnology, GPO, Washington, 1953, p. 134.

10. Frederick Webb Hodge (ed.), *Handbook of American Indians*, op. cit., p. 10.

11. Ibid., p. 318.

12. Ruth M. Underhill, op. cit., p. 211.

13. Tom Bahti, *Southwestern Indian Tribes*, K.C. Publications, Box 14883, Las Vegas, Nevada, p. 8.

14. Andrew Rolle, *California: A History*, Thomas Y. Crowell, New York, 1963, pp. 26-28.

15. John R. Swanton (ed.), op. cit., p. 373.

16. *Wassaja, A National Newspaper of Indian America*, June 1973, p. 4.

17. Tom Bahti, op. cit., pp. 28-29.

18. *Navajo Education*, vol. II, no. 5, p. 8. Diné Bi' Oltà Association, Ganada, Navajo Nation, Arizona, January 1974.

19. Jack Rosenthal, "1970 Census Finds Indians No Longer the Vanishing American," in *The New York Times*, 20 October 1971.

20. Paul Delaney, "Census Statistics Indicate Indians Are the Poorest Minority Group," in *The New York Times*, July 17, 1973.

21. Calvin Trillin, "Reporter at Large," *The New Yorker*, August 5, 1972, p. 35. (The Gallup Intertribal Ceremony.)

22. Jack Rosenthal, op. cit.

23. *Navajo Education*, vol. II, no. 2, p. 2, Diné Bì Oltà Association, Ganado, Navajo Nation, Arizona, October 1973.

Looking Ahead:
Some Considerations and Suggestions

9 When in the summer of 1974 Congress passed and President Ford signed the *Education Amendments of 1974* (H.R. 69), bilingual education programs of the type initiated under Title VII of ESEA were assured of continued federal financial support through 1978. In addition, the new education Act provides for bilingual vocational training, for some adult bilingual education programs, and for fellowships for graduate study in the field of training teachers for bilingual education programs (not fewer than 100 are to be awarded in fiscal year 1975). The legislation calls for the establishment of a Center for Education Statistics (within the office of the Assistant Secretary of HEW), for a national assessment of educational needs "of children and other persons" of limited English-speaking ability, with a report to be made to the Congress by the Commissioner of Education by November 1 of 1975 and of 1977 on the condition of bilingual education in the nation.

The legislation also provides for "forward funding" of programs, so that school districts will not be kept waiting until the opening of a school year to know how much money they will receive from the federal government to carry on programs, as has been the case in the past. Extensions and revisions of education programs for Indian pupils are included in the Act. The composition of the National Advisory Council on Bilingual Education has been modified and the functions of the Council clarified. The Act also authorizes the President to call a White House Conference on Education in 1977.

The complete text of the *Education Amendments of 1974* is far too voluminous to be included here (even as an appendix). Persons wishing to know more about federal aid to public education in general, and to bilingual education in particular, are referred to the text of the Act.[1] The items that have special reference to bilingual education appear in the index to the Act under the headings listed at the end of this chapter in footnote 1.

There are a good many factors which will affect the future development of bilingual-bicultural education and will help determine the direction in which it moves. Among them are money, immigration patterns (including the possibility, though not the likelihood, of Puerto Rico's voting for independence), court decisions (particularly on civil rights matters), and the priorities established concerning *transitional* versus *continuing* bilingual teaching. Other considerations which may enter into decisions will be the measure of success achieved in training competent bilingual teachers for all the language groups in need of them, and in accumulating adequate and suitable materials for teaching the required state-mandated curriculum, especially for the higher grade levels. Another important factor will be the attitudes of various ethnic and linguistic minorities toward acculturation and assimilation, in general, and their feelings concerning the integration or segregation of their children within school districts and in mixed or separate classes within schools. (Mexican-American educators recently—in the spring of 1974—expressed opposition to a court-ordered plan for integrating a school district in Tucson, Arizona, fearing it would disrupt or destroy the bilingual program already in operation there. They stated that although blacks had traditionally pushed for integration, Chicanos had not, and they asked school officials to try to find ways of avoiding carrying out the court order. The school administrators pointed out that legally they could not resist the order to integrate the schools in the district.)[2]

Whether segregation is a good and desirable thing when self-imposed and bad only when it is forced upon a group by someone else is a subject causing some controversy in this decade. It has come up in connection with aspects of the life of black, Puerto Rican, and Chicano students at universities. It is beginning to come up now in relation to bilingual education, and its possible consequences have to be considered.

One of the original reasons put forth in support of bilingual education—providing a setting and an incentive for Anglo pupils to learn a second language—is removed if groups of children are segregated according to language. (The *transitional* bilingual classes are, per se, aimed at just one linguistic target group, but they are conceived of as temporary class assignments, the expectation being that children will be moved into regular classes when their command of English warrants it.) But in other types of bilingual education programs, an integration of two language groups is part of the original concept. It is likely that where federal money is provided, integration of pupils, insofar as it is possible, will be one of the requirements. At present any projects receiving federal money are required to conform basically to regulations calling for integration, not segregation, of pupils. It is true that this presents some difficulties in the organizing of curriculum and the programming of classes within bilingual projects. Conflicting interests, sometimes better served by separation, sometimes by integrated grouping, are not always easy to reconcile.

The phrasing of the revised policy statement prefacing the *Bilingual Education Act* (of the *Education Amendments of 1974*) would seem to place in jeopardy the concept of teaching Anglo pupils a foreign language in federally financed bilingual projects, or to minimize its importance. The federal guidelines for bilingual programs as previously drawn up by the U.S. Office of Education were still being followed during the 1974–75 school year, since formulating and promulgating new guidelines were expected to take a good many months. When new guidelines are promulgated, however, they will presumably have to be in conformance with the legislative intent of the amended Bilingual Act, as interpreted by administrators in the U.S. Office of Education.

There is also by no means unanimity of opinion among minority groups within the United States as to what are desirable degrees of acculturation and assimilation for them, in relation to the nation as a whole. Some members of linguistic minorities express uncertainty about the way their children can best acquire a knowledge of English and also maintain fluency in their first language. Persons who attended all-English schools and are functioning successfully beyond the confines of their original ethnic community, while still maintaining close ties with it, are often inclined to think that the kind of schooling they had is the best kind. A good many individuals have voiced these sentiments to the author. Some, who are actively involved in bilingual programs and sincerely devoted to the interests of the children they are teaching, have asked the author for her opinion as to whether they were doing the right thing. Among the minorities represented by those voicing doubts were Puerto Rican and Mexican-American teachers, Chinese pupils, and a Navajo parent. Such questions are usually asked by persons who come from family environments in which they were encouraged to take advantage of school and to learn both languages, one at home, the other at school. They would undoubtedly have made it academically, no matter what system was used. But their uncertainties as to whether bilingual teaching at school is always the better way points up the desirability of offering families a choice, and continuing with the present policy of making participation in bilingual education voluntary, insofar as the languages of instruction are concerned. Few people now question the need for teaching all children about the history and the differing cultural characteristics and values of the many ethnic and linguistic segments of our society.

As far as money is concerned, an increase or decrease in federal contributions for public education directly affects bilingual projects already in operation or being planned. The complexities in this picture involve how much money Congress authorizes and appropriates, and then, how much is either distributed or impounded. Since the costs of bilingual teaching otherwise are paid out of state and local monies (aside from a few foundation grants), if new methods of financing public schools are devised, bilingual programs will come under review as part of any investigation of the schools' overall financial picture. Undoubtedly there will be an insistence, in any case, on effectuating economies, eliminating waste and inefficiency, and, where it has existed, fraud.

Expenses for programs which are already functioning smoothly need not be as high as in the past, since many teachers and aides have already been trained and materials have been collected and tested. It may be that bilingual classrooms will not be as generously staffed and equipped in the future as some are now. In this respect, it might be worth experimenting to a much greater extent with peer teaching. In the Hawaii English program, as in some other places too, the use of older students to tutor younger ones and of children of the same age group to teach each other what they have learned has been found to be most effective, with both tutor and tutored benefiting from the experience. Bilingual programs would seem to lend themselves particularly well to peer teaching, especially in ungraded and open classrooms in the lower grades, and those at higher grade levels organized to emphasize individualized learning. It would also seem feasible for the Puerto Rican Department of English to make use of the English skills of "returnees" from the States to assist in English classes and to enliven and enrich the English curriculum, and conversely to encourage Spanish-speaking pupils to tutor English-dominant "returnees" in Spanish.

Regarding immigration patterns, various situations have arisen in the past decade which have significantly increased the need for bilingual education and for better teaching of English as a second language. The Castro takeover in Cuba resulted in the opening of doors to Cuban refugees and an influx of Cuban pupils into the schools in the late sixties. A recent decision, in October 1973, agreed upon between the U.S. State and Justice Departments, set in motion a new operation bringing another large group of Cubans into the country from Spain, where they have been waiting to emigrate. An American consular official in Madrid reported in April 1974, that approximately 2,000 refugees were being "processed" each month, and coming to the United States to join family or friends already here. At that time there were approximately 15,000 Cubans in Spain and about 400 more were continuing to arrive in Spain from Cuba each month.[3] A law (P.L. 89-732) previously enacted, in November of 1966, had made it possible for approximately 125,000 Cubans who had been admitted under the "parole" arrangement (with no permanent immigration status) to become permanent residents of the United States.[4]

In 1962, under a presidential directive, close to 15,000 Chinese were "paroled" into the United States from Hong Kong, "to assist in alleviating conditions in that colony caused by the influx of persons fleeing" the Communist regime in China. Chinese relatives of both American citizens and resident aliens, and other Chinese deemed to possess special skills needed in the United States, were considered for "parole" under this directive.

In addition to presidential directives and special arrangements to meet emergency situations, basic revisions in the immigration laws have changed the pattern of immigration into the United States. In the 1960s the principle of national origins in determining immigration quotas, which had been in existence for over 40 years, was abolished. The amended Immigration and Nationality Act, which became effective December 1, 1965, did away with quotas related proportionately to the numbers of immigrants formerly admitted from specific countries, but retained a numerical ceiling of 170,000 annually from the Eastern Hemisphere, with no more than 20,000 allotted to any single country. (There are always, however, certain persons who do not come under these strict visa requirements.) Independent countries of the Western Hemisphere whose nationals were previously not restricted by number, were limited by the amended law to 120,000 a year.[5] Various racial barriers to immigration had been removed earlier. In 1943 Congress had repealed the act which excluded Chinese. (A first quota of 125 was established at that time.) After the war, in 1946 naturalization eligibility was extended to "persons of races indigenous to India, and to all Filipinos."[6] Earlier only Filipinos with United States military service were eligible. All racial bars to naturalization were abolished in 1952.[7]

Anyone who is under the impression that, because Ellis Island is a thing of the past, there are no longer large numbers of people arriving in the United States who don't speak English would be quickly disabused of the idea by studying the immigration statistics, or simply by spending a few days in a public school in one of the large cities on either coast. A teacher may find enrolled in her class Gujerati-speaking children from Bombay, Spanish-speaking South American or Central American pupils, Italians from Calabria or Rome, Portuguese-speaking children from the Azores or the Cape Verde Islands, Cubans, Haitians, Chinese, or Filipinos. The variety is astonishing. Every time there is an economic or political crisis anywhere in the world, many families will look to the United States as a possible haven and a place which offers hope of something better, regardless of how much disillusionment or criticism may be expressed about the U.S.A. at times in various quarters, at home and abroad. And a week or two after their arrival, the children from these families will present themselves at the nearest public school to be educated along with all the other "Americans."

During the decade of the 1960s, over 3 million immigrants were admitted to the United States (3,321,677 to be exact). This does not match the high point of over 8 million for the first decade of this century, or the figures of 5 and 4 million of the two following decades. But it does reflect a steady rise since the thirties when half a million arrived. Each decade since has shown a rise from roughly 1 million, to 2 million, to 3. The highest yearly figure was 454,449 in 1968, accounted for, in part, by the Cuban refugees. The year 1970 had the next highest number, 373,326.[8] A breakdown of the figures by country and by area of the world shows the national origins of the major groups of newcomers to the United States in the year ended June 30, 1970, to be as follows:[9]

North America

West Indies	61,403
Mexico	44,469
Central America	9,343

Asia

Philippines	31,203
China (including Taiwan)	14,093
India	10,114

Europe

Italy	24,973
Greece	16,464
United Kingdom	14,158
Portugal	13,195
Germany	9,684
Yugoslavia	8,575
Czechoslovakia	4,520

In addition to these figures provided by the U.S. Immigration Service, which give some indication of the number of newcomers who may not speak English, there are, of course, the large numbers of Puerto Ricans who are citizens but may be recent arrivals from the island, or born into monolingual Spanish-speaking families resident in the States. The number of Spanish speakers of Mexican origin or background is also not completely covered by official immigration statistics. There are others who have been born in the United States to Spanish-speaking families, and many who slip illegally and uncounted across the border. It is difficult to collect accurate statistics for Puerto Rican and Mexican-American residents, but there is no doubt that they account for the largest group of pupils in the public schools who either speak no English or have a limited command of it.

Decisions about how best to educate all the children who arrive at school handicapped by a lack of knowledge of English must be based, of course, on a consideration of all the facts. Whether bilingual education is the proper course depends on various factors. But *numbers* is certainly a crucial factor, at least in a consideration of need (as distinguished from other factors possibly favoring this approach to education). Justice Blackmun in his concurring opinion in the Supreme Court decision in the *Lau v. Nichols* case, which concerned Chinese pupils in San Francisco, stated:

> . . . I stress the fact that the children with whom we are concerned here number about 1,800. This is a very substantial group that is being deprived of any meaningful schooling because they cannot understand the language of the classroom.
>
> I merely wish to make plain that when, in another case, we are concerned with a very few youngsters, or with just a single child who speaks only German or Polish or Spanish or any language other than English, I would not regard today's decision, or the separate concurrence, as conclusive upon the issue whether the statute and the guideline require the funded school district to provide special instruction. For me, numbers are at the heart of this case and my concurrence is to be understood accordingly.[10]

The Lau decision has been widely interpreted as supporting bilingual education in the public schools. The court decision did not, in fact, specify what kind of remedies the school district should institute, only that some action must be taken to resolve the pupils' language problems. But the thrust of the decision may well lead to more bilingual teaching in certain situations. Some of the key paragraphs of the decision read:

> Basic English skills are at the very core of what these public schools teach. Imposition of a requirement that, before a child can effectively participate in the educational program, he must already have acquired those basic skills is to make a mockery of public education. We know that those who do not understand English are certain to find their classroom experiences wholly incomprehensible and in no way meaningful.
>
> Where inability to speak and understand the English language excludes national origin minority group children from effective participation in the educational program offered by a school dis-

trict, the district must take affirmative steps to rectify the language deficiency in order to open its instructional program to those students.[11]

Whether or not the San Francisco school system moves to offer some instruction through the medium of the Chinese language, in bilingual programs, it is required by the decision to provide much more intensive and effective instruction in English as a second language than it has done in the past for students who do not understand the language commonly used in the classroom. This will presumably apply also to other school districts having similar numbers of pupils who do not speak English.

In those situations nationwide where bilingual programs seem called for, one of the first things to be done may well be to disseminate information to the community at large describing and explaining what bilingual-bicultural education is, and why there is a need for it. Some kind of advance "public relations" is usually advisable to prepare the community for the changes taking place in the school system. One should never underestimate the lack of knowledge on the part of the general public about language abilities, language dominance, and other specifics of the classroom. And "general public" can often be equated with the taxpayers whose dollars will be spent on new and not clearly understood programs.

Even when only ESL classes are being considered, it is essential to explain what the mysterious acronyms ESL, TESL, TESOL, and the like really mean. In an earlier era it was easy to comprehend what "English for Foreigners" meant, but ESL? What on earth is that? Simply spelling out "English as a Second Language" is also not enough. To many people this suggests that someone in the schools is nefariously classifying English as of secondary or minor importance. This misunderstanding has almost cost some programs which had an ESL component the approval of school boards or community members, and consequently the money to pay for them, or even the permission to accept federal money to pay for the programs. "English as a new language" might be a suitable substitute in many situations for the term "English as a second language." The acronym ESL and the ramifications of the concept it stands for, however, are probably too firmly entrenched in the minds of the teachers involved and in the literature in the field to hope that a new expression could take hold.

It is also not a bad idea, when planning a bilingual program in a school which has not previously had one, to prepare the teachers already working in the school for this innovation. An opportunity for discussion, for airing of doubts and fears, in advance of setting up bilingual programs, may be helpful in minimizing opposition and avoiding resentments and hostility between the personnel of the bilingual program and the rest of the teaching staff.

Some principals have also suggested that there should be more coordination, or at least communication, between schools within the same school system regarding priorities, choice of materials, and methods of dealing with common problems. No one believes any more that at a certain hour on a given day of a specified month, all the pupils in a school system should be reciting the same lesson from identical textbooks. But it has been suggested that there might be more cooperation and joint planning among different schools within the same city or school district, since pupils often transfer from one school to another when their families move to a different part of the city. This might be helpful not only in bilingual programs but for all kinds of classes.

When it comes to the actual organization and development of new bilingual programs, the guidelines set up for the federally financed bilingual projects offer valuable ideas and provide possible models. The involvement of parents in various capacities in the bilingual projects and the inclusion of literacy and language classes for parents and other adults in the community are certainly to be recommended. Making use of bilingual persons from the community as aides and encouraging them to upgrade their skills by taking courses leading to academic degrees and certification as regular teachers serves the dual purpose of having members of the community on the staff and helping them further their own education. In most locations there are colleges or universities nearby which offer or can be persuaded to develop suitable courses in educational psychology, language teaching, including ESL, linguistics, anthropology, sociology, history, and other subjects relevant to bilingual education. A good many universities now offer fully developed programs in bilingual education.

In arriving at decisions as to which children or groups of children should be included in bilingual classes, different factors have to be taken into consideration in different places. If there happen to be no Anglo pupils on the school's register, or very few, it will not be possible to have a balanced class made up of half Anglo pupils, half children from some other ethnic group, unless it is feasible and acceptable to transport pupils from one part of a city to another. In speaking of English-dominant children, one has to distinguish between monolingual Anglo children, who can certainly be called "English-dominant," and, for instance, Puerto Rican or Mexican-American children who speak both Spanish and English but are more fluent in English. They are English-dominant bilinguals. If they speak Spanish better, they are Spanish-dominant bilinguals. The amount of time devoted to instruction in one language or the other has to be carefully worked out to provide the best learning conditions for acquiring a better command of both languages, and for keeping up in work in the required curriculum.

Certainly where Anglo children are present, it is a pity not to offer them the opportunity to enroll in the bilingual classes, and the younger the better. Whatever else is not known with certainty about the acquisition of languages, there is absolutely no doubt that age plays a part. It is simply a fact that young children learn a second language more easily and faster than older ones. As a general rule there are marked differences in the ease and speed with which children six or seven years of age, and those of eleven or twelve, or later adolescent years, acquire fluency in a new language. For most children, an opportunity to learn a second language in a bilingual kindergarten, or first or second grade, or even in bilingual pre-school experiences when feasible, is a valuable experience.

The State Department of Education of New York, in May of 1973, set forth some guidelines regarding bilingual education for school administrators whose districts had enough children with no knowledge of or with limited ability in English to warrant this type of program. Among the definitions and descriptions appearing in the memorandum were the following:

> Bilingual education is essentially utilizing two languages, one of which is English, as mediums of instruction for the same pupil population. . . . The major objectives of bilingual instructional programs are to educate all non-English-speaking children and those of limited English-speaking ability in two languages in all areas of the curriculum and to develop an awareness and understanding of the cultural heritage of the ethnic groups within the school.[12]

Four types of possible instructional programs were outlined:

1. *A full bilingual program,* to begin in kindergarten or grade one, planned to extend continuously and sequentially through the grades. For the major portion of the school day instruction would be in the pupil's mother tongue, with the amount of time spent in the target language (i.e., English) increasing as the year progresses. The expectation would be that by the end of the second or third year students would be spending an equal amount of instructional time learning in both languages.

2. *A modified bilingual program* for kindergarten and elementary grades. Here the instructional program for Spanish-dominant pupils would be so designed that learning experiences in all the

major subject areas would be in the pupils' mother tongue, with 20 to 30 percent of the day devoted to learning English as a second language. The amount of "contact time" with English would gradually increase as the year progressed.

3. *A modified bilingual program for intermediate and upper grades (Spanish emphasis)*, the instructional program to provide learning experiences in Spanish in the major subject areas of the curriculum, including Spanish language as a subject, with 10 to 20 percent of the time learning English as a second language. [The reasoning underlying this arrangement is that for older students who know little English, it is essential to provide instruction in the entire curriculum in the language they know, if they are not to fall behind disastrously.]

4. *A modified bilingual program for intermediate and upper grades (English emphasis)*, the instructional program to provide learning experiences in English as a second language 60 percent of the school day, with 30 percent spent on mathematics, science, and social studies taught in Spanish, and 10 percent devoted to instruction in Spanish as a first language [in other words, improving the pupils' command of Spanish]. (Where the word *Spanish* is used, French, Greek, Chinese or other languages may be substituted, if the pupils speak those languages rather than Spanish as their first language.)[13]

The teaching of English (as a second language) is, it goes without saying, a major goal of any bilingual project in the United States. In those situations where a bilingual program is not feasible, because the pupils with a limited knowledge of English in the school speak many different languages instead of the same one, or the school board or the parents of the children themselves do not favor this approach, it is necessary to develop an extensive ESL program. Regarding ESL instruction, the State Education Department of New York provided the following descriptions and guidelines:

The major objectives of the English as a second language programs should be to develop competency in the understanding and speaking (of) English; to orient the student to the mores of his new environment and to provide emotional security for the student through his contact with teachers and other school personnel who speak his language. Depending on the age of the student and the time spent in an ESL class, the development of the skills of reading and writing English are important program objectives. In organizing ESL classes, consideration should be given to the chronological age of students and their competency in understanding and speaking English. It is advisable to have no more than a three-year age differential within a group.

Bicultural educational experiences should be provided in all ESL programs. Present ESL programs generally exclude this important element.[14]

Two different types of ESL programs were outlined:

1. *ESL class and regular classroom programs.* In such programs non-English speakers receive instruction in English for part of the day and are in classes with their English-dominant peers the balance of the day. Minimal instructional time in English should be three hours daily. Emphasis should be on audio-lingual competency in English and English as it relates to curriculum content.

2. *Total ESL Immersion—preferable for lower primary grades.* The instructional program provides learning experiences in English as a second language for 80 percent of the day, instruction in the major subject areas in native language 10 percent of the day, and joint participation in other school programs and activities with their peers for 10 percent of the day.[15]

The memorandum also suggested that bilingual paraprofessionals selected from the community and given special training could be of value in providing support services for the pupils who did not speak English. In conclusion the State Education Department's recommendation was that although two approaches were described for educating children who have a limited knowledge of English, "the major thrust should be the bilingual approach."

Joseph Monserrat of the New York City Board of Education, speaking at the annual International Bilingual-Bicultural Conference held in May 1974 in New York City, reported that within the following month, he expected the New York City Board of Education to declare a policy of supporting bilingual-bicultural teaching in the city schools, and not just the teaching of ESL. He emphasized that ESL classes alone were not "bilingual" programs, and also stated his belief that bilingual education was good education for all children, not only for those who did not speak English.

Dr. John Molina, Director of the Division of Bilingual Education of the U.S. Office of Education, in his opening address at the same conference, predicted that fiscal year 1975 would see a new thrust in bilingual education, with special emphasis given to teacher training and to the development of materials. (At the time of the conference, Congress was debating an education bill which included various measures relating to bilingual education. The Senate had proposed a figure of $145 million with the stipulation that 50 percent of all money above $35 million should be allocated to teacher training. It had also been proposed that $40 million should be appropriated for bilingual vocational training. Included in the amendments to the education bill was also a proposal that a permanent federal Bureau of Bilingual Education should be established to facilitate continuity and long-range planning. The legislation finally enacted in July 1974 as the *Education Amendments of 1974* represented a compromise between the Senate and House versions, arrived at by a conference committee made up of members of both houses. Since the conference committee debated the contested points in closed meetings, it is not easy to ascertain which senators and representatives are responsible for some of the differences between the original proposals and the final text of the Act.)

Dr. Molina expressed the view that there was a need for a more clearly defined philosophy of bilingual education and for promulgating the idea that it can be valuable for all children. Many other speakers at the conference made similar statements, expressing disapproval of the continuing characterization of bilingual education only as a compensatory measure for disadvantaged pupils. Though a point can and should certainly be made of the value of bilingual education for all children, until the concept is assured of unfaltering acceptance and support by broad segments of the society, it would seem desirable, and politic, still to emphasize that bilingual education is a useful and a sometimes necessary compensatory measure for helping pupils who *are* disadvantaged by virtue of not knowing the lingua franca of the country in which they live. If bilingual education can be shown to make the difference between failure and success in academic pursuits and between frustration and a greater degree of fulfillment in personal life, it is more likely to gain approval and financial support than if it is stressed chiefly as a means of bringing about basic changes in the nature of the American society.

There is still resistance to the concept of bilingual education in certain areas, and a widespread lack of knowledge and understanding of what it means, though persons deeply committed to the idea and immersed in the activities involved in operating bilingual projects tend to forget this or choose to ignore it. Successful programs have been terminated when the balance on a divided school board has been tipped against bilingualism by the election of one new member. And when budgets are cut, bilingual programs may be regarded as unnecessary and expendable. A good deal of education of the general public still needs to be done. A better dissemination of information about bilingual education seems to be of major importance.

Additionally, those responsible for the planning of future bilingual programs will have to address themselves to specific problems related to the languages of the ethnic groups involved. In arriving at decisions about bilingual education for American-Indian pupils, for instance, a major factor to be considered is whether the language of the group is vital and flourishing, obsolescing or obsolete.[16] In setting up classes for Haitian pupils, it will have to be determined how much French they speak in addition to Haitian Creole. If it is true, as some Haitian spokesmen claim, that 98 percent of all Haitians (in Haiti) speak only Creole and that for Creole-speaking Haitians, French is as much a foreign language as Spanish[17] (or English), then the logical procedure in teaching Haitian pupils in the United States might well be to move from Creole to English in the bilingual (or English-language) classroom. But it does appear that since the Haitian Creole lexicon (though not the grammar and syntax) is French-based, French can not really be called a totally foreign language for the majority of Haitians. The step from Creole to French, in both speaking and reading, would seem easier and more logical than from Creole to English. As one example among many, Creole *ti* (little) is closer to standard French *petit* (p'ti) than it is to English *little* or Spanish *pequeño*. It is simply an example of the drastic reduction that occurs in pidgins and Creoles. (It may be that there is a need, in Haiti, for the schools to use Creole as a medium of instruction, as some educators have proposed, and teach children to read and write it. But that is not our concern here.)

One problem which has arisen in preparing materials for the Spanish-English bilingual programs concerns the variations in vocabulary and idiom in the Spanish spoken by Cubans, Puerto Ricans, and Mexican Americans. This subject has already received some attention. Materials which have been produced by various curriculum-development centers under the auspices of the U.S. Office of Education have been field tested for their suitability and acceptance among the different Spanish-language groups, and revisions made, taking into account the criticisms and recommendations. Undoubtedly, giving recognition to these variations is important in materials designed for the elementary grades, especially in testing and evaluation. At higher grade levels, and in high school classes, it would seem reasonable to expose students to such variations, as a matter of policy, through readings in the literature of different Spanish-speaking countries, in order to make them aware of the differences and to develop a broader knowledge of the language.

In designing bilingual programs for Chinese pupils in the United States, certain facts about dialects and the differences among spoken versions of the language have to be taken into consideration, since they can have a bearing on what it is feasible to include in the program.

Some bilingual programs have confined the Chinese component chiefly to the use of the spoken language as a medium of instruction. Others have given considerable attention to teaching the pupils to read and write Chinese. But learning to read and write Chinese is not an easy task, and once learned there is no simple transfer from Chinese characters to written English, as is the case with European languages which make use of the same alphabet. (Even though there are different values for most vowels and some consonants, most children who have learned to read French, Spanish, Italian, or Portuguese—who have learned what the technique of reading is—can make the transfer once they have learned to speak English. Of course, some Chinese educators claim that for children who have mastered written Chinese, learning to read and write English seems simple, by comparison.)

The problems in planning Chinese bilingual programs are also compounded by the fact that most of the Chinese families in the United States, at least in the past, have spoken the Cantonese dialect, which is totally different from Mandarin. Now a good many newcomers speak a Hong Kong dialect and some speak Mandarin (or the standard Han dialect being taught in schools in the People's Republic of China). All of these facts have to be taken into consideration in developing bilingual education for Chinese children in the public schools. Another problem which has arisen in San Francisco is the withdrawing of Chinese children from public schools and their enrollment in private schools by parents who oppose the forced busing of their children out of the neighborhood schools as a method of integrating schools in the San Francisco school system.

In developing bilingual programs for pupils from any of the language minority groups, the teaching of English (as a second language) is of great importance. As has been made clear in many statements, ESL alone is not bilingual education, but it must be a major component of any bilingual program. And in situations where bilingual teaching is not being introduced, it is essential that pupils who do not speak English be given the best possible instruction in the second language they are learning. Wherever possible, ESL specialists should be provided. Language laboratories equipped to permit students to work on their own, listening to the spoken language and checking themselves against proper models are useful and can save a teacher's time and energy for other instructional activities. Some principals, concerned with budget priorities, claim that ESL specialists are not necessary, that their classroom teachers can handle the problem of teaching English to their pupils. Though it is certainly desirable for all teachers in schools with large numbers of children whose first language is not English to have some understanding of the problems and some training in some techniques of teaching English as a second language, it is certainly better to have skilled ESL teachers in addition.

Much greater use could be made of music, poetry, and drama in ESL classes—and in the teaching of other languages too—than is found in most schools. To be useful as language-learning techniques, performance doesn't necessarily have to be on a professional level. The singing of traditional folk songs, contemporary popular songs, rounds, even carefully chosen commercial jingles, can establish language patterns indelibly in the memory. Memorizing verses of many kinds, humorous poems, doggerel, limericks, and aphorisms (as well as poetry of a better quality) can also be of value in language learning. In dramatization, both free expression in acting out stories and the memorizing of scripts for presenting scenes from well-written plays can be both useful and fun for students. Language classes don't have to be dull. The more pupils enjoy them, the more they are likely to learn.

At most conferences of language specialists, statements are made about the need for more research in the field of linguistics and language learning. Though this is undoubtedly true, perhaps the more pressing need—as far as bilingual-bicultural teaching in public schools is concerned—is for an application in the classroom of what is already known. There is a need to train more specialists to work in bilingual programs and also, if not to re-train, at least to give additional training to already certified and active teachers so that they will be better equipped to teach children whose first language is not English. This means not only taking specific courses in educational psychology and techniques but broadening their backgrounds in many general ways, studying a second language if they have not had the experience themselves, and acquiring more knowledge about cultural differences throughout the world, so many of which are reflected right here at home in our American society.

One of the potential sources of greatness of the United States has always been the multilingual-multicultural character of its people. These diverse strains which make up the American nation should not be squandered or wilfully destroyed, but carefully cultivated and encouraged to thrive, so that each can make its contribution to the society. Bilingual-bicultural education—which in its varied manifestations in this country becomes multilingual-multicultural education—can add to the richness and the enduring strength of the United States by nurturing mother tongues and cultural diversity and by furthering understanding and respect for one another among persons who may have differing origins and points of view but who are always fundamentally more alike than they are different. For we all share the same basic hopes and desires and needs inherent in our common humanity.

Notes

1. Available as Senate Report No. 93-1026, 93d Congress, 2d Session.

See: Title I—Amendments to the Elementary and Secondary Education Act of 1965. Sec. 105. Bilingual education programs.

    Title V—Education Administration
      Sec. 501. National center for education statistics.
      Sec. 502. General provisions relating to officers in the education division.
      Sec. 508. Publication of indexed compilation of innovative projects.
      Sec. 516. Appointment of members of and functioning of advisory councils.
      Sec. 517. Other amendments relating to advisory councils.

    Title VI—Extension and Revision of Related Elementary and Secondary Programs.
              Part A—Adult Education
      Sec. 607. Amendments relating to bilingual education.
              Part C—Indian Education
      Sec. 631. Extensions of programs for the education of Indian children.
      Sec. 632. Revision of programs relating to Indian education.
              Part D—Emergency School Aid
      Sec. 641. Extension of emergency school aid.

    Title VIII—Miscellaneous Provisions
      Part A—Policy Statements and White House Conference on Education
      Sec. 801. National policy with respect to equal educational opportunity.
      Sec. 802. Policy with respect to advance funding of education programs.
      Sec. 804. White House Conference on Education.
              Part B—Educational Studies and Surveys
      Sec. 821. Study of purposes and effectiveness of compensatory education programs.
      Sec. 822. Survey and study for updating number of children counted.
              Part C—Amendments to the Higher Education Act of 1965
      Sec. 833. Bilingual education amendments.
              Part D—Other Miscellaneous Provisions
      Sec. 841. Amendments to the Library Services and Construction Act and the Vocational Education Act of 1963 relating to bilingual education and vocational training.
      Sec. 845. Extension of advisory councils.

2. *Arizona Daily Star*, March 1974.

3. *New York Times*, 15 April 1974, p. 14. (Henry Giniger, Special to the *New York Times*, "U.S. Opens Doors to More Cubans," Madrid, 13 April 1974.)

4. U.S. Department of Justice, Immigration and Naturalization Service, "Our Immigration, A Brief Account of Immigration," M-86 (Rev. 1971) N. p. 18.

5. Ibid., p. 17.

6. Ibid., p. 16.

7. Ibid., p. 10.

8. United States Department of Justice, *1970 Annual Report, Immigration and Naturalization Service*, Report of the Commissioner of Immigration and Naturalization, June 30, 1970, Washington, D.C., p.35. (Superintendent of Documents, GPO, Washington.)

9. Ibid., p. 40.

10. U.S. Supreme Court Reports 39 L Ed. 2d p.8.

11. Ibid., p. 4.

12. The State Education Department, Albany, N.Y., May 24, 1973, a directive sent to selected school district administrators.

13. Ibid.

14. Ibid.

15. Ibid.

16. William Slager and Betty Madsden, "Introduction," *Language in American Indian Education*, Winter, 1972, a newsletter of the Office of Education Programs, Bureau of Indian Affairs, U.S. Department of the Interior, University of Utah, William R. Slager, ed., Betty M. Madsden, Assistant Editor. Also, Wick R. Miller, "Obsolescing Languages: The Case of the Shoshoni," pp. 1-12 in Language in American Indian Education.

17. Irvel Gousse, Assistant Coordinator, Brandeis High School Bilingual Program, speaking at the International Bilingual-Bicultural Conference in May 1974, New York.

Appendix:
Sources of Information and Materials

A good deal of material pertinent to bilingual-bicultural education has been written or compiled by both commercial publishers and non-profit organizations or institutions supported by the U.S. Office of Education or private foundation grants. Articles and reports on various aspects of bilingual education also appear frequently in scholarly journals and government-sponsored publications. No evaluation of materials will be attempted here, but the following list of organizations and periodicals providing information about curricular materials and teaching techniques may be of interest, though it makes no claim to being complete.

American Council on the Teaching of Foreign Languages (ACTFL), 62 Fifth Avenue, New York, New York 10011, publishes "Foreign Language Annals," a quarterly, subscription $10.

Asian Newcomer Parent Program, 2 Waverly Place, San Francisco, an HEW project sponsored by the Education Center for Chinese, has prepared a beginning ESL curriculum for recently arrived Chinese (and other Asian) parents.

BABEL (*Bay Area Bilingual Education League*) of the Berkeley (California) Unified School District publishes a newsletter and a catalog of materials produced by BABEL, Bilingual Project, Berkeley Unified School District, 1414 Walnut Street, Berkeley, California.

Bilingual Resources Center, New York City Board of Education, Office of Bilingual Education, 110 Livingston Street, Room 224, Brooklyn, New York 11201, functions as a clearinghouse, resource library, and dissemination center on bilingual education.

The Bilingual Review/La Revista Bilingue, devoted to various aspects of Hispanic life in the United States, is to be published, under special grants, by faculty members of City College of the City University of New York, first issue announced for the fall of 1974.

Building Bilingual Bridges, a Title VII project at P.S. 2, New York City, serving Spanish-, English-, and Chinese-speaking pupils, has prepared several illustrated trilingual booklets for use at the elementary level.

Bureau of Indian Affairs has published an *Annotated Bibliography of Young People's Fiction on American Indians*, Curriculum Bulletin No. 11, 1972, Office of Education Programs, U.S. Bureau of Indian Affairs, 1951 Constitution Avenue NW, Washington, D.C. 20242. The BIA also publishes, several times a year, a newsletter (a substantial journal), "Language in American Indian Education," prepared for the BIA by the University of Utah, Salt Lake City 84112. It is intended for teachers and other educators who are involved in the educational system of the BIA. It contains much information about bilingual education.

Center for Applied Linguistics, 1611 North Kent Street, Arlington, Virginia 22209, Rudolph Troike, director (1974), publishes newsletter, "The Linguistic Reporter," subscription $2.50. The center organizes conferences, disseminates information about studies in linguistics, and has prepared bibliographies of materials for specified grade levels, single copies of which are available free, on request.

Chicano Education Digest, Box 5802, Riverside, California 92507, subscription (12 issues) $6. (Started publication in the spring of 1974.)

Chinatown Planning Council, Inc., English Language Center, 27-29 Division Street, New York, New York 10002.

Chinese Bilingual Pilot Project, San Francisco Unified School District, ESEA Title VII, has produced a number of illustrated story booklets in Chinese and English, "Winter Festival," "The Story of Ching Ming," "The Moon Festival Is Here," and "Preparing for Chinese New Year," and some information pamphlets, "Background Materials on Ching Ming Festival" and "Chinese New Year Resource Material."

Dissemination Center for Bilingual Bicultural Education, 6504 Tracor Lane, Austin, Texas 78721, telephone: (512) 926-8080, Juan Solís, director. Established under grants from ESEA, this is a major distribution organization for materials prepared by various government-sponsored units. The Dissemination Center publishes "Cartel," a monthly annotated bibliography of materials published by commercial publishers as well as government-supported agencies, which are suitable and recommended for bilingual programs. The December issue is cumulative for the entire preceding year. Yearly subscription is $10. The cumulative issue may be purchased separately for $3.70. (Editorial communications and materials for inclusion should be sent to "Cartel," Research Librarian, at the Dissemination Center's address.) The Center is also the distributor of the *Proceedings* of the annual National (1972) and International (1973) Conferences on Bilingual Bicultural Education.

Among the many materials available from the Dissemination Center are *Spanish Curricula Units, 1973,* prepared by the Spanish Curricula Development Center, Dade County Public Schools, Miami, Florida; *Estudio Cultural de Puerto Rico,* developed by Bilingual Program ARRIBA, Philadelphia; *Escucho, Digo y Aprendo,* developed by the Englewood Independent School District, San Antonio, Texas; and *The Texan, Man of Many Faces,* Laura Carter Higley, Del Valle Bilingual Program, Del Valle, Texas.

Also available from the Dissemination Center is a list of college and university programs among state education agencies which offer an undergraduate major, a graduate-level major, or teacher training programs of various types designated as bilingual education. Information has been compiled for the following states: Arizona, California, Colorado, Illinois, Massachusetts, New Mexico, New York, and Texas (as of Feb. 27, 1973).

Educational Resources Information Center (ERIC). ERIC is described in *Foreign Language Annals* as a "nationwide information system designed to serve and advance American Education," and the following information is provided about its structure and services. "It is sponsored by the National Institute of Education. The system's basic objectives are to provide information on significant current documents and to make them available, either through normal publication channels or through the ERIC Document Reproduction Service. ERIC Clearinghouses, each focusing on a separate subject-matter area, seek to acquire, select, abstract, index, store, retrieve, and disseminate information about educational research and resources.

About MLA/ERIC. *The Modern Language Association of America* conducts the ERIC Clearinghouse responsible for the collection and dissemination of educational information on languages and linguistics. This includes information on instructional methodology, psychology of language learning, presentation of the cultural and intercultural content, application of linguistics, curricular problems and developments, and teacher training and qualifications specific to the teaching of languages. Also included are reports or documents concerned with the language teacher and researcher in the language sciences and those dealing with psycholinguistics, theoretical and applied linguistics, language pedagogy, bilingualism, and instructional materials related to commonly and uncommonly taught languages, including English for speakers of other languages.

Regular Communication Channels. "The official journal of the American Council on the Teaching of Foreign Languages, *Foreign Language Annals,* regularly includes a section on ERIC-related activities prepared by the MLA/ERIC Clearinghouse. This material reviews significant developments in foreign-language teaching and is of interest to teachers, administrators, researchers, and public officials, commercial and industrial organizations, and the public. The *TESOL Quarterly* also contains regular listings of ERIC accessions dealing with the teaching of English to speakers of other languages."

International Center for Research on Bilingualism, Laval University, Quebec, Canada.

Institute of Bilingual Bicultural Services, Mercy College of Detroit, 8200 West Outer Drive, Detroit, Michigan 48219.

Linguistics Society of America, 1611 North Kent Street, Arlington, Virginia 22209, a membership organization of some 6,500 persons interested in the field of linguistics. John Hammer, executive director (1974).

Materials Acquisition Project, San Diego City Schools, 2950 National Avenue, San Diego, California 92113, telephone (714) 232-6864, functioning under an ESEA grant, publishes *Materiales en Marcha,* which lists and evaluates materials in Spanish and Portuguese published abroad suitable for use in bilingual programs in the United States. *Materiales en Marcha* also contains articles on bilingual education.

Multi-Culture Institute, 693 Mission Street, Rm. 311, San Francisco, California 94105, a non-profit organization, publishes *MCI News.*

New York State Education Department, Bilingual Education Unit, Albany, New York 12224, has prepared a booklet "Programs Providing Bilingual Education, Title VII, ESEA, 'Questions and Answers,' 'Participating Schools,' 'Contact Persons,'" for use in the schools of New York State. Free copies are available to New York State school personnel when ordered through a school administrator. Also "Educación Bilingüe, Una Declaración del Plan y Acción que Proponen los Regentes de la Universidad del Estado de Nueva York," State Department of Education, Albany, New York, August 1972.

Northwest Educational Cooperative, Bilingual Education Service Center, Mt. Prospect, Illinois, publishes a newsletter monthly during the school year, "to inform readers on bilingual-bicultural issues and activities outside and within the state of Illinois. Persons wishing to receive the newsletter will be added to the mailing list on request."

Southwest Educational Development Laboratory has developed materials for Spanish/English bilingual programs for early childhood and elementary grades, which are available for purchase through National Educational Laboratory Publishers, Inc., Post Office Box 1003, Austin, Texas 78767.

Spanish Curricula Development Center, Dade County Public Schools, 1420

Washington Avenue, Miami Beach, Florida 33139, functioning under ESEA grants, has prepared, field-tested, revised, and published materials for Spanish/English bilingual programs for Cuban, Puerto Rican, and Mexican-American pupils. Ralph Robinett, director.

Summer Institute of Linguistics (SIL), main headquarters, Box 1960, Santa Ana, California 92702, founded in 1934, is a collaborative arm of Wycliffe Bible Translators, of the same address. "The Summer Institute of Linguistics has as its goal the study of the languages of the world's aboriginal groups, and the preservation of a record of these languages for linguistic science. SIL is also concerned with the practical application of its linguistic findings in helping speakers of these languages. For each language a practical alphabet and materials for making the transition from the mother tongue to the national language are prepared. SIL provides linguistic training for those interested in working toward these goals. ... The Institute currently [1974] conducts field research in twenty countries and in four hundred and fifty minority languages. SIL holds seven annual institutes in the United States at the Universities of Oklahoma, North Dakota, and Washington (Seattle). ... A session consists of ten to twelve weeks of intensive university work. The sessions are especially designed for those preparing to serve pre-literate people, to do some specific linguistic task such as translation or literacy work, or to study languages for which linguistic materials are inadequate. The courses therefore deal with the general principles basic to all languages."

TESOL, "a professional organization for those concerned with the teaching of English as a second or foreign language," School of Languages and Linguistics, Georgetown University, Washington, D.C. 20007. The acronym stands for *Teachers of English to Speakers of Other Languages*. TESOL publishes a quarterly and a newsletter. Membership includes subscription to the quarterly and newsletter. Dues, regular membership, $14, student (at least half-time study) $7.

The Texas Education Agency, Austin, Texas (in collaboration with the *Regional Educational Agencies Project on International Education*) has produced "A Resource Manual for Implementing Bilingual Education Programs."

Bibliography

America's Educationally Neglected: A Progress Report on Compensatory Education (Annual Report to the President and the Congress), 1973, the National Advisory Council on the Education of Disadvantaged Children, 425 Thirteenth Street NW, Suite 1012, Washington, D.C. 20004.

Analytical Bibliography of Navajo Reading Materials, Curriculum Bulletin No. 10, *Indian Education*, Bernard Spolsky, Agnes Holm, Penny Murphy, prepared by the Navajo Reading Study, the University of New Mexico, for the Bureau of Indian Affairs, United States Department of the Interior, June 1970.

Andersson, Theodore: *The Teaching of Foreign Languages in the Elementary School*, Heath, Boston, 1953.

——, and Mildred Boyer: *Bilingual Schooling in the United States*, 2 vols., Southwest Educational Development Laboratory, Austin, Texas, 1970. For sale by the Superintendent of Documents, U.S. Government Printing Office, Washington, D.C. 20402.

Bahti, Tom: *Southwestern Indian Tribes*, K. C. Publications, Box 14883, Las Vegas, Nev., 1971.

Benítez de Rexach, Celeste: Address delivered at the Seventh Annual Convention of TESOL, San Juan, Puerto Rico, May 10, 1973. Printed in Puerto Rico by the Printing Services Division of the Department of Education, Commonwealth of Puerto Rico, 705 Hoare Street, Santurce, Puerto Rico.

Cabrera, Ysidro Arturo: *A Study of American and Mexican American Culture Values and Their Significance in Education*, University of Colorado, Boulder, 1963. Reprinted by R. and E. Research Associates, 4843 Mission Street, San Francisco, Calif., 1972.

Canada Yearbook, published by the authority of the Minister of Industry, Trade and Commerce, Division of Statistics, Ottawa, Canada, 1972.

China Recontructs, published monthly by China Welfare Institute, Wai Wen Building, Peking 37, China. Guozi Shudian, general distributor, P.O. Box 399, Peking, China.

Cleland, Robert Glass: *From Wilderness to Empire: A History of California*, Glenn Dumke, ed., Knopf, New York, 1959. (A combined and revised edition of *From Wilderness to Empire, 1542-1900* and *California in Our Time, 1900-1940.*)

Connecticut Education, Connecticut State Board of Education, Hartford, October 1973.

Conwell, Marilyn: *Louisiana French Grammar*, Janua Linguarum, Series Practica, Mouton, The Hague, 1963.

Debo, Angie: *And Still the Waters Run: The Betrayal of the Five Civilized Tribes*, rev. ed., Princeton University Press, Princeton, N.J. 1972.

Desheriyev, Juri: "National Languages and Interlingual Communication," *Soviet Life*, no. 8 (203), August 1973, Pushkin Square, Moscow, U.S.S.R. (Washington Editorial Board, 1706 Eighteenth Street NW, Washington, D.C.)

Dickson, Frederick S.: "A Famous Indian Dictionary," Yale Review, New Haven, Conn., 8° vol. 8 (1919), pp. 770-783.

Dillard, J. L.: *Black English*, Random House, New York, 1972.

Dissemination Center for Bilingual-Bicultural Education, *Guide to Title VII ESEA Bilingual Bicultural Projects in the United States*, 1972-1973, Austin, Tex., 1973.

Ervin-Tripp, Susan M.: *Language Acquisition and Communicative Choice*, Stanford University Press, Stanford, Calif., 1973.

Finocchiaro, Mary: *Teaching Children Foreign Languages*, McGraw-Hill, New York, 1964.

Fishman, Joshua: *Language Loyalty in the United States*, Mouton and Co., London, 1966. (Janua Linguarum—Studia Memoriae, Nicolai Van Wijk Dedicata, edenda curat, Cornelis H. Van Schooneveld, Stanford University, Series Maior XXI.)

Francis, Convers: "Râles, Sébastien," in the Library of American Biography, conducted by Jared Sparks, 2d ser., vol. 7, Hilliard, Gray and Co., Boston; R. J. Kennett, London, 1834-1848.

Fries, Charles: *The Structure of English*, Harcourt Brace, New York, 1952.

Gaarder, A. Bruce: "The Organization of the Bilingual School," *Journal of Social Issues*, vol. XXIII, no. 2, 1967.

Galarza, Ernesto: *Barrio Boy*, University of Notre Dame Press, Notre Dame, Ind., 1971.

Gomez, Rudolph (ed.): *The Changing Mexican American. A Reader*, Pruett Publishing Co. Box 1560, Boulder, Colo. 80302.

Hall, Robert A., Jr.: *Pidgin and Creole Languages*, Cornell University Press, Ithaca, N.Y., 1966.

Handlin, Oscar: *The Newcomers: Negroes and Puerto Ricans in a Changing Metropolis*, Anchor Books, Doubleday, Garden City, N.Y., 1962.

Haugen, Dr. Einar: *Bilingualism in the Americas*, a Bibliography and Research Guide, American Dialect Society, University of Alabama Press, University, Ala. 1956.

Hodge, Frederick Webb (ed.): *Handbook of American Indians North of Mexico*, 2 vols., Bulletin 30, Smithsonian Institution, Bureau of American Ethnology, GPO, Washington, D.C., 1912.

Horner, Vivian, and Vera John: *Early Childhood Bilingual Education*, prepared by the Early Childhood Bilingual Education Project, Materials Center, the Modern Language Association of America, 62 Fifth Avenue, New York, 1971.

Inhalder, Barbel, and Jean Piaget: *The Psychology of the Child*, Basic Books, New York, 1969.

John, Vera P., and Vivian Horner: see Horner, Vivian.

Kelley, L. G. (ed.): *Description and Measurement of Bilingualism: An International Seminar*, published in association with the Canadian National Committee for UNESCO, by the University of Toronto Press, Toronto, 1969. (Seminar at University of Moncton, June 6–14, 1967.)

Kenton, Edna (ed.): *The Indians of North America*, 2 vols., Harcourt Brace, New York, 1927. (Selected and edited from *The Jesuit Relations and Allied Documents: Travels and Explorations of the Jesuit Missionaries in New France, 1610–1791*, edited by Reuben Gold Thwaites, Burrows Brothers Co., Cleveland, 1896, 1897, 1898, 1899, 1900, 1901.)

—— (ed.): *The Jesuit Relations*, Vanguard, New York, 1959.

Keyes, Frances Parkinson: *All Flags Flying*, McGraw-Hill, New York, 1972.

Kip, Reverend William I. : *The Early Jesuit Missions in North America*, compiled and translated from the letters of the French Jesuits, with notes, vol. XIV, Wiley and Putnam, London, 1847.

Kroeber, Alfred: *Handbook of the Indians of California*, GPO, Washington, 1925.

Lado, Robert: *Linguistics Across Cultures*, The University of Michigan Press, Ann Arbor, 1957.

——: *Language Teaching: A Scientific Approach*, McGraw-Hill, New York, 1964.

La Enseñanza del Español a Estudiantes Hispano-parlantes en la Escuela y en la Unversidad, Office of Education, U.S. Department of Health, Education, and Welfare. Publication No. (OE) 72-135, 1972. (Prepared by a committee commissioned by the American Association of Teachers of Spanish and Portuguese, A. Bruce Gaarder, Chairman.)

Lamb, Ruth S.: *Mexican Americans: Sons of the Southwest*, Ocelot Press, Claremont, Calif. 1970.

Lambert, Wallace: "Psychological Approaches in the Study of Languages," *The Modern Language Journal*, no. 47, 1963, pp. 114-121.

——, and Elizabeth Peal: "The Relationship of Bilingualism to Intelligence," in Norman Munn (ed.), *Psychological Monographs, General and Applied*, vol. 76, no. 27, The American Psychological Association, Inc., 1333 Sixteenth Street NW, Washington, D.C. 1962.

——, and G. Richard Tucker: *Bilingual Education of Children*, Newbury House, Rowley, Mass., 1972.

Mackey, William F.: *Language Teaching Analysis*, Longmans, London, 1965.

Maine Indians: A Brief Survey: prepared by the (Maine) State Department of Indian Affairs, Augusta, Maine, 1971.

Malherbe, E. G.: "Commentaries/Session I," in L. G. Kelley (ed.), *Description and Measurement of Bilingualism*, published in association with the Canadian National Committee for UNESCO, by the University of Toronto Press, Toronto, 1969.

Materiales en Marcha, published monthly under a grant from the U. S. Office of Education by Materials Acquisition Project, ESEA, Title VII, San Diego City Schools, 2950 National Avenue, San Diego, Calif. 92113.

McKown, Robin: *The Image of Puerto Rico: Its History and Its People: on the Island—on the Mainland*, McGraw-Hill, New York, 1973.

McWilliams, Carey: *North From Mexico*, Greenwood, Westport, Conn. 1968 (reprint of 1949 edition).

——: *Brothers Under the Skin*, rev. ed., Little, Brown, Boston, 1964.

——: *The Mexicans in America*, Teachers College Press, Columbia University, New York, 1968.

Meier, Matt S., and Feliciano Rivera: *The Chicanos: A History of Mexican Americans*, Hill and Wang, Inc., New York, 1972.

National Advisory Council on the Education of Disadvantaged Children, *America's Educationally Neglected: A Progress Report on Compensatory Education,* Annual Report to the President and the Congress, 1973.

Navajo Education, published monthly by Diné Bi' Oltà (*Navajo Education*) Association, College of Ganado, Ganado, Navajo Nation, Arizona.

Navajo Times, published weekly by the Navajo Tribe, P.O. Box 310, Window Rock, Arizona 86515. (The official newspaper of the Navajo Tribe.)

Negrón de Montilla, Aida: *Americanization in Puerto Rico and the Public School System,* Editorial Edil, University of Puerto Rico, Rio Piedras, Puerto Rico, 1970.

New Brunswick, Province of: *Schools Act and Regulations* (consolidated to 1972), Fredericton, New Brunswick, Canada. Printed and published by authority of the Queen's printer for the Province.

Olivares, José de, *Our Islands and Their People,* 2 vols. (In the General Library of Puerto Rico, 500 Ponce de Leon Avenue, San Juan.)

"The Organization and Administration of Public Schools in Quebec," 3d ed., Dominion Bureau of Statistics, Education Division, Ottawa, Canada, 1966.

Osuña, Juan José: *A History of Education in Puerto Rico,* Editorial de la Universidad de Puerto Rico, Rio Piedras, Puerto Rico. Copyright 1923, 2d ed., 1949.

Parkman, Francis: *The Jesuits in North America in the Seventeenth Century,* vol. II, New Library Edition, Corner House Publishers, Williamstown, Mass., 1970.

Peal, Elizabeth: see Lambert, Wallace.

Pelletier, Wilfred, and Ted Poole: *No Foreign Land: The Biography of a North American Indian,* Pantheon, New York, 1973.

Piaget, Jean, and Barbel Inhalder: see Inhalder, Barbel.

Proceedings, National Conference on Bilingual Education, April 14–15, 1972, Austin, Texas, published by the Dissemination Center for Bilingual Bicultural Education, Austin, Tex.

Rasles, S.: Lettre à Nanrantsouak, 12 octobre 1723, in *Lettres édifiantes,* Paris, 1717–1776, 16° vol. 23, pp. 198-307.

——: Account of the savages in New France in *Lettres édifiantes,* Lyon, 1819, vol. 4, pp. 95-138.

———: Lettre, 15 octobre 1722. La Mission auprès des sauvages Abnakis in *Lettres édifiantes*, Paris 1717–1776, 16° v. 17, pp. 285-324.

Report with respect to the House Resolution Authorizing the Committee on Interior and Insular Affairs to Conduct an Investigation of the Bureau of Indian Affairs, H. R. 2503, Dec. 15, 1952, 82nd Cong., 2d Sess., GPO, 1953.

Republic of South Africa, Department of Information, *This Is South Africa*, Pretoria, South Africa, 1971.

Republic of South Africa, Department of Information, *South African Yearbook*, Pretoria, South Africa, 1973.

Reference Paper No. 45, Information Division, Department of External Affairs, Ottawa, Canada, 1972 (revised).

Rolle, Andrew: *California, A History*, Thomas Y. Crowell, New York, 1963.

Ruhl, Bartlett (ed.): *Records of American Diplomacy*, Knopf, New York, 1947.

Samora, Julian (ed.): *La Raza, Forgotten Americans*, University of Notre Dame Press, Notre Dame, Ind., 1966.

Sanchez, George: *Forgotten People: A Study of New Mexicans*, University of New Mexico Press, Albuquerque, 1940.

Saville, Muriel, and Rudolph Troike: *A Handbook of Bilingual Education*, Center for Applied Linguistics, Washington, D.C., 1971.

Schuyler, H. C.: "The Apostle of the Abnakis: Father Sebastien Rale, S. J.," *Catholic Historical Review*, Washington, D.C., 1915, 8° vol. 1, pp. 164-174.

Sprague, John Francis: *Sébastien Rales: A Maine Tragedy in the Eighteenth Century*, The Heintzemann Press, Boston, 1906.

Steiner, Stan: *The New Indians*, Dell, New York, 1968.

———: *La Raza*, Harper & Row, New York, 1970.

Swanton, John R. (ed.): *The Indian Tribes of North America*, Smithsonian Institution, Bureau of American Ethnology, GPO, Washington, Bulletin 145, 1953.

Teaching Spanish in School and College to Native Speakers of Spanish, U.S. Department of Health, Education, and Welfare Publication OE-72-135, 1972. (Prepared by a committee commissioned by the American Association of Teachers of Spanish and Portuguese, A. Bruce Gaarder, chairman.)

TESOL Newsletter, published by the national TESOL organization, Ruth Wineberg (ed.), School of Languages and Linguistics, Georgetown University, Washington, D.C. 20007.

Thwaites, Reuben (ed.): *The Jesuit Relations and Allied Documents: Travels and Explorations of the Jesuit Missionaries in New France, 1610–1791*, 73 vols. reprinted in 36, Rowman, Totowa, N.J., 1959. (This is a reproduction of the 76 volumes published by Burrows Brothers Co. between 1896 and 1901.)

Tucker, G. Richard, and Wallace Lambert: see Lambert, Wallace.

Turner, Paul R. (ed.): *Bilingualism in the Southwest*, University of Arizona Press, Tucson, 1973.

Underhill, Ruth M.: *Red Man's America: A History of Indians in the United States*, rev. ed., The University of Chicago Press, Chicago, 1971. (Paperback edition.)

UNESCO Institute for Education, *Foreign Languages in Primary Education*, Hamburg, Germany, 1963.

United States Commission on Civil Rights, *Mexican American Education Study*, 1971. Available from Superintendent of Documents, Washington, D.C.

Viñas de Vasquez, Paquita: "The Teaching of English in Puerto Rico," *TESOL Newsletter*, vol. VI, no. 3, American Language Institute, Georgetown University, Washington, D.C., April 1973.

Vivas Maldonaldo, José Luis: *Historia de Puerto Rico*, 2d ed. (rev.), Las Americas Publishing Co., New York (Biblioteca Puertorriqueña 3), 1962.

Wall, Anne: "Reminiscences of Life in Puerto Rico," unpublished, Bayamón, Puerto Rico, 1973.

Wassaja, A National Newspaper of Indian America, published monthly by the American Indian Historical Society, 1451 Masonic Avenue, San Francisco, Calif. 94117.

Weinreich, Uriel: *Languages in Contact: Findings and Problems*, Linguistic Circle of New York Publications, no. 1, 1953.

Willink, Elizabeth: "Bilingual Education for Navajo Children," part II, *American Indians, Assumptions and Methods*, in Paul R. Turner (ed.), *Bilingualism in the Southwest*, University of Arizona Press, Tucson, 1973.

Zhamin, V.: *Education in the USSR: Its Economy and Structure*, Novosti, Moscow, 1973.

Index

Cajun French, 6, 30, 32, 37, 45–47
Cajuns, 46–47, 117
Calais, Maine, 153
Caldwell, Idaho, 134
Calexico, Calif., 8
California, 13, 132
    American Indian and Mexican American program, 161
    bilingual programs, 17, 49, 56, 130, 131
        summary, 132
        (See also San Francisco)
    history, 14–15
    Mexican Americans in, 16
Cambridge, Mass., 124
Canada, 101–106, 118, 119n.–120n.
    American Indians, 105, 153, 155
    bilingual schools, definition of, 104
    bilingual teaching experiments, 105–106
    bilingualism, 101–102
    class distinctions, 116
    educational system, 102–104
    English-speaking people, attitude toward bilingualism, 101–102
    Eskimos, 105
    ethnic groups, non-French, 102, 104–105
    French language, 6, 30, 32, 37, 42, 101–106
        in schools, present system, 102–104
    French-speaking people (see French Canadians)
    Public Service Commission, 101
    separatist movement, 24, 101
Caribou, Maine, 40
Carnegie Foundation, 167
Carolina, P.R., 92, 93
Castro, Fidel, 8, 180
Catholic Church, American Indians and, 152, 154, 155
Catholic schools (see Parochial schools)
Catholics, French-Canadian, 38, 42, 102, 103, 105
Census Bureau, 172
Center for Applied Linguistics, Arlington, Va., recommendations on American Indian programs, 170–171
Center for Education Statistics, 177
Ceylon (Sri Lanka), 117
    languages, 108–109
Chacon, Pete, 132

Chamorro language, 19n., 151
Chapline, Elaine, 58n.
Chelsea, Mass., 124, 125
Chen, Jack, 121n.–122n.
Cherokee Indians, 152
    in North Carolina, 129, 142
Cherokee language, 151
    publications in, 152
    written, 152
Cheyenne Indians, 151
Chicago, 17, 135
Chicanos, use of term, 16, 31–32
    (See also Mexican Americans)
Chicopee, Mass., 124
China, People's Republic of, 71, 109, 117
    ethnic groups, 113, 118
    language policy, 113–115, 191
    refugees "paroled" to U.S. from Hong Kong, 181
Chinese language, 6, 7, 113–115, 122n.
    bilingual programs, 49, 56, 77, 124, 130, 131, 141, 183–184, 190–191
    Chinese-Spanish program, 47–49
    dialects, 190–191
    standard (Han, Mandarin), 71, 113, 190
    writing, 114–115, 191
Chinese people, 2, 137, 179
    immigration laws on, changed, 181
Chinle, Ariz., 167
Chippewa Indians, 155
Choctaw Indians, 131
Choctaw language, 151
Chula Vista, Calif., 56
Church Rock, N. Mex., 162
Cincinnati, 7
Civil Rights Commission, U.S., 77, 172
Class distinctions:
    in bilingual programs, 128
    in language, 30, 35, 116–117
    upward mobility, 35–36
Cleveland, 7, 142
Clinton, Mass., 124
Cochiti Pueblo, N. Mex., 159
Colorado, 13, 16, 128, 131, 133
    American Indian programs, 133, 161–162
Coloured people in South Africa, 107, 120n.
Comprehensive Bilingual Education Amendments Act of 1973, 78–79

217

San Felipe Pueblo, N. Mex., 159
San Fidel, N. Mex., Acomita Day
  School, 159, 160
San Francisco:
  Chinese bilingual programs, 49, 56,
    77, 130, 183–184, 191
  Puerto Ricans in, 17
San Juan, P.R., 93, 94
  TESOL Conference, 1973, 34, 86, 97
San Juan, Utah, 145
Sanchez, George, 19n.
Sanostee, N. Mex., 164
Santa Ana Pueblo, N. Mex., 159
Santo Domingo Pueblo, N. Mex., 159
Sapir, Edward, 174n.
Save the Children Federation, 169
Scandinavian countries, 116
School integration, 178, 191
Schwyzertütsch, 35, 108
Scituate, Mass., 124
Seminole Indians:
  in Florida, 158–159
  in Oklahoma, 131
Seminole language, 151, 158–159
Sequoya, Cherokee writing invented by,
  152
Service de Liaison des Projects Bilin-
  gues Français-Anglais, 39, 40
Shoshonean languages, 159, 161
Sinclair, Maine, 136
Sindhi, 109
Sinhalese, 108–109
Sioux Indians:
  Lakota, 144, 151
  Oglala, 130
Sisters of Mercy, 154
Slager, William, 194n.
Snowflake, Ariz., 163
Socio-economic status:
  in bilingual programs, 128
  language and, 116–117
Somerville, Mass., 124
South Africa, 120n.–121n.
  bilingualism, 68, 106–107
  schools for Indian, Coloured, and
    Bantu pupils, 107
South Carolina, 143
South Dakota, 129, 143–144
  American Indian programs, 130, 170
Southbridge, Mass., 124
Southwest Board of Cooperative Serv-
  ices, 161

Soviet Union, 71, 109, 117
  ethnic groups, 110–112, 118
  languages, 110–113
Spain:
  conquest of America, 15
  Cuban refugees in, 180
  Spanish people in European labor
    force, 117
Spanish-American War, 12, 82, 86
Spanish language:
  bilingual programs, 6–8, 11–18, 20–
    24, 47–57, 61, 67–70, 77–79
  court decisions on, 77–78
  evaluation of, 52–56
  guidelines on, 186–187
  in Puerto Rico, 81–99
    (See also Puerto Ricans)
  state-mandated, 123–127, 130–134,
    137–142, 144–146
  in China, 115
  Chinese-Spanish project, 47–49
  in FLES programs, 27
  of immigrants, 181–183
  non-standard or variant types, 30–
    33, 190
  Puerto Rican, 6, 30, 33, 190
  in Soviet Union, 112
  in U.S., importance of, 69–70
    (See also Mexican Americans)
Springfield, Mass., 33, 78, 124, 125
Sri Lanka (see Ceylon)
Stamford, Conn., 133
States, bilingual-bicultural programs
  supported by, 119, 123–147
  list of, 131–146
Stoughton, Mass., 124
SUN project, 161–162
Supreme Court, U.S., 77, 183–184
Swahili, 109
Swanton, John R., 175n.
Switzerland, languages, 35, 108
Syracuse, N.Y., 141

Taino Indians, 15
Tamatave dialect, 109
Tamiami Trail, 156, 157
Tamils, 108–109, 117
Taos Pueblo, N. Mex., 159
Taunton, Mass., 124
Teachers:
  in bilingual programs, 25, 30, 180,
    184–185